CW00960174

SWEENEY
AN INTERTONGUING

SWEENEY

AN INTERTONGUING

RODY GORMAN

First published by
Francis Boutle Publishers
272 Alexandra Park Road
London N22 7BG
Tel 020 8889 8087
Email: info@francisboutle.co.uk
www.francisboutle.co.uk

ISBN 978 1 7394256 1 6

Acknowledgements

I am grateful to the Arts Council of Northern Ireland, Colmcille, Dublin City University, the Royal Literary Fund, Skye & Lochalsh Talent Development Initiative and the Trustees of the Katherine Kavanagh Estate for awards that helped me to develop this work.

Special thanks to my family, and partner Annie who suggested the name Sweenese. Thanks also to Atlas Arts, Meg Bateman, Liam Carson, Tom Fitzgerald, Bryan Frykenberg, Donna Geervliet, Ireland Literature Exchange, Fergus Kelly, Margaret Lonergan, Seán Lynch, Robert Macfarlane, Fearghas MacFhionnlaigh, Hector MacInnes, Eoin Mac Cárthaigh, Eoghan Mac Giolla Bhríde, Caoimhín Mac Giolla Léith, Ciarán Mac Murchaidh, Seán Mac Risteaird, Peter Mackay, Kath MacLeod, Lorcán Mac Mathúna, Andrew McNeillie, Noel Monahan, Caitríona Ní Chléirchín, Colm O'Boyle, Feargal Ó Béarra, Lillis Ó Laoire, Cearbhall Ó Síocháin, Liam Prút, John Purser, Sarah Smyth, Victoria Smyth, John Storey, Greg Thomson, Alan Titley, Gearóidín Uí Laighléis, Peter Urpeth, Toni Velikova, David Walker, Colin Waters and Moray Watson.

Parts of this work have been published in *A' Mheanbhchuileag/An Cormhíol* (Coiscéim, 2018), *Aneas, Atlanta Review, Causeway, Cyphers, The Deep Heart's Core* (Dedalus, 2016), *EarthLines, Edinburgh Review, Feasta, Fras, Glasgow Review of Books, Gutter, Haiku Spirit, Into the Forest* (Saraband, 2013), *Irish Pages, Irish Poetry Reading Archive, Irish Review, Knots, Thistles and Thorns: Challenges and Benefits of Translating Into and Out of*

Gaelic and Irish (Aberdeen University Press, 2024), *New Writing Scotland*, *Northwords Now*, *Ó Bhéal*, *Poetry Ireland Review*, *Poetry Proper*, *Poetry Review*, *Southwords*, *The SHOp*, *The Stony Thursday Book*, *Strokestown Poetry Anthology 2017*, *The Time Horse* (Festuniel, 2021), *Trafika Europe*, *Windows*, www.oranbagraidh.com; www.pure.uhi.ac.uk/publications/window-to-the-west, www.scottishpoetrylibrary.org.uk and www.knockengorroch.org.uk/the-real-merlin/

Rody Gorman
Cruard, Skye 2024

Dramatis Personae

The Unstable Narrator
Sweeney Gelt – deranged ex-king
Ronan Finn – Cleric
Sweeney's Men – Sweeney's retinue
The Eight Psalmists – Ronan's retinue
Congall's Gillie
Donald Mackay – King of Ireland
Columba – Gaelic saint
Angus McArdle – Kinsman of Sweeney
Congall McScanlon – King of Ulster
The Madmen of Ireland
The Flax Women
The Clerics of Cloonburren
Erin – Sweeney's estranged wife
Lynchehaun – Sweeney's half-brother
Hag of the Mill – Lynchehaun's mother-in-law
Mrs. McInerney – Steward's wife
The Great and Good of Dalnaria
Fing Shang Findalay – Wife of steward Forbes Forde-Daly
Allan – Scottish madman
The Voice
The Madwoman of Glenbalkan
The Women of Erin
Another Madman
God
The Five Heads – Hoodlums from the Fews
O'Cleary, the Clerk, Sexton and Altar-boy from Cape Clear
The Justmen of Alternan
Moling – Cleric

Enda McBracken – Church warden
Muriel – Mangan's wife
Moira – Mangan's sister
The Other Woman
Mangan – Moling's swineherd
Michael O'Cleary – Scribe
Daniel O'Duigenan – Scribe

[Unstable Narrator]

Faisnéis: I nDiaidh Fleá Dhún Gé

An lá sin i gCath Mhaigh Rath
I ndiaidh Fleá Dhún Gé,
Líonadh rí Dhál nAraidhe, Suibhne,
De ghinideacht is de ghráin,
D'fháinneáil is d'fholuain,
De bhuairt, d'uamhan is d'uafás
Nó nach raibh alt ar bith aige
Ó bhonn go baithis
Nach raibh ar crith nó faoi sceimhle.

Chreathnaigh a chosa, chlis a chroí
Agus a anam, líonadh é
Le mearbhall is le mearaí,
Luathadh doirse na héisteachta
Le gábh na gealtachta
Gur thug sé léim lúfar uaidh
Gur thug sé droim le daoine
Gur imigh sé leis ar foscadh
Le fianna is ar feis i bhfásaigh.

Pre-text: After the Fleadh in Dungay

At the Battle of Moira that day
After the Fleadh in Dungay,
Sweeney of Rasharkin
Was filled with madness and hatred,
With bewilderment and dread
So that there wasn't a bit
From the tip of him to the top
That wasn't shaking or in terror;

His legs trembled, his heart failed,
And his soul, he was filled with confusion
And craziness and he leaped up,
Turning his back on mankind,
Sheltering in the shadows with the Fenian deer
And sleeping in the wild at night.

[Sweeney]

M'aireaglán i dTuaim Inbhir

M'aireaglán i dTuaim Inbhir,
Níl aon áras chomh seasta leis –
Réaltaí agam de réir mo thola,
An ghrian is an ghealach ann.

An fear a rinne dom é Gobán
(A eachtra siúd go n-instear daoibh),
Mo chroíán an Fear Thuas i bhflaithiúnas
An tuíodóir a chuir díon air.

Teach ar nach dtiteann an fhearthainn,
Mar nach bhfuil eagla roimh na sleánna,
Teach gan scolb gan sonnach,
Soilseach mar a bheifeá i ngairdín.

Nam Aonar Dhomh am Bàrr Eidhne

M' àirigh ghlan an Tom an Inbhir,
Chan eil taigh làn cho seasmhach –
Rionnagan agam do mo rèir,
A' ghrian ris is a' ghealach.

An Goban Saor a rinn e dhomh
(An eachdraidh aige gun innsear dhuibh),

Mo chridhean, Dia air nèamh,
'S e 'n tughadair a chuir suaineadh air.

Taigh far nach bi 'n t-uisg' a' cur,
Far nach eil eagal ro na gathan,
'S e gun sgolb gun chliseach ann,
Soillseach mar gum b' eadh an gàrradh.

The Man Above

My neatclean plumpasturesummer-shieling in Tom an Inbhir, there's not a safetidefull uterusvesselmansionhouse as longstanding or ingenious as it, stars arranged for me at will, the seabottomsunland knowledge-exposed and the brightwhite turnipfrenzymoon. The Great Artificer, the son of the freemason made it for me (may his adventureshistory be told to you), my gallant dear heart little playboysuperman, the man above, the Thatcherist God in the kingdom of blissheaven put a ropetwistroof on it. A homehouse in which riverwaverainwater never putpourfalls after wanting for all that, where there's no fear of shredskinpromontorypointed spokeknotbarbsnubstingrayjavelins, with never a splinterskirmishpricklewattle or wattlewicketwall-work or a notchnickscallopscollop or palisade, as eyebright-clear as though you were in a cattle-stallcourtpalaceforthouse*lustgarten* without a dyke-mound.

[Unstable Narrator]

1

Dála Shuibhne Mhic Cholmáin Chuair, rí Dhál Araidhe, d'fhaisnéis muid romhainn (i gCath Mhaigh Rath) a dhul ar fáinneáil agus ar foluain i gcath, seo ann fachain is tucaid trína thángadar na hairíonna is na habairtí fualaing is foluana sin faoi siúd thar chách i gcoitinne is *to hell with that for a game of soldiers*. So that's some of the stories and of the goings-on of Sweeney, the son of MacColman from Corr, king of Dalnaria so far. *Finis*.

BULLY SWEENEY ON SHOW HERE!

1

Aboutlike the daily circumstances of Sweeney, the son of Coleman Corr, king of Dalaradia, we have already given a pre-account (in the Battle of Moira) of his going fannelflutterloitering and full-on floathovering in catbattalionbattle. Here is the fightingcrycause and motivereason that the plentydeservingnoble-personsymptoms and phrasetricks of frenzydistractionfooling and full-on floathovering came underabout him beyond the everyonerest in common and what battletravelmet with him west-thereafter.

2

There was a certain *cetera* ornery adornenthroneorderordained noble holypatronagepatronsaint-saint in the ruraldry-landstate of Ireland, viz. Ronan Finn McBerry of Dromiskin, Primate of All Ireland, (and with a long pedigree, including Creedons, Faircloughs, Macarkleys, McKernans, Crohans, Shaughnessys, McColum of Coole, Murrays and O'Learys, going back to the O'Neills and Niall of the Nine Hostages).

Aye, he was a fair man that fulfilled
The Daygod's swear-wordtestamentcommand
And kept the neck-of-land-narrow championsupportobligation
Of piety and propendured inbitegraspoppression
For the fearshadowprotectionsake of Coifi's co-god.

He was a deargenuinefaithful confirmedworthy bond-man for God
As he would pot-hookhangcrucify his corpsehulkbody
For God's charitylovedegree and earn recompense for his lifebreathsoul.

He was a wingshield of abodeprotection
Faceagainst evil grabattacks of the devil
And joylessvices, that finefamiliarfriendly
Fair-miened gentlegenial industrious man.

[Sweeney]

ag siúl i m'fhearann
is mo chríocha, go tobann
ceolán Rónáin Fhinn

walking in my land and territory suddenly Ronan's bell

3

One hostingjourneyflowtime, fact, he-it was roodmarking a cellchurchyard in Dalanaria, viz. conamed Killaloony, in the fifth province of Ulster.

[Ronan]

Stand

Christ the High King's my treasuregiftdarling
In non-skyheaven. Here in Oriel at Dromiskin
Between the cedars and elders, the Lagan and Fane,
Between the old pagan sacred and profane,
I've dedicated my secularworldlife to my flock of men
As their sublunary father,
Giving them, as I must, the Roman line
Predicated on the new searoadorder
Of not just agapeistic love
And devotion but geopolitical power.
Here where I've marked the border
On this hillquarryrock I'll build my round tower
For all the world like Apollo Eight or Nine
Or Sueno's Stone with masonry from Darver
And high crosses like bird stands,
The handiwork of a master woodcarver
But still if I could choose I'd rather
Stand alone here and not move an inch
For a common sparrow or starling,

A dunnock or a sillydwarfwren
A robin or aberdevinesiskin,
A nuthatch or speckledivy-bush-turtle-dove
Or yolkyyellowwhingoldennib-blackbird or bramble-finch
To alight on my stretched-out orant hand

[Unstable Narrator]

thall ag an teorainn,
gáir is dordán an daimh doinn
agus guth clogáin

over at the border the humming and cry of the brown stag and the sound of a bell

The king of Dalaradia at that time was, aye, the Sweeney, the son of Coleman, that we saidmentioned. Then Sweeney heard where he was the reproachvoice-sound of Ronan's blisterclockbell as he roodmarked the cellchurch-yard and asked his countrycommunityretinue whatwho it was they heard. 'Ronan Finn McBerry', they said 'that's beating the bounds and roodmarking his cellchurch-yard in your sovereign state endboundaryterritory and quarterland from Creagh Demesne to Farran, it's the reproachvoice-sound of his blisterclockbell that you're hearing now'. (It's clear from that that the holy saint didn't tip-catpermit Sweeney to try and establish the gizzardchurch in Aglish.)

[Sweeney's Men]

Guth

Sin an fear sin Rónán Finn
Le muintir Mhic Cholaim Chúile,
Mhic Criodáin, Mhic Mhuirí, Mhic Laoire, Mhic Néill

Nach bhfeiceann tú le súil de d'shúile
Ag teorainn chille thar a n-eol
I gCill Loinne, gan chonn gan chéill,

Is ní crónán, gáir ná ceol
Ná dordán an daimh doinn sa sruth
A chluintear i d'chríoch is i d'fhearann anois

Ná ceiliúr an loin den bhinn ach guth
A chloigín agus a cheoláin bhinn
Ó Shliabh Mis go Sliabh Mis.

Censurevoice-sound

There's that fair man Ronan Finn with his long pedigree that you don't see with your hope-eyes marking the boundaries of a cellchurch-yard beyond his ken in Killalooney, without a titter of wit, and it's not droning or a famecry or songmusic or the hum of the Jovelordwoodbrown championox-stag in the stream you hear in your endterritory and quarterland now or the farewellcelebrationwarble of the the elkouzel from the sweet gableregardpeak but the censurevoice-sound of his little clusterbell and his gableregardpeaksweet tinklingwhimpererbell from Slemish to Slieve Mish.

Civitas

An té Rónán Fionn ag an teorainn
I do chríoch is i d'fhearann,
Is é guth a chloig
A chluineann tú anois.

Is é a bhfeiceann tú tiarna
Nó rí ina *civitas*
Áit a raibh díthreabh
Lena chuid cléireach i mbun leabhar

Le do scéala is d'imeachtaí a scríobh
Agus le sliocht is lorg a fhágáil ar an tír
Ó Shliabh Mis go Sliabh gCuilinn go Cuailgne

Go Doire Cholm Cille go Binn Ghulbain go Sliabh Bladhma
Go Dún Sobhairce go hInis Muirígh go hInis Bó Finne
Agus faoi dheoidh Tobar na nGealt ag Tigh Moling.

Civitas

Your man Ronan Finn at the border in your endterritory and quarterland, it's the censurevoice-sound of his blisterclockbell you're hearing now. What you're seeing is a lord or a king in his *civitas* where there was a hermitagewilderness with all his altar-boyclerks at their books to write down your journey and narrative and leave a progenytracemark on the ruraldry-landstate from Slemish to Slieve Gullion to Cooley to Derry to Benbulben to the Slieve Blooms to Dunseverick to Inishmurray to Inisboffin and at last the Madman's Well at St. Mullin's.

[Sweeney]

Mo Bhunús

Maith dom as gach a ndearnas ort, a Eorann,
A ríon ós tú é, agus ort féin, a rí,
Nuair a nochtas i mo réim i gCill Loinne –

Ní raibh fúm ach go leagfainn síos claí teorann
Mar bhunús mo chríoch is m'fhearainn is mo thí
Le súil go seasfadh sé go brách na broinne.

My Almostmajoritywealthessencebasisorigin

Goodforgive me for all I did to you, Erin, queenquine, and to you, your majesty, when I nakedviewappeared in my swaycourse in Killalooney – all I wanted to do was knocklay a borderboundary fencewall as the almostmajoritywealthessenceoriginbasis of my endterritories and my quarterland and my househome in the eye-hope it would stand until the crack of doom.

[Unstable Narrator]

Your man Sweeney was boastgreatly hauntangered and he gotupwent impatientfastfuriously to eject the altar-boycleric from the cellchurch-yard. His wifewomanpartner, Erin, one of the McQueens/Quinns from Keenaght, diffibulates the featherwing or bannerend of Corkery's purple-lilacbordered curtainmantle which was around him, hiretrapping him, so that the moneysilver buckle or broochspinespike all brightwhite and finely put together in gold in the curtainmantle round his wombbelly escapebouncefly-upsprung underaround the house-holdhouse. With that he failingbequestleaves his curtainmantle with the queenlady, he became barenaked in his racerun to put out the altar-boycleric from the cellchurch-yard until he reached a place where Ronin was.

4

[Ronan Finn and the Eight Psalmists]

Ranna Rónáin

♪♪

Molaim an rí is a mháthair mhín
Gach lá ó mhaidin go moch
I rann de chuid Leabhar Chaoimhín
Sa mboth taobh leis an loch,

Amuigh sa raon is thíos faoin ngleann,
Sa gcoill chiar, sa trá
Is go hard i mullach na mbeann
Go molaim an rí gach lá.

Ronan's Partitionverses

I mollypraise the king and his meangentle mother every day from dawn to dusk in a partitionverse right out of St Kevin's Psalter in the booth-hut beside the fiordlough, out on the range and down in the smoke-cloudhollowglen, in the waxdark castrationdesecrationwood and up on the rooftop of the gableregardhornpeaks.

[Unstable Narrator]

It phantom-markhappened that the altar-boycleric was in headendfront of Sweeney that time mollyjudgepraising the highking of non-skyheaven and dry-landsurface-earth, viz. flamelightbright solaceclear-reciting his psalms and his tidefull lovely linenlined tramplepsalter in witnesspresence before him. Sweeney got hold of the tramplepsalter and sound-condemnthrew it into the underworld infradepths of the phlegmale-cold pondlake that was beside him and it sympathybay-quenchdrowned in it. Sweeney got hold of Ronan's hand westafter that and drewpulled him for all that after him outpast the cellchurch-yard and didn't let go of the altar-boycleric's hand from him forby till he heard a bah!complaintcry. The one who made the bah!complaintcry was aye viz. the gillieboy belonging to squint-eyed Congall McScanlon from Clane, king of Ulster, who holdcame from Congall himself for Sweeney to snow-fall-burywage catbattalionbattle at Moira. Fromsincewhen the gillieboy reached the place of multicolloquy with Sweeney he tells him the storynews from choiceforwardbeginning to laststernend. Sweeney goes with the gillieboy and perishleaves the churchman in darkmelancholy and blackafflicted after the sympathybayquench- drowning of his tramplepsalter and the contempt and hardshipindignity done to him.

[Ronan]

Dobrón

Ní raibh mé ach ag moladh
Rí neimhe agus talún
Agus ag gabháil na rann
As mo leabhar álainn
Go ndearna an té Suibhne a dhiúracadh
Agus a theilgean uaidh
Agus a bhá i ndomhain faoin loch
Agus mo tharraingt ina dhiaidh
Gan mo lámh a ligean as a láimh
Le mo chur thar an gcill amach
Gur fágadh mé mar chléireach

Go dubhach dobrónach
Ina fhianaise ag éamh
Le heasonóir is dímhigin.

Blackaffliction

All I was doing was mollyjudgepraising the king of non-skyheaven and dry-landsurface-earth and recitegoing partitionverses out of my lovely book when your man brandishcast and soundcondemnthrew it and it swathstripsympathybayquenchdrowned in the depths of the fjordlough and then drawpulls me for all that after him without letting go of my hand in his hand to put me out of the cellchurchyard and I'm left there as an altar-boysextonclerk darkmelancholy and blackafflicted in his witness-presence bah!crycomplaining for the contempt and hardshipindignity.

[Unstable Narrator]
5

An Clèireach agus an Dòbhran

An dèidh là 's oidhche,
Thàinig dòbhran a bha san loch
Nam fhianais agus breac bàn
Agus mo shaltair leis gun mhilleadh
Loinne no litreach innte,
Lìneach, làn, àlainn.

Agus thug mi altachadh-buidhe
Don dòbhran gun choire
Trìd na mìorbhaile sin
Agus an dèidh sin mo ghuidhe
'S mo mhallachd air Suibhne
'S mo bheannochd air Èirinn.

At the end of a psalmday and a night backwest after that a Dover-hound waterotter that was in the pondlake came to Ronan with his tramplepsalter without a linenline or letter contraryruined in it. Ronan gavetanboy thanks to the Daygod for that miracle and cursed Sweeney then, saying:

[Ronan]

My Will

My will with the will of Coifi's powerful co-god,
As he came barenaked to put me out,
That he shall be likewise forever skyclad
Fannelflutterloitering and full-on floathovering throughout the world
And that death by a last-wordplanetpoint of a spear
Bears him off to Ring or Ringsend in the end.

My curse attend Sweeney again and my blessing on Erin
Who trywent to hiretrap him and stillagain
I failingleave for Coleman's clanchildrenfamily
The day that they see this tramplepsalter
That was sympathybayquenchdrowned by Sweeney
That destruction-need and extinction is their lot.

[Unstable Narrator]

And he recitesang the Leerudderexhortationlay:

[Ronan]

An Breac Bán

I m'fhianaise, nach dubhach, an breac bán,
Cathach álainn Chaoimhín
A choimeád mo laoch, an fear mín,
An cléireach cráifeach ina lá
Is é ag gabháil a shalm is ag léamh

Á theilgean i ndomhain sa loch
Idir an choill chiar
Agus an chill agus á bhá,
Gníomh nach suairc
Oíche dhubh dhorcha dhuairc.

Agus ina dhiaidh sin aniar
Á thabhairt ar ais ag dobhrán
Ar maidin go moch
I ndiaidh lae is oíche is ag filleadh
I bhfianaise cách gan mhilleadh

Gur chualathas ar fud an raoin
Gáir mhór agus éamh
A rinne giolla Chongail Chlaoin:
Fág Cill Loinne liom atha,
Tar go Maigh Rath chun an chatha.

The Fallowblank Speckledtroutcopybook

In my witnesspresence, the fallowblank speckledtroutcopybook, St. Kevin of Glendalough's lovely temptingsorrowfulbattle-reliquaryCathach which my layhero, the gentlepious altar-boycleric used to guardkeep in his day as he recited his psalms and read being lastingthrown in the depths of the lough bothbetween the waxdark Kalendsdesecrationwood and the cellchurch-yard and sympathybaydrowned – evil deed! – on a black dark night. And back wanting after that for all that being brought back by a dim-witotter early in the morning after a day and a night and foldreturning in the witnesspresence of everymanChristbody without oppositedamage and then a bah!cry and fameshout were heard all over the routrange that the gillieboy of Conall from Clane made: *Leave the church at Killalooney with me for a while, come to Moira to the battalionbattle.*

[Congall's Gillie]

Èigh

♪♪

Tar don chath, tar don chath
Gun caill thu do chiall 's do chonn,
Go gclaochlóidh tú deilbh is dath
Ann an craobh droighinn dhonn

Is gun tèid thu às do riochd
Trí gháir mhór an tslua
Le mallachd air do shliochd
Ó Shliabh Mis go Sliabh gCua,

Ag teitheadh romhat sa ród
Na do ruith theann
Gan troigh a chur ar fhód
Le sneachda cruaidh nad cheann

Nó coicís ar mhí san iúr
Gan chodladh sámh gan suan
Gan sos gan tionnúr
Ó Loch Léin go Loch Cuan

Go bhfaighidh tú bás de rinn
Le gath tro do chneas
Trí bhriathra Rónáin Fhinn
Aig Taigh Moling aig deas.

A Tingling Cry in the Ear Portending News of Death

Comereturn to the battalionbattle, comereturn to the battalionbattle and misslose your darlingdeathsenses and bodyreason and change warpshape and colour in a dunbrown lumberblackthorn cloudrelationtreebranch and go out of ghostplaceairhueform through the armyhostcrowd's famecry and a curse on your tracktrooptribedescendents from Slemish to the Knockmealdowns, shunfleeing on the road, running close, never putting a foot on a sodstripspot with a hard snow headendagainst you, and in the roofsummit of a yew tree without stuporslumber or snooze-sleep from the Lakes of Killarney to Strangford Lough until you die by the last-wordplanetpoint of a spear with a dartraybeardsnubspokesting through your neckbreastwaistskinbody through the words of Ronan Finn in St. Mullin's in the rightreadysouth.

[Ronan]

6

Mo Bheannacht is Mo Mhallachd

Suibhne Mac Colmáin gam chràdh,
Tharraing e mi ar leith de láimh
Gus Cille Luinne fhágáil leis
Gus a bhith atha ina héagmais.

Thàinig e thugam ina rith grod
Nuair a chuala sé mo chlog,
Thug sé leis fearg aibhseach
Gam chur a-mach, dom ionnarbadh.

Ba leasc liom mo chur a-bhos
Bhon chiad bhall ina rabhas,
Ged gur leamsa ba leasc,
Do Dhia tháinig a thoirmeasg.

Cha do leig e mo làmh as a láimh
Gus an cuala e an t-éamh
'S gun abradh ris: 'Tar don chath,
Shroich Dòmhnall Magh Rath'.

Chaidh math domsa de,
Ní ris a rugas buidhe,

Nuair a shroich fios mun chath
Esan a dhol leis an bhflaith.

D'ionsaigh sé 'n cath bho chèin
Dar chlaon a chiall is a chonn,
Siridh e Èirinn ina gheilt ghlas
Agus de rinn gheibh e bàs.

Mo shaltair ghabh e na làimh,
Dhiúraic sé í fon linne làin,
Thug Críost thugam e gan choir
Is cha bu mhiste 'n saltair.

Là gus oidhche faoin loch lán
Is cha bu mhiste 'n breac bán,
Dòbhran de dheòin Mhic Dé,
Thug e thugam arís é.

An tsaltair a ghabh e na làimh,
Fàgaidh mi sin ag Clann Cholmáin,
Gheibh Clann Cholmáin olc
An lá a chífidh siad an saltair.

Tháinig sé anseo lom nochd
Gam chràdh is dom thafann,
Is e a nì Dia de
Bidh Suibhne lom nochd de shíor.

Ghabh ga fhastadh a bhrat,
Èirinn iníon Choinn Chiannacht,
Mo bheannachd ar Éirinn
Is mo mhallacht air Suibhne.

My Blessing and My Curse

Sweeney's paintormenting me, he pulled me to one side by the hand to leave Killaooney with him and be missingaway from it a long time. He came to me in a mad rush when he heard my blisterbell, he was angry, he surrenderexpelled and banished me. I didn't want to be put out from the place where I was first and so God saw to it to prevent that. He didn't let go of my hand from his hand until he heard the bah!cry saying to him 'Come to catbattalionbattle, Donald has reached Moira'. Good became of it for me, no yellowthanks to him, when word arrived of the catbattalionbattle and that he was to go with the high prince. He attackapproached the theatre of war from afar in which he lost his wits, he'll seekwander Ireland as a green fool and die by the point of a spear. He took my tramplepsalter in hand, he threw it into the tidefull generationpond, Christ brought it back to me without a blemish and the psalter was none the worse for it. A day and a night under the tidefull loch and the copybook like a white trout was none the worse for it, by God's will a dim-witotter brought it back to me. The psalter which he took in his hand, I'll leave that with Sweeney's Klanchildren, they'll see the evil day the day they see the psalter. He came here stark naked tormenting and harassing me, God will see to it that Sweeney is stark naked forever. She tried to hold him in his bratcloak, Erin daughter of Quinn of Keenaght, my blessing on Erin and my curse on Sweeney.

[Columba]

An Fháistine

An lá sin a gcuirfear an cath claon
Go bhfágfar tusa le Congal faon
Folamh fann ar an má seo mar aon
Is ar an maighean ar chlaíomh ghlas beidh braon.

Claochlóidh do chéadfaí, creathnóidh do bhaill,
Seachnóidh tú daoine, feoil agus saill,
Gheofar thú ag an gcailleach ar faill
I do dhamh ina dhíthreabh ar aill.

Meirbhleoidh do mhéara, cobhsóidh do chéim
Is i do raon maidhme is i do réim
Reatha baoise go mbéarfar ort béim
Ina bhuille díleann ina léim.

[Unstable Narrator]

7

Ronan went backwestafter that to Moira to engage in the peace process between Donald MacKay (Hanberry) from Dungay, viz. king of Ireland, and squint-eyed Congall McScanlon from Clane, king of Ulster, but he couldn't peacify them so there was no deal. The altar-boycleric would be brought however as a frith-and-grith patronagesecurity between them every layday so that not one apparitionperson would be deadkilled from the hourtime the temptationlonging catbattalionbattling would be mischiefstopped to when they were tip-catpermitted again. But Sweeney would temerate the securityprotection of Ronan the go-between otter-boycleric and exceeded his handpart before rising meal-time every day for every fairyforgivenesspeace and relieftruce-eirenicon that Ronan would make, he would deadkill a man before the mealtime of the fight every layday and another man at the final rock-pinnacle-slashcessation every noonevening. On the day it was stepsurpassdeter-mined to givedo boastgreat catbattalionbattle royal, Sweeney came into the theatre of war ahead of all the others.

8

Regaelia

He was decorated like this: a filmy tullesilk albshirt
Next to his brightwhite handsomebodyskin
And a royal ruched satin loinkilt around it

Congall had made for a sovereign and gave him at the battle
Of Moira that day for overthrowing the army
Of L. L. Phelan, Olav of Keady,
And a lilacpurple innertuniclayer
Coloured with warpclose stripselvage well plaitwoven
With delightbeautiful findrinny gold goldburnished
In layers of dearsmooth gemstones of carbunclescabmesh-husk
From one headend of that stripselvage to the other
With arcbillowloops of silkvelveteen over
Smoothshining studbeadbuttons to rallydamclose
And open it and a glebecuttingtroutspeckling
Variegation of all whitebright moneysilver
Everywhichway and every havenjourneywaypass
He went and a needlenarrow spearpointhard
On that innerlayertunic, two exceedingly long
Broadflatsurfaced splinterspears in his hands,
A speckledtroutpoxyellow buffalohornbugle
Corniculated wingshield on his topvineback
And a fistgolden glaivesword on his left chestside.

[Ronan]

Gan Folach

Ón mbrat cortharach corcra
Le dealg airgid nó sioball
Eagartha mín,
Ó léine shreabhnaí shíoda
Le taobh do chnis ghil
Agus fuathróg de shról rí,
Ón ionar le ciumhais dhlúth
Fite d'ór álainn le sraith
Mogall ó cheann go ceann
Le lúba thar na cnaipí
Le breacadh geal airgid
Is rinn chrua snáthaide

Le cumhdach caol glan
Go clúmh ar do cholainn
Nó gan chlúmh i gcoill
I gceirt na caillí gan chonn
Is gur lom í snáth do cheirte,
Gan éadach is gan bhróg,
Gan leann is gan chochlán
Gan folach féin ort
Ó bhonn go baithis
Ó do chúl go do dhá chos,
Ó rí go gealtán
Ó m'ionad aréir i Ros Earcáin
Go m'ionad anocht i dTigh Moling
Is go dté tú mar aon fheithid
Ar foluain agus ar fáinneáil
Le síon is le sneachta go nocht
Ar fud Éireann is an domhain.

Without a Hidingsack

From Corkery's fringed purple curtaincloak with a fine silver ornamentarranged spinespikebrooch or sybilfibula, from Sheedy's finefilmy silk shirt against your brightwhite sideskin and a girdle of satin for a king, from the innerlayertunic with a warptight stripedge woven in gold with a spreadstretchswath of shellmeshes from headend to headend with hasphooploops over the buttonstuds troutpocked with brightwhite argentum and a hard needlepoint with a kylethin pureclear shrinecovering to foliagefeatherfurhair on your trunkpersonbody or without foliagefeatherfurhair in the castrationwood in the hussyhaglad's threadbare apple-treerags, without clothclothes or brogueshoes, without a beermantle or Coughlan's hoodcloaklet, without as much as a hidingsack on you from head to toe, from king to lunatic from my place last night in Rasharkin to my place tonight in St Mullin's and may you go off like any serpentinsectbeast, fannelfluttering and full-onflitting appearingnaked in the snow all over Ireland and through the universe.

[Unstable Narrator]

9

He went on and came before him in that proceedgaitmanner and haulgarnerhappened on Ronan and eight psalmreciters of his countrypeoplecommunity beside him shakesprinkling churchconsecrated rainurinetearswater on the fairyarmycrowds and they shakesprinkled on Sweeney in the same form, no matter, as every other Christperson. As he thought that they were casting aspersions on him, he gambolkickthrew his branchfinger in the amentum of the riveted splinterspear that was in his hand and dartshot a psalmreciter of the men of Ronan and deadkilled him with that one shot. He gambolkickthrew the second tanist shot of the keenedged sharpangled shortdashdart at the altar-boycleric himself and foraminated the blisterclockbell that was on the face of his lapchest and the penistreevaultshaft of it escapebounceflyupsprang out of it uphigh in the air and the saved-by-the-bell altar-boycleric said: 'I pray to powerful Coifi's co-god' he said 'the co-height that the penistreevaultshaft of the shortdashshot went in the air and the trancenebulae of non-skyheaven that you go in paniclunacy like every tinywildserpentinsectbeast and may the death that you inflicted on my dearnovicefosteracolytestudent be what you get in the end, viz. death by the last-wordplanetpoint of a spear off Ring or Ringsend and my curse on you and my blessing on Erin and I invoke Oran and Telly for me faceagainst your seedrace and the clanchildren of Coleman Corr', and he said the Leerudderexhortationlay:

[First Cleric]

Gabháil na Salm

Ní ag fochaid ort a bhí mé
Ach ag croitheadh uisce coisreactha ar an slua
Ó Shliabh gCuillinn go Sliabh gCua
Nuair a dhiúraic tú orm sleá
Gur maraíodh mé d'aon urchar ar an má
Agus ag gabháil na salm mar is cóir

As leabhar álainn Chaoimhín, a Dhia mhóir
I néalta neimhe, is ag moladh Dé.

The Psalms

I wasn't mocking you but shakesprinkling holy water on the armycrowd from Slieve Gullion to Slieve Mish when you brandish threw a splinter-spear and I was deadkilled by a single shot on the mazeplain and gosinging the psalms as is proper from Kevin's lovely book, great God, in the trancenebulae of non-skyheaven, and and mollypraising the daygod.

[Ronan]

10

Cionta

Mo mhallachd air Suibhne,
Rium is mòr a chionta,
Shàth e gath na sleagh' aige
Tro mo chaolach-aifrinn.

An clag sin a rinn thu a ghonadh,
Cuiridh e thu ri craobhan
Gus am bi thu mar-aon ris na h-eòin,
An clag naomh ro naoimh.

Mar a chaidh 'n craosach
Air an uair an-àirde,
Gun tèid thu fhèin, a Shuibhne,
Ri gealtachd gun chàirdean.

Ghoin thu mo dhalta,
Dhearg thu do ghath na bhroinn,
Bidh agad mar chumha dheth
Dol bàs de rinn.

Mas e 's gun tig rium fhìn
Sìol Eòghainn an teinne,
Thèid an cur an cranndaidheacd
Le Òdhran 's an tè eile.

Òdhran 's an tè eile,
Chuir iad an cranndaidheacd iad,
'S e mo ghuidhe tron t-sìorraidheachd,
'S leatsa mo mhallachd.

Beannachd bhuam air Èirinn,
Èirinn chaomh gun charachd,
Gun donas is gun duilghe
'S air Suibhne mo mhallachd.

Transgressionguiltblame

Curses on Sweeney, he's guiltblametransgressed me greatly, he thrust the dartshaft of his spear through my mass-bell. That clackbell you lanceblasted will send you among the treebranches till you're one with the birds, the saintholy holysaint clackbell saintholy to holysaints. As the dartshaft went straight up, so may you, Sweeney, go in cowardskittishness without friends or relations. You've wounded my disciplechild, you woundreddened your dartshaft inside his breast, your lamentreward for this will be death by the planetpoint of a spear. If I should be opposed by Clan MacEwan, they'll be exposed to the severewithering blast by Oran and the other woman. Oran and the other woman have put them out in the coldwithering blast, my cursewish through eternity is to curse you. I bless Erin, dear Erin without wrestledeceitfulness or devilbadness etc. and on Sweeney my curse.

Curse

My curse upon Sweeney,
He has transgressed me greatly,
He thrust his smooth dart
That made my sanctus bell fall apart.

That holy bell you pierced
Will send you raging mad
In the heather and branches of the wood,
One among the birds of the air.

Just as the javelin-shaft went
Like that up into the firmament,
May you go insane in the wild, Sweeney,
Without respite, without human company.

You wounded my dear disciple and foster-child,
Your javelin has left him red,
May you have as your reward
Death by the point of a spear.

★

God bless Erin I say,
Dear Erin whose beauty will never decay
And curse Sweeney
Throughout all eternity.

Dán Doiligh

Mo mhallacht ar Shuibhne,
Chuir sé ó chion mé go mór
Nuair a thug sé fogha
Le ruibhne buile faoi mo chloigín.

An clog caoin a rinne tú a ghoin
Is ba naofa ná na naoimh,
Cuirfidh sé mar a dhéanfadh dlaoi fulla
Le craobhacha thú ag Snámh dhá Éan.

Mar a chuaigh ar dtús báire
Crann an fhogha in airde,
Go dtite sé ar do chrann, a Shuibhne,
Tú imeacht ar gealtacht gan chairde.

D'imir tú an bás ar mo dhalta,
Dhearg tú é d'aon fhogha,
Is éard is dán duit féin dá bharr
Dul i gcré de rinn, a chrandacháin.

Má thagann ann i mo choinne,
Sliocht Eoghain úd na gaile,
Is iad Uarán agus an té eile
A sciúrsfaidh iad uile.

Beannacht uaim ar Erin,
A bhean dhil de shliocht Uí Chaoimh
Agus go deo na díleann,
Gan bhláth gan bhiseach ar Shuibhne.

A Distressfulhard Dawnfategiftpoem

My curse on Sweeney, he-it loveshareoffencedestroyed me the hourtime he javelindashattacked my little clusterclockbell in a javelintroopray frenzy. The gentlekeencry blisterclockbell you wool-wastedeathwanestabbed which was saintholier than the holysaints will burysend you like a delusionmadness thatchnoosewisp into the branchtrees as a nakedwood-grazingbattle-fugitivebirdbeastpaniclunatic at Swim-Two-Birds. As the tall handleshaft of the splinterjavelin rose up at the start of contestplay to the penistreeshaftvaults of non-skyheaven, may it befall you as your treelot, Sweeney, to go and become a nakedwood-grazingbattle-fugitivebird-beastpaniclunatic without fast friends without respite. You played death with my darlingdalitnovicefosterstudent, you bare-redwounded him in a javelindashattack, your dawnpoemgiftfate is to claydie at last-wordplanetweapon-point off Ring or Ringsend, you witherling. If anyone there from the warfitvapour Clan MacEwen should stand faceagainst me, Oran and the other one will flog them. God bless Erin, dear wifewoman of the passagetraceline of O'Keefe and until the inexhaustible chattelDeluge comes, no blossomprospering for Smashall Sweeney.

[First Cleric]

Cléireach Gan Ainm

Chroith mé clog is uisce coisricthe,
Ghabh mé mo chuid salm
I bhfarradh mo mhuintire
Gur tugadh fogha fúm
Le faobhar i bhfianaise an tslua
Nó gur scinn m'anam in airde
San aer d'urchar neimhe.

Ach mairfidh mé más marbh
Fós i gcuimhne mar dhalta
Do shíol mo chlainne
Nó fós mar an cléireach
Gan ainm de chuid Rónáin
Ar tharla dó gur tháinig ar a chrann
Gur tharraing sé buile Shuibhne.

Anonymous Sextonaltar-boycleric

I wavesprinkleshook a blisterclockbell and rainurinetearswater and sang my psalms along with my communitypeople until I was rushrundart-dashattacked in witnesspresence of the fairyarmycrowd with sword-pointzeal and my lifebreathsoul springflew up in the air like a bolt. But I'll live on though I'm dead still in memory as a petpupilfoster-child-darling to my clanfamily's seed-descendants and again as the anonymous sextonaltar-boycleric belonging to Ronan to whom it garnerhappened that it fell on his penisvaultshaft-treelot that he brought about Sweeney's supernaturalrevelationpoetry-inspiringfrenzy.

[Unstable Narrator]

11

Cathanna

Ó chuala Suibhne na cathanna
Agus na trí gártha móra
Agus a bhfuaimeanna
Is a bhfreagraí i néalta neimhe,
D'fhéach sé suas in airde
I bhfraitheacha na firmiminte
Go ndeachaigh sé sna glinnte
Amhail gach feithid aerga.

Soldier's Heart

Sincewhen the catbattlebattalions on everyboth sides encounterfought
They oncethmuslowroared like a vast
Dowryherd of championox-stags back and forth
And pummellpounded three heavy hakashouts on high.
Fromsincewhen Sweeney heard those boastgreat cries
And their sounds and outcropreverberations in the trancenebulae
Of non-skyheaven and in the welkinrafter
Of the firmament he trylooked up in the hallucinationspheresky
And was filled with nementonwar-goddesstormentilbattle-fury
And dourobnubilation and suddenviolent madness
And flutterloitering and floathovering and fumblerestlessness
And double unsteadyrestlessness and strifemalice for every place
Where he used be and *Sehnsucht* for everywhere he hadn't reached.
His branchfingers were deadened, his legfeet trembled,
His heart quickened, his bodily senses and perceptions
Were cleave-subdued, he lost the power of vision,
His arms fell skyclad from his hands
And he *verda-at-gjaltied* with the wordcurses of Ronan
In double woodpanicmadness and goblinlikeness
Like any tinywildserpentinsectbeast of the air.

Ronan's Curse
(*Après* Thanos Didaskalou)

After his sense of foreboding, Sweeney has an apoplectic event:
He loses his balance and suffers a collapse.
He experiences extensor hypertonia,
Then a brief cardiac arrhythmia.
His senses are overcome.

He suffers ophthalmoplegia, then hypotonus
As his weapons fall naked from his hands.
He undergoes depersonalisation
With a possible out of body experience
And an altered appreciation of body image.

There is evidence of depressive reaction, fugue, social isolation and drift.
He has a suspicious interpretation of offers of assistance
But preserves intellect and memory
And affective warmth and partial insight into his condition.
He has panic feelings and a persistent disorder
Of a disturbed body schema and image.
There is a brief episode of emotional hallucination,
Third person auditory, tactile (probably) and visual.
There is evidence of peculiar behaviour.

The course becomes chronic despite the occasional remission.
He feels strange and unreal.
His body feels as if it were too light, as if it could fly
Like any bird of the air and perch in the tree-tops
As *spiritualizatio agilitas* or *subtilitas*.

He has suffered severe sensory deprivation and change.
He sees his face distorted. His own voice seems strange.

[Sweeney]

Bua Shuibhne

Sa gcath cé gur chrith mo chosa,
Gur luathaigh mo chroí, gur mheirbhligh mo mhéara
Nó go ndeachaigh mé sna néalta,
Rug mé i ndiaidh sin an bua
Le gach ar fhág mé de scéalta
Agus d'imeachtaí agus de laoithe
I mo dhiaidh mar a bhí i mo dhán,
I m'*homo viator*, i m'Shuibhne sirtheachán
Is mar mo chuid na dearcáin is na sméara,
Gan chodladh gan cheol ach osna gaoithe
Thar gleann ar mo *via dolorosa*
Ó Shliabh Eachtaí go Sliabh gCua.

Sweeney's Destinyvirtuevictorygift

In the battalionbattle though my legfeet trembled, my heart quickened, my branchfingers deadened and I went off in trancenebulae, I gained destinyvirtuegiftvictory for all that with all the stories and goings-on and Leerudderlays that I left after me as was my dawnpoemfate as a *homo viator* and as Sweeney the wee travelseeker with thistlecavityacorns and blackberries for my lot, without sleep or songmusic but the sighing of the estuarywind across the hollowglens on my *via dolorosa* from Slieve Aughty to the Knockmealdowns.

[Sweeney]

Machaire

Ag machaire Mhaigh Rath
Mar ar cuireadh an cath mór
Inar tuairgeadh mo mhuintir,
Airím uaim ceiliúr an loin,
Búir na ndamh is donáil na gcon
Is leadradh na mac tíre

Seachas méileach is meigeallach
Cléireach is mac léinn is daoine.

Battlefield

At the battlefield of Moira where the great battalionbattle was fought when my people were hammerpummelled, I missfeelhear the farewell-celebrationwarbling of the ouzelelk, the howling of the hounds and rending of the landsonwolves and not the bleating of clerics and students and manpeople.

[Unstable Narrator]

aig Magh rath sa bhlàr,
an lèine-sròil 's am brat-òir
aig Suibhne fon ùir

at Moira in the field Sweeney's silk shirt and golden cloak under the ground

sa má mar ar thit
na laochra maidin Dé Máirt
caoga bó ag geilt

in the plain where the heroes fell on Tuesday morning fifty cows grazing

12

Tadhall

Ansin i ndiaidh dó teitheadh
As an gcath amach
Níor mhinic dá chois
An lár a thadhall ar luas
A réime is an t-am a thadhladh féin
Ní bhainfeadh drúcht d'uachtar an fhéir
Ar éadrom is ar aeracht a chéime.

Níor fhan sé den réim reatha sin
Nár fhág sé machaire ná maoil sléibhe
Ná móin ná muine ná mothar,
Cnoc ná cabhán ná coill
Chluthar dhlúth in Éirinn gan taisteal
An lá sin gur ráinigh Ros Earcáin
Go ndeachaigh san iúr sa ngleann.

Then when he came out of catbattalionbattle, his legfeet veryunoften transientvisit-touched the dry-landearth and the centreground for the Luas-like earlyspeed of his runningsway and when he did transientvisit-touch it he wouldn't remove the dewdrops from the cropcreamhin-drancetop of the haygrass in Barroughter for the lightness and airiness of the rabbetravinehiketrackstep he'd surpass-step. He didn't stintstop on that headlong runningsway and didn't fail-leave a pithplain from the Moy to the Maze or linksbattle-field in Maghera or mamelon in Moyle or Jovemoormountain in Moolieve or turfbog in Moor or Jovecover-thicket in Muineagh or blunder-busscloudclusterclumpswampthicket-tanglejungle in Moher, a hill in Knock and Knockan and Knickeen or a maimcavity in Cavan and Navan or dargle and dingle in Dingle and Dargle, a wold in Oldbawn or a knob or knoll in Nobber or Naul and knowe in Knowth and Dowth and Howth or a secretivewarmwarp-solid Kalendscastrationwood in the Irelandworld unhackletravelled that day[1] till he came to in Rossberry in Glendarken and went into a yewtree that was in the smoke-cloudhollowglen.

[1] **Gluais an Chléirigh, 1629:** Agus chaith sé aois is a aimsir ar gealtacht / In Éirinn agus i mBreatain i gcéin / Gur mhair gan fortacht gan fóirithint / Gan taobh a thabhairt le duine /Amhail a dhearbhaíonn an leabhar a scríobhtar air féin / Darb ainm *Buile Shuibhne*.

Gluais a' Chlìrich, 1629: Agus chaith e aois is aimsir air ghealtachd / Ann an Èirinn 's ann am Breatainn an cèin / 'S gun do mhair e gun fhòirinn gun fhurtachd / Gun taobh a thoirt ri daoine / Amhail a dhearbhas an leabhar a sgrìobhar air fhèin / Dham b' ainm *Boile Shuibhne*.

(**O'Cleary's Clerical Gloss, 1629**: And he hankercompulsionthrowspent his agetime and weathertime in pan-iclunacy in Ireland and in Britain faroff and lived without help or healing, without trustsiding with menpeople (as is confirmed by the book written about himself reputation-named *Sweeney's Supernatural Poetry-inspiring Rev-elationvisionfrenzy*.)

13

The turfwar was won by Donal Magee that day *amhail a dúramar agus a d'fhaisnéis muid romhainn*. There was yea verily a male clown relative-in-law of Sweeney's in the catbattalionbattle, viz. Aeneas McArdle of the northcountryfarmpeople the MacNees or McNeeneys in Dalaradia. He came in defeateruption rangerouteflight out of catbattalionbattle with a band of his house-holdcountrypeople with him via a havenjourneyway-pass in Glendarken. He and his house-holdcountrypeople were famediscussing Sweeney and were saying it was most strange that he wasn't to be seen quickalive or numbdead since the catbattalionbattle was encounterfought but still they were sure that it was because he was bell-shocked by Ronan's swearcurse that there was no fortuneknowledge of his violentdeathtragedyfate. Sweeney heard what they chantsingsaid in the Newry yew above them and said this piteous *lai*:

[Sweeney]

Ototototoi

Here I am in the Mourne Mountains, a wood-kern
Without a mantle or tunic, my clothes torn,
Without a spear or sword, without a brother,
Without a serving-man, running away
From the summit of one hill to another
And on rough ground up in the wild country.

But do you remember the time, Aeneas
And his men, when we were the king and polis
With so vast and great a company then,
Ten thousand foot and three times fifty horse
And the horsemen following me throughout
And fifty chattel helots guarding my flank

And I myself was the supreme hypatos
And in my hands were two riveted spears,
Black, sharp, shod with broad iron and at my side

A gleaming tusk-hilted sword and on my back
A yellow mottled horn shield and how we fought
On level ground that Tuesday at Moirathon?

[Angus McArdle and Band]

Ré

♪♪

Tháinig sinn go luath
As an gcath mór claon
A d'fhág sinn gan tuath
Gan fine sa raon

Is inár raon madhma,
Cuid go dtí Maigh Lí,
Cuid go Sliabh Bladhma
Is cuid go Loch Rí,

Sinn ag gabháil na rann
Go hard inár dtriúr,
Sinn féin mar bhuíon sa ngleann
Is é féin san iúr.

Ní ceird geilte bheith sáil.
Rith leat, as ucht Dé,
Le damh rua Mhaigh Fáil
Thairis ar an ré.

Nach orainn a bhí an rath
Nár thug tú an lá
I ndiaidh sin sa gcath
A cuireadh sa má.

[Angus McArdle]
Plainmoonera

We came fastsoonout of the great battalionbattle which left us without kith or kin on the plain, routed, some of us to Moylee, some to the Slieve Blooms and some to Lough Ree, singing our partitionverses uphighloud all three, ourselves with our band in the smoke-cloudhollowglen and your man in the yew. Weren't we the lucky ones that you didn't win the dayofbattalionbattle in Moira on the battlefield. It's not a panicwoodlunatic's business to be heelcosy. Run, in the name of God, with the red ox-stag of Moyfail across the mooneraplain.

[Angus McArdle]

Canadh

Chuala sinn canadh san iúr os ár gcionn
Agus ceiliúr an loin den bhinn,
Crónán is gáir an daimh doinn
Is cúichearán an bhéiceadáin bhinn,
An chuach a dhéanann cuach Bhanna,
Slua an tí ag coirm leanna,
Guth feadóige is téada crot dá míne
Is níl ceol ar talamh níos binne.

Chantsingcalltalking

We heard chantsingcalltalking in the yew above us and the farewellcelebrationwarbling of the elkouzel from the regardpeak, the humming and crycall of the Jovelordwoodbrown championox-stag and the croodleruckling of the gluttonbrawler, the tuftembracequaichbundlefalsetto cuckoo of the tuftembracequaichbundlefalsettocuckoo of the Bann, the house crowd at a beerfest, the censurevoice of the whistleplover and the strings of humpharps however smallsmooth and there's no peaksweeter songmusic on earth.

[Sweeney]

ag gabháil rann i mbile
mar iarsma mo mhuintire
os cionn tobar na cille

singing verses in a tree as the last of my line above the churchyard well

14

Ogie

Ah, Ogie! jiggy a lay!
Ah, Errigal! are ye?
Fuck Havey is in villa I will,
Unfair for settee eeri e.
Duh! Y'oney! she a goose, a son,
Better I'm not him, coon!

Gone Cole is, gone Colla same,
Gone Banchory, gone band all.
Miss so soon egg, Rosemary?
Dumb red rowan on foe vole.
Rooms cardiac ray, not roe.
Scary rave owl! Ah, ogre!

Mo Dhealbh

Tagaigí i leith, òganachaibh,
Ó guerreiros, venham para cá,
A fhearaibh Dhail Àirigh,
'S ann a gheibh sibh anseo sa chraoibh
Vós encontrareis na árvore na qual está
An fear a tha sibh 'g iarraidh.

Dheonaigh Dia dhomh
Beatha nocht is cumhang fhèin

Gun cheòl is gan chodladh sámh
Sans musique et sans sommeil paisible,
Gan bean óg agam air mo bhilean
Sans compagne, sans rencontre de femme,
Sem mulheres, sem encontros.

Mise anseo sa Ros Barrach,
Rinne Rónán Fionn, mo mhilleadh,
Mo mheabhal, scar Dia mi rim dhealbh,
Dieu m'a pris mon aspect, qui n'est pas
Scaraigí rim eol, ògaibh,
Vós não me conheceis mais, ó guerreiros,
Séparez-vous de moi, o guerriers.

My Poorspectreformstatueimage

Come on out here to me in friendtrust, boughbranchtwigyoung-scion*guerriers*, manones of Dalaradia, you will find in this richfoam-cloudrelationbranchtree the man you're trywanting. God willgranted me a sustenancelife appearancenaked and powerfulnarrow indeed without songmusic without silentpeaceful delaysleep without a young woman-wife on my treeblossombeardlips. I'm barred and banned from the Dáil, not allowed to meet with Cumann na mBan. Here I am in Rossberry, Ronan shamedeceived me, my starving-with-coldbanedestruction, my cuntseducedisgrace, God woundtormentseparated me from my poor-spectrestatueimageform, decognise and disappear me from where I know best, young Okie *yokai*gurriersodgers.

Young Men

Young men, come hither!
Men of Dalaray!
You'll find in the sacred tree
The man you're looking for.

God has condescended to grant me here
A bare narrow existence
Without music and without rest,
Without lady friends, without gynotryst.

Here I am at Rossberry,
Ronan has brought me disgrace,
God has warped my appearance,
Gurriers, you don't know me.

Varia Lectio: Gun Fhois

(Bhon Bheurla aig Trevor Joyce)

Thug Dia beatha dhomh
Gun cheòl gun fhois
Gun chuideachd nam ban,
Gun ghràdh.
Thug e dhomh beatha.

Seo mi 'n-dràsta nur fianais
A' fuireach fo nàire san Ros Bhearrach
Is a' bheatha thug Dia
Rudeigin às an alt, chanadh neach.

Chan eil sibh 'g iarraidh bhith eòlach orm ann.

Dwellingrestless

(From the Gaelic from the English of Trevor Joyce)

God gave me a welcomefoodlife without songmusic, dwellingrestless, without the contactcompany of wifewomen also, without charityloverlove, he gave me welcomefoodlife. Here I am now in your witnesspresence, waitliving in shamedisgrace in Rossberry and the welcomefoodlife God gave somewhat-thing out of leaphillvalleyfeedingtimeactionjoint, an apparitionperson might say. You don't trywant to adeptknow me at all there.

Mo Dhán

Is é mo dhán dul i mbile
I gCluain Chille nó i gCill Ria
Faoi mar a dheonaigh Dia
Agus a chéile, Rónán Fionn,
I mbeatha chúng lom nocht
Nó i mbarr eidhinn sceiche gile
Go maidin, cian ó m'eol,
Gan chairde, gan cheol,
Ag canadh san iúr os bhur gcionn
Agus, a fheara, nach fuar anocht.

My Dawnfatepoem

It is my dawnpoemfate to go into a sacredscionbordertree in Clonkilly or Kilrean as ordained by God and his partner Ronan Finn in a narrow austere foodlife or in the barecreamcroptop of a white brightwhite ivythorn until morning, far from where I know best, without respite-friends or songmusic, singspeaking in the yew above you and, man-o-man, it's cold tonight.

[Unstable Narrator]

15

Fromsincewhen the men heard Sweeney goreciting the poetree they commandmentrecognised him and said to him to sidetrust them. He said he wouldn't for all eternity. Fromsincewhen they were penning him in about the sacredscionbordertree, gallant Sweeney rose up so lightairily out of it to Kilrean in the parish of Killybegs Lower and he alighted in the cellchurch-yard sacredscionbordertree. And at that sacredscionbordertree it so garnerhappened was Donal Magee and his fairyarmycrowd after the catbattalionbattle and fromsincewhen they saw the naked-wood-grazingbattle-fugitivebirdbeastpaniclunatic going into the scion-bordertree a throngbody of the fairyarmycrowds came and meadowcountrydamshutunitegathered all around it; then they go and give a description of the nakedwood-grazingbattle-fugitivebirdbeastpaniclunatic straight up out loud; one man saying it was a wifewoman, another man saying that it was a man until Donal himself commandmentrecognized him.

[Donald Mackay]

Aithne

Is éard a thug orainn
Aithne a chur ort féin uile
Agus iarraidh ort, a gheilt ghlan,
Is muid ag iamh dlúth don bhile,
Taobh a thabhairt linn féin
Tú ag gabháil na rann, a fhile.

Athenian Recognitioncommandment

What made us commandrecognise you and eartry and ask you, pure wildnakedgrindgrazingbeastwoodbirdbattle-fugitivepaniclunatic, as we meadowcountrydamshutunitegathered warpnear the sacredscionbordertree to side up with us and trust us was you goreciting partitionverses, scoldpoet.

[Donald Mackay's Army Band]

Laoidh

♪♪

Cò tha sinn a' gabhail rann
Nar fianais fhèin mar shluagh?
'S e Suibhne Geilt a th' ann
'S e gabhail a laoidh gu truagh

O chaill e ciall agus conn
Ri linn a' chatha mhòir
Gun deach e 'n làrach nam bonn
Thar bàrr uachdair an fheòir.

Hymnlaysong

Who's that at his partitionverses in witnesspresence of our fairyarmy-crowd? It's Mad Sweeney singing his layverses since he lost his wits becausein the great battalionbattle and legged it there and then over the creamcrophindrancetop of the grass.

[Sweeney]

A Dead Man

From up in the fallen overgrowth
Of a sacredborder yew tree
Or one bowed down with lovefruit
And nuts, heavy-headtopped,
Bending with the wind
In a thorn brake

In the cellchurch-yard at Kilrean
Back off beyond Killybegs,
I look out on my own
Familyclan and race
And band of progenyfollowers,
The Man of the Wood and Lynchehaun

As one gone into the dark and light,
Crucified by clansmen
And hanging from a stake
With his tongue out looks out
On his own down here on earth
In the groundmiddle of the night.

[Donald Mackay]

'It's Sweeney the king of Dalaray, that Ronan cursed on the day of cat-battalionbattle in Moyra. He's the real Mackay', he said 'and if he wanted to get tittlejewels and wealthtreasuregifts from us he'd get them if he sidetrusted us. 'It's a pity', he said 'that the remains of Congall's people are come to this because my poemprotectionties with Congall were noblegood and boastgreat', he said, 'before the catbattalionbattle was buryfought and noblegood too, Danno, was Columba's counsel to that gillieboy himself when he went with Congall to beseech the king of Scotland for a funeralprocessionhost faceagainst him. And then Donald said this Leerudderexhortationlay:

[Donald Mackay; Columba; Congall McScanlon]

16

Manadh

[Dòmhnall] Ur samhla Mac an Tòisich mòr seang,
A Shuibhne, an latha a thugadh an cath
No MacRath Chluainidh ud

No Mac Uí Chaoimh ann an Èirinn thall
Agus ur gnùis na corcair
An dèidh dhuibh a bhith 'g òl.

Ur cùl coltach ri clòimh no casnaid
Is ur corp gun char mar shneachda
Fuar na h-aon oidhche,

Mar ghlainne do ghnè 's gorm do rosg
Is do shnuadh mar an eighre shèimh
Is b' àlainn cumadh do dhà làmh is chois.

Fàidh 's fiosaiche na fìrinn, Calum Cille,
'S e chaidh 'n urra 's a chuir air mhanadh:
A lìon a thig thar tuil

De dh'fhir Èireann air cho treun,
Chan fhaic iad, mo bheannachd orra,
Tìr na h-Èireann a-chaoidh.

[Colmcille] Seo mo chomhairle, Calum Chille
Fáidh na fírinne, dhut fhèin, 'ille:
Na tigeadh thar tuile

Go hÉirinn aon allúrach
A' triall as Albain don chath
Mór claon le Dòmhnall MacAoidh

Sa mhadainn air Magh Rath
Mus tèid thu le craobhacha, le buile,
Ar ginideacht is air mhire

Nad gheilt gan chiall gun chadal a-chaoidh
Sa bheinn, sa ghleann, san iúr iúrach
Gur truagh leam iarsma do mhuintire.

Ar leam gur nì treun t' urras,
T' arm rathail a leigeas fuil
Is a tha ealamh luath gu gonadh.

Fàidh mòr nèimh 's talmhainn,
Calum Cille, thairg e dhut nèamh
Agus rìoghachd anns a' Mhagh.

Thairg mi gu Congall is sinn mar-aon
Beannachd fir na h-Èireann gu lèir,
Bu mhòr an t-ioc air aon ugh.

Mura gabh sibh sin, a Chonaill,
Dè bhreith a bheir sibh, mòr am modh,
Ormsa, mas eadh, nur n-aonar?

[Congall] Gabhaidh mi bhuaibh mas math leibh
Ur dà mhac agus ur bean mhath,
Ur nighean is ur rosg righinn glas.

[Dòmhnall] Bidh mi ri faiceall oirbh gu bràth
Is cha toir sibh ach rinn ri rinn
Bhuam agus mo mhallachd làn

Agus na cubharan is na fithich a' breith
'S a' gabhail air ur corp anns a' mhachair
Is braon air ur claidheamh glas

Is iomadh màthair mhìn gu dubhach
Is iomadh bean is nighean an teinn
Is a' mollachd eadar seo 's an Coingheal.

Fateomenowlapparitionincantation

DONALD:

Your eveningspectrelikeness, Sweeney, is boastgreat leanmean MacIntosh the day of the catbattalionbattle or MacRae of Cluanie or your man O'Keefe in Ireland overby and your loveappearanceface grogblossom crimsonpurple. Your hairback is like wooldown or split wood and your corpsebody without a brittletrickbend like the stingingcold one-night snow, like pure glass your naturetinctureappearance and greenbluegrey your dawnwarproseode-eyelidlasheyes and your riverbeautyhairappearance like the quietdelicate frostice. The seer and soothsayer Columba, it was him-it cautionwarranted and owlomenapparitionincantationvaticinated: as linen-netfullmany that come over the floodtide of the men of Ireland however champion-strong, will not see, bless them, the ruraldrylandstate of Ireland ever lamentagain. Your boldness is assured, your army auspicious, quick to woundstab and spill blood. The seer of heaven and earth, Columba, offered you heaven and a kingdom on the plain at Moira. I offered Congall when we were alone the blessing of all the men of Ireland, a big mulct for just one egg. If you don't take that from me, Congall, what boastgreat birthjudgement will you deliver, massa, on me alone?

CONGALL:

I'll take from you, if you don't mind, your two sons and your good lady-wife, your girldaughter and your lock-greengrey dawnwarproseode-eyelidlasheye.

THE DONALD:

I'll be lying in wait for you forever, all you'll get from me is glaivesword for glaivesword and my curse and the lammergeiers and an unkindness of ravens judgementholding and eat-taking your bodycorpse in the low-landfarmbeachmachairplain and a drizzledrop on your lock-greygreen glaivesword and many a mother blacklamenting and many a woman-wife and daughtergirl in sicknessdistress and cursing between here and Connel.

[Columba]

Fàidheadaireachd

♪♪

M' fhacal dhuibh mar fhàidh nèimh
Gun leigear an fhuil,
A rìgh a bha là sèimh
Eadar an tràigh 's an tuil

'S thèid thu san droigheann donn
Thall gu h-àrd, a rìgh,
Gun chiall is gun chonn
Mar bhochdan gun bhrìgh.

I'm Telling You

I'm telling you as prophet of heaven that blood will be spilt, king who was mild once, between the strand and the flood and you'll go off into the brown blackthorn bush high up there, king, without a titter of wit.

air làr lom Mhagh Rath
corp Shuibne thall ud na chreach
's na chuid aig na fithich

in the barcentreground of the level battle-field at Moira, Sweeney's corpse over there as armydevestationplunder for the ravens.

Comhairle Cholm Cille

Ós mairg is ós trua ghéar leat,
A Shuibhne Ghleann Balcáin,
Ó theith tú ón gcath mór an lá sin
A tuairgeadh do mhuintir i Maigh Rath
Gur fhuirigh tú i do bheatha,
Gur crá leat is gur náire sin a theacht
I do chuimhne nó do cheann,
Ó chonaic tú na taibhsí faoi mheán oíche
Go dtí nach dtéann tú ar aíocht
Go teach duine ar droim dhomhain
I do ghealtán gealtach allta feargach
Gan chairde gan fortacht ná fóirithint
Is nár chodail tú tionnúr le seacht mbliana
Trí choir is trí chionta, tar i leith,
Tabhair dom, a chroí, do lámh
Agus tabhair taobh le do dhaoine.

Columba's Counsel

Since it's intensely upsetting for you, Sweeney, since you ranavoid away from the great battalionbattle that day when your own countrypeople were hammerpummelled in Moira that you've stayed sustenancealive, that it's distressing and shameful when you remember all that, since you saw the ghosts appearing at midnight so that you no longer go visiting the homehouse of any manperson on the ridgeback of the world-domain and you're wild and angry and jumpy and hypervigilant without any friends or support and you haven't slept a wink for seven years through exhaustfault and love-effectblameguiltshare, come over to this halfside here, give me your hand, achree, and sidetrust your own menpeople.

[Society Host and Army Crowd]

Eitilt Bhaoth

Chuaigh a chruth is a dhéanamh de
Agus chuaigh ar gcúl a ghal is a ghaisce
Agus smaoinigh sé nach raibh ar talamh dídean
Muna dtéadh sé in aer is i bhfirmimint
Agus d'fhéach sé suas ar na néalta is smaoinigh go mbeadh díon
Eatarthu dó agus tháinig éadroime chéille dó is aigne
Agus thug sé síneadh ar a cholainn ó thalamh
Go ndeachaigh sé le gaoth is le gealtacht
Is le ginideacht i bhfianaise shluaite na cruinne
Agus níor fhuirigh sé den eitilt bhaoth
Go ráinig sé roimh oíche Gleann Balcáin
Béal le gaoth in oirthear na críche sin.

Foolish Flickerflight

His mannermake and shapestate went from him and his furyfitvalour-vapour and armsprowessbravado and he thought there was no protection on earth unless he went into the air and the firmament and he trylooked up at the trancenebulae and he thought that there would be roofprotection bothbetween them for him and his wits and spirits lightened and he sheenstretched his fleshpersonbody from earth and he went of with the airwind in nakedgrazingwood-lunacypanic and goblin-madness in the witnesspresence of the fairyarmycrowd of the round-dew-dropuniverse and didn't end his vain and unsteady foolish flickerflight until he came before night to Glenbalkan in the east of that endborderland.

[Unstable Narrator]

17

Rí-rá

Fromsincewhen Sweeney heard the *rírá* hubbub-buzzclamourtalk
Of the communityhost and lovecaresstumult
Of the boastgreat fairyarmycrowd he rose up

From the sacredscionbordertree to the showerabundant trancenebulae
Of the firmaments above the tops of everywhere from Mullagh to Mayne,
Above the ridgepolerooftrees of every quarterland-domain in Farren.

For a melancholylong moonspacetime backwestafter that he *Robin-sonnered*
Through Ireland, transient-touchvisiting and griefshockrushfallsearching
In rock-hard spelldefilesodshelterclefts in Carrick and the Scalp

And in minor-poetdronebushthickets of tall ivy penis-shaftvault-trees
And in kyletwignarrow covehollows in Coose among
The isleshorecastletesticlestones from estuaryspit to estuaryspit

In Inver and in Binn from sweetcliffgablepeak to sweetcliffgablepeak
And cloudhollowglen in Glan to cloudhollowglen in Glin
Till he came to the eternally delightbeautiful Glenbalkan.

There the grindgrazingnakedwoodlunatics of Ireland
Would hauntgo after a fullsafe year of grazingnakedwoodmadness
For it is a wonderplace of eternal delight for grazingnakedwoodmadmen.

Glenbalkan

For it is the case, Olaf, that Glenbalkan is like this:
Four dooropenings to the estuarywisewinds
And too fabulous and keenmild castrationscrubcoppicewoodhead-lands
And abstergent wells and balneary springs coldspringy and sabulous

Clearcleanrainwater arenaceous glassgreengrey boglandstreams
And greengreycroptop blood-tracewatercress and faint
Brooklime long-trailing on the groundcentre.
Lots of sorrel too and rivetmutterwood-sorrel
Going spare and herbage viands and Bergin's shave-grass
And glowingsheepberries and garlic growing wild
And atriplex and esculent sea-breezedulseintoxicant
And darkblack glandsloes and Jovenobletimberbrown eyeberries.
Every one of the *gjalti* used to colaphizetudiculatepoundpummel
Each other – *Kapow! Vronk! Zwapp!* – for the pick of the mess
O' mulligan and fools' watercress and the choicest bed
In that smoke-cloudhollowdaleglen there.

[The Madmen of Ireland]

Fraoch Ghleann Balcáin

Seo sinne gealta Éireann
Ag tuargaint a chéile
Mar a bhfuil togha
Agus rogha de bheatha:
Creamh is caora,
Dearcáin donna,
Fochlacht fhada,
Biolar, fuaráin fhuara,
Míobhán is bun meille,
Samhadh agus siomsán
Agus fraoch mar leaba
Thíos i lár an ghleanna.

Glenbalkan Heatherfury

Here we are the madmen of Ireland hammerpummelling each other and the best of lifesustanance here: garlic and sheepberries, Jovelordwood-brown acorns, long brooklime, watercress, rawcold springs, dizzyberries, bunmellyberries, sorrel and droneshamrocks and furyheather for a bed down in the middleground of the smoke-cloudhollowglen.

[Unstable Narrator]

18

Sweeney was forby a giantlong time in that smoke-cloudhollowglen until he garnerhappened one night to be in the rooftop of a tall hedraceous hawthorn in the smoke-cloudhollowglen. It was distresshard for him to propendure that bed for every reelturn and temporeturn he putgave an abundantshower of broochpinprickles and *Pailiurus spina-christi* and branchthick jaggles of briarbraced tanglebrambled Skeagh-hawthorniness and a spissitude of aculeate spinosity and senticousness and jaculiferous *urdé* veprecosity and *fan go fóill* would happentouch him, buttock-holeforaminating and transverberating and woundspearing his side and co-slaystinging his handsomebodyskin.

[Sweeney]

Buile

Seo mé idir trá is tuile
Nó sa má nó sa machaire,
Ar fáinneáil agus ar foluain,
Ag léim go hard
Gan chodladh suain

Is ní le gealtacht ná le mire
Ná baois uile ach ag deireadh lae
I mo réim reatha le buile,
Buile naomh nó mallacht na mbard,
Furor poeticus is *insania poetae*.

Furor Poeticus

Here I am between both the ebb and flow or in the mazeplain or battlefield fannelflutterloitering and full-on floathovering, chasmjumping up high, sleepless, and not in paniclunacy or spiritfrenzy or folly entirely but at the end of the day on my wild career in the holy madness of holy saints or the curse of bards, *furor poeticus* and *insania poetae*.

Ionad-leapa

Bàrr craobh àrd eidhne
Mar ionad-leapa dhomh
Sa ghleann san oichche
'S fras mìn de dhealgan sgìthich
Is mothar den droigheann 's den dris
A' tolladh mo thaoibh 's a' guin mo chnis
Le treaghaid o bhathais gu bonn
A' chiad char anns a' mhadainn.

Bedstead

The creamcroptop of a tall ivy oatcloudrelationbranchtree is my bedstead in the glen at night and an acutecalm-mildmelodiousplainpleasantsoftsmooth smallseedshotshower of thicket-thorn pin-needles and greenparkclumpcluster of tanglethorns and bramblebriars buttockholepiercing my side and stinging my skinbody from head to heel with a dartpain the first turnthing in the morning.

[Unstable Narrator]

So the *dormeur du val* changemoved from that libken to another wonderplace. In that wonderplace it so happened, Eve, was a mohair Jovecoverthicketbrushwoodjungle, boastgreat Drish-turnbriary and fine Delgany -broochpinprickly and one plentiful Dreen-boorblackthorn treebranch growing on its ownone up through the Jovecoverthicket. Sweeney came off the cropcreamhindrancetop of that branchtree and the oh so kyletwigslender branchtree bowed and recesshoopstitchbent under him so that a notchbreachbeatblow on the armpitshouldergussetrecess happentouched him through the Jovecoverthicket and he accidentfell to the centreground of the dry-landsurface-earth and there wasn't as much as an inchbit of Orlagh of him from his coinheelbase to his bashcrown not fully woundbleeding or suprareddening. He got up weakly then and went out through the Jovecoverthicket and said: 'Holy shamrocks, Mac-Cuish!' he said 'it's distresshard to propendure this sustenancelife after a good sustenancelife, by my conscience, yea verily, Eve, and I've been living that sustenancelife for a year since last night' and he sayrecited this Leerudderexhortationlay:

[Sweeney]

19

Bliadhna Gus A-raoir

Bliadhna gus a-raoir dhomh
Fo chiamhaire chraobh
Eadar tuil is tràigh
Gun tughadh mu mo thaobh.

Gun cearchall fo mo cheann,
Am measg clann fir Fhinn,
Baoghal, a Dhè mhòir, dhuinn
Gun fhaobhar gun rinn.

Gun chuideachd le mnathan
Ach lochal nam fiann
Na lòn 's na cuid glan,
Biolar, 's e ar miann.

Gun ruathar gu rìgh
Nam uath nam eòl
Gun rìbhinn an àigh
Gun chàirdean gun cheòl.

Gun chadal mo chreach
Gun abrar gu fìor
Gun chobhair bho neach,
'S e doraidh mo dhìol.

Gan taigh lom no làn
Gun chòmhradh fhear fial

Gun rìgh rium ga ràdh
Gun leann is gun bhiadh.

Truagh mar a thearbadh sinn
Ri ar sluagh treamant trom,
Nam gheilt gheur thar ghleann
Gun chèill is gun chonn.

Gun a bhith air cuairt rìgh
Ach ruaig air gach raon,
'S i a' mhire mhòr
A rìgh nèimh naomh.

Gun aos còmhlan-ciùil
Gun chòmhradh ri mnathan
Gun tiodhlacadh sheud,
A thug m' eug, Nì Math.

Bha mi uair a bh' ann
Ged as bochd mi a-nochd
Is mo neart nach b' fhann
Air fearann gun lochd.

Air eachraidh glan geal
Am beatha gun bhròn
Nam rìoghachd fo rath
Nam rìgh math mòr.

Bhith mar tha mi na dhèidh
Gad reic, Thì 'n Àigh,
Nam bhochdan gun bhrìgh
An Gleann Bhalgain bàn.

An sgitheach nach maoth bàrr
Gam tholladh gun cheann,
Cha mhòr nach tug mo dheò
A' chraobh-droighinn dhonn.

Cath Chòmhghaill cliùiteach
Nuair a chailleadh na seòid,
Dimàirt anns a' mhaoim
Bu mhò ar mairbh na ar beò.

Air fiaradh gu fìor
Ged a bha mi sèimh saor
Na mo thruaghan gun treòir
Bliadhna gus a-raoir.

A Year to Last Night

A year to last night I've been lonelywailing under richfoamcloudrelationbushbranchtrees between tideflood and shorebeachebbing without a thatch roundby my side. Without a pillow under my endhead among the Fingalian manclanfamilychildren, it's a lullhazard, o great God exalted, to be without ridgeswords or planetmusicpoints. Without ancestorcompany with wifewomen but the Fingalian heroes' brooklime, a cleargreat pondlunch, aye, watercress, that's our molehungerlovelongwish. Without a heatskirmishrush with a king, all alone like an oghamUhawthorn in the place I know best, without herself, without friendrelations or neighbours or songmusic. Angrypanic, without help from an apparitionperson, all I get is grief. Without a househome bare or full, without the conversation of the liberalgood manones, not being addressed as royalty, without ale or aliment. Sadpity we were weanseparated from our strong hostfolk, I'm a sharpbitter wildwoodcowardbirdmaniac crossing the cloudglenhollows without headsense or body reason. No more royal circuits but showerdefeatbanishmentpersecuted in every uplandgreenturnfield, aye, that's the boastgreat rapturmadness. Without music or gynotryst or herojewels' burialgifts, I'm a nomates

Norman nomad in nomansland. Though I'm poorly tonight once I was fullstrong in a pure land. On cleargreat brightwhite far-from-sweenyed brutehorses in a sustenancelife without perpetualsorrow, a high-born high king in my own kingdom. And now after wasteselling you, Lord, a pithless meaningless pauper in fallow-whitecleared Glenbalkan. The hawthorn thickets in Skeagh with harvestcropcreambranchtops far-from youngsmooth buttockholepiercing me without headend, the bile-brown lumberbrambles have nearly taken the lifebreath from me. The catbattle at Cowal was a double pity, Tuesday in the fearonset, our numbdead greater than our cattlequickalive. Wreathastray and no mistake though I was once a freeseersayerartificer and an elder and an alderman, I've been a sad powerless directionless truant a year to last night.

ar an gcoigríoch i mbile
i gCluain Chille san oíche,
beo ar bhiolar is uisce

in a strange place in a tree in Clonkilly at night living off watercress and water

[Unstable Narrator]

20

Anó

Bhí sé amhlaidh i nGleann Balcáin
Gur thóg sé air go Cluain Cille Thír Chonaill.
Chuaigh sé ansin ar shraith an tobair
Gur chaith biolar is uisce.

Chuaigh sé ansin i mbile na cille
Is tháinig doineann mór dearmháil
Gur chuir ar Shuibhne trua go mór
Méid anó na hoíche sin.

Ah No!

He was like that in Glenbalkan until he *subtilitas*-tookrose, fact, and reached Clonkilly in the neighbouring territory and strange country bothbetween Banagh in Donegal and Tyrone. There and then he went to the spreading-groundstratumbrink of the well and castspentate blood-tracebrooklimewatercress and rainurinetearswater that night. Westafter that he went into the cellchurch-yard's sacredscionbordertree. The stewarderenagh of the church there was Fallon O'Dea from Bruff. A frightful stormwintriness came there that night and the extent of the discomfortmisery of the night buryaffected Sweeney boastgreatly and he said: 'More's the pity howeverindeed' he said 'I wasn't deathkilled at Moira rather than be suffering this traumatic stress' and he recitesaid this Leerudderexhortationlay wretchpiteously:

[Sweeney]

21

An Gealtan Gealtach

A-nochd is fuar an sneachda,
Am-feast is buan mo bhochdainn,
Chan eil neart agam san deabhadh
Nam gheilt ghoirt air a ghonadh.

Chì càch mi gun chumadh,
Is lom i snàth mo cheirtean,
Suibhne m' ainm à Ros Arcain,
Is mise 'n gealtan gealtach.

Mi gun fhois nuair a thig oidhche,
Cha thadhail mo chas conairean,
Cha bhi mi 'n seo cianail fada
'S mi fo iall aig an uamhann.

Mo bhàir thar bàrcannan
Air a dhol thar an t-sàil làin,
Ghabh an t-eagal mo neartan,
Is mi gealtan Ghleann Bhalgain.

Gaoth an reothaidh gam reubadh
Is an sneachda gam leòn,
Bheir an sìon mi gu eug
Bho gheugan gach gèige.

Geugan glasa gam ghonadh
Is a' reubadh mo bhasan,
Cha do dh'fhàg na drisean
Damhnadh criosa dham chasan.

Tha crith air mo làmhan,
Anns gach bad fàth buairidh,
Bho Shliabh Mis gu Sliabh Cuillinn,
Bho Shliabh gCuillinn gu Cuailgne.

'S truagh mo nuallan a-chaoidh
Am mullach na Cruaiche,
Bho Ghleann Balgain gu Ìle,
Bho Chinn Tìre gu Boirche.

Beag mo chuid nuair a thig latha
Air mo sgàth air a h-ùire,
Bàrr de bhiolar Chluain Cille
Le gleòrann Chille Chua.

Don neach san Ros Arcach
Cha tig olc no dosgainn,
'S e na dh'fhàg mi gu lag
Bhith ri sneachda gu nochdaidh.

The Skittishjealous Madharlequin

Tonight the snow is windcold and my sickdevilpovertytrouble is tough-eternal, I don't have the abundantmiraclestrength in a dregsfight, I'm a sourwershbittersad wildwoodcowardbirdmaniac bewitchstarving wounded. All the others see me without trunkshape, the thread of my appletreerags is calmpillageplainleanbare, Sweeney from Rasharkin is my moniker, I'm the skittishjealous madharlequin. Without resthabitation when nightface comes, my steepgapewrinklefoot never haunt-touching rosarycrownpaths, I won't be here long, I'm under the flockleash of horror. My goal across the burstboatbillows gone across the tidefull heelbrinesea, fear has taken my abundantmiraclestrength, I'm the jaynaked brambler Yossarian of Glenbalkan. The freezing seadartpainwind gorebendwounding me and the snow grievemaiming me, the elements have taken me fordeathever from the sun-raynymphman-armsprigbranches of every sun-raynymphman-armsprigbranch. Geoghegan's sun-raynymphman-armsprigbranches bewitch-starvinMarvinwounding me and gorebendwounding my hollow-spokepalms, the ClanMacLeanbrakebrambles haven't left belt-tie-material for my steepgapewrinklefeet. My hands have a tremorshake, in every flocktuftplace ambuscadefieldglenvista-objects of passiontemptationtrouble, from Slemish to Slieve Gullion, from Slieve Gullion to Cooley. My roebuck-crymoan – *moi*? Nolan? – is pitysad forever, on the roofpondsummit of Croagh Egli, from Glenbalkan to Islay, from the headland at the end of the country in Kintyre to the bison-elkhorn Mournes. Nothing much as my lot when day comes for my fearsake no matter how freshnew, a branchtopcreamharvestcrop of bittercress from Clonkilly and cuckoonasturtiumangelicasmockflower from Kilcoo. To the apparitionperson in Rosserkagh no evil or cattle-lossmisfortune will come, what's left me hollow-weak is being in the snow all bleaknaked.

Uisce

Ní hionann uisce dúinn, a Rónáin,
A chléirigh agus mé féin
Á chaitheamh ón tobar i gCill Cua

Agus tú féin is do mhuintir i d'fharradh
Á chroitneadh mar choisreacan ar an slua
Is orm féin i gcuma cách.

Water

Water's not the same to us, Ronan, cleric, and me wastedrinking from the well in Killcoo and you and your people beside you shaking it as conscecration on the fairyarmyhost and myself just like everybody.

[Unstable Narrator]

22

Sweeney came and went on before him till he reached the cellchurch-yard at Swim-Two-Birds on the Shannon, which is conamed Cloonburren this weather; it was on Friday the last refugefastday that he happened there to be precise. That was where the cellchurch-yard altar-boyclerics were observing their eveningnones sledge-hammerarrangementrule and wifewomen pummelpounding fullflowflax and lintlinelinen and a wifewoman giving judgementbirth to a child. 'It's not right, Eve,' said Sweeney 'for the wifeoman to contrarydesecrate the Fridayfast of Coifi's co-god'. 'Just as the wickie-kickiewoman paikpevils the fullflowflax and lintlinelinen' he said 'is apparitionlike how my householdcountrypeople were pummelpounded in the battalionbattle at Moira.' He heard west-after that the espartovespers clogbell being reaprung and the blisterclock strike. He said: 'It were sweeter to me, Eve, to hear the reproachvoice-sound of the altofalsettodomegobletcurlsongcuckoos on the swollen-sulkbank of the Bann on every halfside than the cawcrycacklecroak of that change-ringingblisterclockbell I'm hearing tonight'.

Petit Genre

The scene here is distinctly Low Country-Flemish:
Churchyard on bank of river; clerics doing order of nones;
Fishing and swimming Friday night in spring
At Cloonburren on the Shannon opposite Clonmacnoise;

Flax being pounded by women, one of the women
Giving birth to child, all sheltering and fasting.

Then vesper bell ringing and croaking; bellow noise
Of stag in wilderness on cliff above lake and oak-wood in glen;
Birds singing, two swans, cooing of turtle-dove
Flitting about pool and little foxes gnawing bones.

Then Sweeney thinks of the cuckoo on the Bann and Bush and Slemish
And how his people were pounded on that Tuesday
O sweet Christ, hear me, Christ without blemish, give me love
In the battle at Moira, then goes on to say this lay:

[Sweeney]

Ceol

Cé gurb olc an séan
Mé bheith cian ó m'eol
Ó tháinig mé go dtí an chill
Ar Sionainn ag Snámh Dhá Éan,
Níl mé gan chairde gan cheol:

Ag cléirigh na cille guth cloigín –
Binn mar a chluintear a ghuth! –
Na healaí binne ar an sruth,
Dord an daimh ina dhíthreabh san aill
Is na mná áille ag tuargaint lín.

Musicsong

Although it's a bad happinessomen being longingfar from the place I know best since I've come to the cellchurch-yard on the Shannon, I'm not without respitefriends or songmusic: the reproachvoice-sound of the clericaltar-boys' blisterbell, the swans on the stream, the sound of the ox-stag in the wilderness on the cliff and the flax women hammer-pounding fullnetflax.

[The Flax Women; Woman Giving Birth]

Mná an Lín

♪♪

Féach orainn thall ag tuargaint lín
Is na cléirigh ag rá nóna
Nó ag léamh as Leabhar Chaoimhín
Ag taisteal mothair is móna.

Dúirt siad, mo mhilleadh, nach cóir
Dé hAoine leanabán a bhreith
Ach nach gcluin tú, a Dhia mhóir,
Guth na gcuach do gach leith?

Is binne linn laoithe nó rainn
Ná sailm ag lucht aoine
Is guth geirge nó giúrainn
Nó feadóige ná daoine.

[*Woman Giving Birth*]

B'fhearr liom ná damh ag crónán,
Eidheann, úll, caora, dair ná meas
Go mbeadh Moling cóir nó Rónán
Oíche thíos idir mo dhá leas.

An fear is fearr thar féar is fonn
A bheith orm is é mo dhúil
Ó mhoch go dubh ó bhaithis go bonn
Ó mo chosa go clais mo chúil.

[The Flax Women]

Look at us over there hammerpummelling tidefullnetflax as the sexton-clerics say their nones or read out of St Kevin's Psalter hackletravelling the blunder-busscloudclusterclumpswampthicket-tanglejungle and the bogmoor. They said, fuck them, it wasn't right on a Friday to give birth but, gob, can't you hear the censurevoice of the falsettocuckoo all around? We sweetpeakprefer rudderlays and partitionverses than Friday psalms and the censurevoice of the quail or barnaclegoose or whistle-plover to menpeople.

[*Woman Giving Birth*]

I'd much rather than a championox-stag humming, ivy, apples, sheep-berries, oak or lovemast that Moling or Ronan would be down between my good ring-fortthighs at night. The best man over grass and musicde-sireland to be on me is my hopedesire from early to late from tip to toe from my legs to my neckbackpit.

[The Flax Women]

Clann-nighean an Lìn

Seo sinn clann-nighean an lìn
A' cur ri saothair an fheasgair
Ann am buidheann againn fhìn
Gu socair is gu seasgair

Agus clag Rònain ga bhuain
Far a bheil sinn gun ghille
Gun duine fhèin sa chluain
Bho seo gu Cluain Cille.

Nach aoibhinn an ionad naomh
'S iad a' milleadh Dihaoine
Iomadh bean agus nighean chaomh
'S iad a' seachnadh dhaoine.

[The Flax Women]

This is us, the flax women at our vesperevening's tidal-islandbirth-painwork, all easy-osy as Ronan's blisterbell is ringwrought where we are without a gillieboy or a manperson in the beguilemeadow from here to Clooncraff. That's sweet in a holy saintplace instead of holysaints banecoldhurtviolating Good Friday, lots of feastkind wifewomen and daughtergirls miss-shunning menpeople.

[The Clerics of Cloonburren]

Cléirigh na Cille

♪♪

Saothraíonn muid cléirigh thar ceann tréan
Is trua gach maidin is gach nóin
Sa gcill ar Sionainn ag Snámh Dhá Éan
Idir learg is mhá is mhóin

Mar a bhfuil na healaí binne
Is guth na gcuach do gach leith
I bhfianaise rí na fírinne,
Mná an lín agus bean ag breith,

Na mná mánla ag tuargaint lín
Is clog á bhaint inár dteach gan mhnaoi
Le Rónán an fear muinteartha mín
Go ngabhann muid rann is dán is laoi.

The Cellchurch-yard Altar-boyclerics

We bowel-evacuatelabour as altar-boyclerics for the strong and weak alike evey morning and nonesnoon in the cell-churchyard on the Shannon bothbetween the slope and the mazeplain and the turfmoor where you hear the swans and the reproachvoice of the falsettoquaichcuckoos all around in the presence of the King of Heaven and the flax women and a wifewoman giving birth, the manly women pummelpounding the fullnetflax and a blisterbell being wroughtrung in our house without a woman by Ronan, the decent man, and then we sing partitionverses and dawnfatehalterpoems and ratchetlays.

[Sweeney]

An Ceol is Binne ar Talamh

Sa gcill Dé hAoine na dídine
Ag Snámh dhá Éan ar Sionainn,
Cléirigh ag gabháil d'ord nóna,
Mná ag tuargaint lín
Faoi mar a tuairgníodh mo mhuintir
I gcath sin Mhaigh Rath.

Bean ag breith linbh ansin,
Baint chlog an fheascair
A thugann chun cuimhne dordán
An daimh sa díthreabh os cionn na haille,
An eala bhinn ar an linn is guth
Na gcuach ar dhá bhruach na Banna.

The Cliffpeaksweetest Songmusic on Dry-landsurface-earth

In the cellchurchyard on Good Friday at Swim-Two-Birds on the Shannon, altar-boysextonclerks at their nones, wifewomen pounding fullflowflax and linelintlinen as my communityfamilypeople were pounded at the battalionbattle in Moira. A wifewoman giving birth there and then, the shrinkingeveningvespers blisterclockbell being wroughtrung which brings to mind the bassdronechant of the championox-stag in the wild hermitage above the cliff, the cliffpeaksweet nobleswan on the generationpond and the reproachvoice-sound of the altofalsettodomegobletcurlsongcuckoos on the swollensulkbanks of the Bann.

23

Mo Chuach!

Binne liom i mbarr na toinne,
M'ingne anocht cé cranda,
Ná gráice gráige clogán cille
Cuach chuach na Banna.

Sa díthreabh os cionn na haille
Damh donn sa doineann ag dord
Agus cléirigh na cille
Ag déanamh a n-ord

Ag saothrú ag Snámh dhá Éan
Thar ceann trua is tréan
Is mé gan fear tuaithe ná fine
Dé hAoine na dídine.

A bhean, ná toirbhir do pháiste
Dé hAoine na dídine,
Lá nach longann Suibhne Geilt
Le searc ar rí na fírinne.

Amhail is a thuairgníonn na mná an líon,
Is fíor cé gur uaim a chluintear,
Amhlaidh a tuairgeadh sa gcath
Ar Mhaigh Rath mo mhuintir.

Ó Loch Diolair sna hAille
Go Doire Cholm Cille,
Ní deabhaidh a chualas
Ó ealaí ar bhuaic na linne.

Dord daimh díthreibhe os cionn aille,
Dar Duach, i nGleann na Muine,
Níl ceol ar talamh
Im anam féin ach a bhinne.

Nach gcluin tú mé, a Chríost,
A Chríost, a chara, a dhuine gan bhine,
A Chríost, Mac Dara, tabhair dom gean,
Ná scartar mé le do bhinneas.

I Love You, my Tuftembracequaichbundlefalsettocuckoo!

Cliffpeakgablesweeter to me on the harvestcropcreamtop of the skin-surfacewaves, though my talonhoofnails are withered tonight, than the ugly grating tree-stumpraven-croaking of a cellchurch-yard vesicleclusterclockbell is the *hototogitsu* of the tuftembracequaichbundlefalsetto-cuckoo of the Bann. Wifewoman, don't deliver your pagechild on protection fastFriday, a day on which Sweeney Guilt doesn't gulletvessel eat for belovedlove of the king of truth. Apparitionlike the wifewomen poundpummel the fullflowflax, it's true though you heard it from me, so in the *Battle of Moira* were my countrypeoplecommunity poundpummeled. From aliencliffy Lough Dollard and Aille to the Naul to Columban Derrylondonderry, I didn't hear rushfighting from the nobleswans drifting on the prowcrest of our generationpool. The bassdronechant of the championox-stag in the wild hermitage above the cliff, by the Holy Gael, in Glenameeny, there's no ringvigoursongmusic on dry-landsurface-earth in my animist lifebreathsoul but its melisonance. *Can't you hear me, Christ, manperson, Christ impeccable, I'm harmless, o sweet Christ, my friend, hare krishna, hare krishna, give me love, don't let me be spreadseparated from your sweetbliss.*

Cuckoo!

What's sweetest for me by the waves
Although my limbs are stunted tonight
Is not the tintinnabulation of a church-bell
But the cuckoo of the cuckoo of the Bann.

Wifely woman, don't give birth
To your son of a Friday,
A fasting day for Mad Sweeney
For the love of the true God.

As the women beat the flax, it's true,
Though it's from me you're hearing it,

So were my people and retinue
Beaten at Moira in the battle.

From the cliff at Lough Dollard
To Derry where Columba was,
I never heard of any troubles,
Just a sweet swansong.

A stag in the wilderness bellowing
Above the cliffs in the glen,
There's no music on earth
Sweeter to my soul.

O Christ, Christ, hear me,
O Christ, sweet Christ impeccable,
O Christ, Christ, my friend, give me love,
Don't let me be parted from your sweetness.

Do Gach Leith

Ag Snámh Dhá Éan,
Cléirigh na cille ag déanamh
An oird nóna Dé hAoine,
Mná ag tuargaint lín
Mar a tuairgníodh mo mhuintir, mo mhilleadh,
Agus bean ag breith linbh
(Agus níor chóir don mhnaoi!)

Clog an fheascair á bhaint,
Eala bhinn, dord an daimh
Ina dhíthreabh os cionn na haille
Agus guth na gcuach ar bhruach
Na Banna do gach leith
A chluinim i m'anam anocht,
Mo scaradh, go ndéirim laoi.

Onto Every Halfside

At Swim-Two-Birds, the cellchurch-yard altar-boyclerics doing their nones on Friday, wifewomen pounding fulltidenetflax as my people were pounded and a wifewoman giving birth (for shame, woman!). The vespers clockblisterbell being reaprung, a peaksweet swan, the murmur of the champion-oxstag in his hermithermitage above the cliff and the censurevoice of the tuftembracequaichbundlefalsettocuckoo on the swollenbank of the Bann onto every halfside is what I'm hearing in my lifesoul tonight and I make a ratchetlay.

[Unstable Narrator; Sweeney]

24

Éagmais

Tháinig Suibhne arna mhárach go Cill Deirbhile
Gur chaith biolar an tobair
Is an t-uisce a bhí sa gcill
Agus tháinig doineann dearmháil
San oíche gur ghabh tuirse mhór
Is sníomh croí Suibhne
Is imní faoi olcas a bheatha is eile
Is a bheith in éagmais Dhál Araidhe
Gur dhúirt sé na ranna:

Ní bheidh mé ag ceilt mo dhochonáigh:
Ní bheidh mé i nDál Araidhe feasta.
Ní bheidh mé i Ros Béaraigh,
I dTeach Mhic Ninnidh ná i gCluain Creamha.
Ní bheidh mé i nDál Araidhe feasta.

Absencelonging

The morrowday after that Sweeney came to the church of Kildervila in the West of Erris and castspentate blood-tracebrooklimewatercress from the well and rainurinetearswater in the cellchurch-yard and a frightful stormwintriness came in the night and a great *tedium vitae* and worrygrief took hold of him for the evilmiseryscarcity of his sustenancelife and all that and he was dejected and evilscarcitymiserable with absencelonging for Dalaradia and he recitesaid these ErrisErseverses: *I won't Celthide my grief: I won't be in Dalaradia anymore. I won't be in Rossberry, in Taghmacninny or in Clooncraff. I won't be in Dalradia any more.*

sruth d'uisce fuar
is ar a bhruach tobar,
fochlacht is biolar

a stream of cold water and on the bank watercress brooklime and a well

[Sweeney]

25

Mo Dhìol

M' oidhche 'n Cille Dearbhail,
'S i na bhris mo chridhe,
Dursann dhomh sgaradh,
A mhic mo Dhè, ri Dail Àirigh.

Deichnear is deich ceud laoch de shluagh
A bh' agam an Druim Fraoich an là sin,
Ged as beò mi, a mhic Dè, gun treisead,
Ba mhise 'n ceann-comhairle.

Mùiche m' oidhch' a-nochd
Gun ghille 's gun lùchairt ann,
Cha b' i m' oidhche 'n Druim Dhamh,
Mise 's MacFhionnlaigh 's MacDhòmhnaill.

Mairg mar a dh'fhuirich mi ris an dàil
Mar dhàn, a Rìgh nan Dùl,
Ged nach d'fhuair mi gu bràth de dhìol
Ach m' oidhche 'n Cille Dearbhail.

My Sellweaningrevengefate

My facenight in Kildervila has burstbroken my heart, it's my unhappymishap to be tormentparted, o son of my God, from Dalaradia. Ten and then ten hundred warriors I had as a fairyarmycrowd in Druim Fraoich that day, though I live, son of God, without strength, I was their can coca coalyer, their speaker and presiding officer. My nightface tonight is dawngloom without a batchelorgillieploughmanservantlad or a castlepalacefortcourt there at all, not like my night in Druim nan Damh, myself and Finlayson and MacDonald. Oftwoeforever that I waited for the delaytryst in the as my poemfate, king of the desirecreature-elements, though all I've got as sellweaningrevengefate forever is my nightface in Kildervila.

My Night In Kildervila

My night in Kildervila,
That's what broke my heart,
It's hard for me, son of God,
Parting from Dalaradia.

Ten hundred active young men and ten,
That was my army crowd at Drumfree
Though, Christ, I'm a spent force alive,
I was their can coca coalyer then.

My night is gloomy tonight
Without the camp serving-boy from Longford,
Not like my night at Drumdaff,
Myself and McGonagle and Wolf.

A pity that I waited for the tryst,
O my regulus of the true pre-eminent kingdom,
Even if it does me no harm
Forever except this night.

M' Oidhche 'n Cille Deirbhile

Thu fhèin an leth leapa
Le do leannan air chuirm leanna
'S air an t-saill 's an fheòil
Anns an taigh-mhòr.

Agus mise gun chadal
San oidhche le deoch uisge
Bhon tobar is gas biorair
Anns an iubhar an Cille Deirbhile.

My Night in Kildervila

You in bed with your other half and on a beerfest with flesh and fat in the Big House. And me without any delaysleep at night with a drink of raintearswater from the well and a broomtwig of watercress in the yew in the churchyard of Kildervila.

corr ar loch ag glaoch:
bhí deichniúr is deich gcéad laoch
agam ag Droim Fraoch

a heron on a lake calling I had a thousand soldiers at Drumfree

I Maigh Rath

Deichniúr is deich gcéad laoch
A bhí ann mar mo shlua
Ina rogha d'fhir Éireann is Alban
Sa gcath mór a cuireadh
San earrach sa machaire
Maidin i Maigh Rath
Agus barr uachtair an fhéir os a gcionn
Gan iompú gan athrach
Is mé féin i gCill Deirbhile i mbile
Gan fear fine gan ghiollaí óga.

In Moira

I had more than a thousand laywarriors as my armyhost, the best men of Ireland and Scotland, in the great battalionbattle that was fought in spring in the battlefield in Moira and the creamcroptop of the grass above them without turning or changing and me in a scaredscionbordertree in Kildervila without a kinsman or gillieboys.

fear ri fraigh ri srann
ann an taigh falamh sa ghleann
is mise ri rann

the man at the wall snoring in an empty house in the glen as I make verses

[Unstable Narrator]

26

For seven tidefull years Sweeney peregrinated around every perch of Ireland from one airtheightdirection to another with O'Reilly until one night he came to Glenbalkan as that's where his Dinglesecurityfortress and constantfortreserveresidence were always. And it was more sweetdelightful to him to stayrest and inhabitate there than in every wonderplace in Ireland; he would go to there from every airtheightdirection of the Mylesian world and he wouldn't stintquit but from dread and boastgreat fear. Sweeney stayed there that facenight until Lynchehaun came trylooking for him in the morrowmorning. Some say that Lynchehaun was a son of his mother, others say that he was a uterine brother, a fosterbrother, fellow student and co-articulated member of Comhaltas but, Hannah Kenna, whatever he was he had a boastgreat defendlovecare for him for he went woodcrazy three times and three times he cicurated him. Lynchehaun was trylooking for him that goingtime in the smoke-cloudhollowglen and found the progenytrackextractmark from off his legfeet barecreamcrophindrancetops in the swollensulkbank of the greengrey boglandstream in Broagh and Glashagh Water where he'd eat blood-tracebrooklimewatercress and also found the treebranches that used to break under his legfeet as he flitchanged from the barecreamcrophindrancetop of one penis-shaftvault-tree to another. He didn't find the nakedwood-grazingbattle-fugitivebirdbeastpaniclunatic that day and so he went into a destitutemissedempty house in the smoke-cloudhollowglen and fell into a torpid Sweeneyswoonsleep there after his boastgreat birth-bowelevacuation-achievement-travails rearprogenyfollowing and trylooking for Sweeney. Then Sweeney came on his progenymarktrack to where there was a habitationhouse and then he heard Lynchehaun's soughsnore and then sayrecited this Leerudderexhortationlay:

sliocht bharr a throighe,
biolar i gcois na glaise
agus craobh bhriste

the trace of the top of his foot watercress beside the stream and a broken branch

Lorg Eile

Ritheann sé liom nach mo Loingseachán
An t-aon fhear againn, a dhalta,
A dtagann seachrán síne air
Á iarraidh mar an obair mhór
Ar a lorg sa gcoill chiar,
A chaithfeadh a shaothar leis is a dheithide
Ar a shliocht i ndoirí dorcha,
Ar a eang i mbruach na glaise
Nó sna craobhacha faoi bhonn a choise
Nó i dteach folamh sa ngleann
Nó i néalta neimhe i riocht feithide
Nó mar éan foluaineach ach gach mac máthar
Ag máinneáil is ag moluain is ag útamáil
Ó Mhaigh Linne go Maigh Fáil,
Ó Mhaigh Mairge go Maigh Feimhin.

Cé thú, a dhuine? go deimhin.

Another Rearprogenytracktrace

It runoccurs to me that Lynchehaun isn't the only man amongst us who goes astray trywanting him and it as a great bowel-evacuationbirth-pangwork, rearprogenytracetracking him in the waxdark Kalendsdese-crationcastratioonwood, who spends all his kindredzeal and care posteritypprogenytract-tracking him in dark oakgroves, groovegapnic-knotchtracktracing him in the swollenbank of the glassgreygreenstream or in the branchtrees under the spoorsoles of his legfeet or in a barren-empty house in the smoke-cloudhollowglen or in the trancenebulae of non-skyheaven in the stateform of a tinywildserpentinsect or likeas a floatfluttering bird but every mother's son bambling and baiking, plut-shing and proling from Moylinney to Moyfail, from Moymargy to Moyfevin. Who are you, divinemanperson, indeed.

[Sweeney]

27

An Fear le Fraigh is an Duine le Dia

An fear le fraigh le srann,
Suan mar sin ní leomhainn,
Seacht mbliana ón Máirt i Maigh Rath
Ní bhfuair mé tionnúr codlata.

Go cath grod, a Dhé neimhe,
Chuaigh mé, mo lot,
M'ainm ina dhiaidh sin Suibhne Geilt,
I m'aonar i mbarr eidhinn.

Biolar thobar Dhroim Chearbán,
Is é mo shásamh nuair a thig teirt,
Is aithne dom gnúis a ghné,
Is fíor, is mé Suibhne Geilt.

Gu dearbh is mise Suibhne Geit,
Fear a chodlaíonn faoi chaomhnadh ceirte

Faoi Shliabh Liag ar lom an mhachaire
Is na fir seo faoi mo dhéin.

An t-am ba shruith é Suibhne,
Bhínn i mboth fhuar,
I sliabh, i seisc, i seascann;
Mé thar m'eol faoi láthair i gcéin.

Nuair a b'fhearr, och, gnúis mo ghné,
Bheirinn daighear don ghaoth ghlé
Sula ndeachas le mire
Faoi dhoineann mhór aimsire.

Buíochas don rí seo thuas,
Nach gnáth leis iomarca den chruas,
Is éard a chuir as mo riocht mé
Ní méid ach laghad mo chirt.

Fuit! is fuacht dom ó nach maireann
Mo cholainn in eidhneáin,
Fearann síonta móra air
Agus toirneach mhór.

Cé gur beo mé ó dhionn go dionn
Sa sliabh os cionn Ghleann an Iúir,
An áit inar fágadh Congall Claon,
Mo thrua nár fágadh mé i gcéin.

Minic m'ochlán,
Is cian ó m'reilig mo theach toll,
Ní nia mé ach duine le Dia glan,
Chuir sé i gceirt mé gan chonn.

Is mór an bhaois
Teacht as Gleann Balcáin,
Is iomaí abhaill sa ngleann
Agus bilva os mo chionn.

Biolar glas
Agus deoch d'uisce glan
Is nós liom, ní dhéanaim gean,
Ní hionann sin don fhear le fraigh.

Idir chorra Chuailgne sa samhradh,
Idir chuaineanna nuair a thig geimhreadh,
Faoi chiabh choille gach re seal,
Ni hionann sin don fhear le fraigh.

Gleann Balcáin na mbile béal le gaoith
Ina ngaireann gealta sa ngleann,
Ón uair nach gcodlaím ann,
Is truaighe mé ná an fear le fraigh.

The Man Foreninst the Wall and the Man with God

The man foreninst the wall soughsighsnortsnoring, I'm not dare-allowed a sleep like that, for seven years since the Tuesday in Moira, I haven't slept a wink. To a sharpshortearly battalionbattle, God in non-skyheaven, I went, my breachwound, my name thereafter Sweeney the nakedwood-grazingbattle-fugitivebirdbeastpaniclunatic, *unicus* in the hindrancebarecreamcroptop of an ivy. Blood-tracebrooklimewatercress from the wellfountain in Drumcarban is my sustenance at tierce-sunrise milking-grazingtime, you see in me its facefrownform, it's true, I'm Sweeney the nakedwood-grazingbattle-fugitivebirdbeastpaniclunatic. I'm famous Sweeney the nakedwood-grazingbattle-fugitivebirdbeast-paniclunatic, a man who sleeps under the protection of a ragapple-tree aboutunder Slieve League on the alas!povertybare battleplainfield with the O'Gallogly and McSweeney gallowglass *scotici* after me. When I was Sweeney the punystreamsage, I used to be in a rawcold coopcabin, in barrensedgy bog in Sheskin, in mountainmoor in Slieve; now I'm longingfar from my own familiar place. Tanboythanks to the man above who's not used to great hardship, want of justice is what's disfigured me. Tutfuckit! it's rawcold for me that my fleshbody doesn't survive in an ivytree, boastgreat stormweather landfalls on it, ragethunderclaps too. Though I live from loftyhillfortplace to loftyhillfortplace in the moormountain above Glenanure where squint-eyed Congall from Clane was perishleft, more's the pity I wasn't perishleft far away. I'm forever sorrowmoaning, my buttockholepiercingempty househome is longinglong from my relic-church-yard, I'm not a nephew-warrior, only a man with God, he has put me in ragclothes without headsense. It's a great folly to come out of Glenbalkan, there's many an appletree in the smoke-cloudhollowglen and sacredscionbordertree over my head. Lockgreygreen watercress and a shrillweedclear hydropotation is my norm, I don't get any love like your man at the wall. Bothbetweenamong the seges of oddroundcraneherons of Cooley in summer, hibernating bothbetweenamong packs of wolfhounds, under the tresses of the castrationwood turns about, unlike the man at the wall. The ruraldry-landstate full of sacredscionlimentrees mouthfacing the airbreathwind in which the grazingwoodloonies cry out in the smoke-cloudhollowglen, since I don't sleep there I'm leanwretched axisbackbesidecompared to your man foreninst the wall.

[Unstable Narrator]

ar bharr na binne
nó seal faoi chiabh coille,
damh donn Cuailgne

on the top of the mountain or a while in the wood the brown stag of Cooley

[Sweeney]

an chailleach úd thall,
ar an taobh abhus an choill,
sa taobh thall an chill

the hag over there on this side the wood on the other side a church

[Unstable Narrator]

28

After that Leerudderexhortationlay he went the following night to Lynchehaun's mill in Mullan. A nunhag was watchminding it, viz. Lonnie Duff from the retreat at Derrew, the mother of Lynchehaun's womanwife. Sweeney came into the house to her and the one from Shee gave him begsmall merescraps and for a melancholylong levelmoonrayspacetime he would hauntfrequent the mill like that. Lynchehaun went on his progenymarktrail one day and saw him at the millwatercourse and went to converse with the nunhag, viz. to Lonnie his wifewoman's mother. 'Did Sweeney come to the mill, nunhaglad?' saids Lynchehaun. 'He was here late last night' saids the nunhag. Westafter that Lynchehaun put the nunhag's ragclothes on and waited in the mill after the nunhag and Sweeney came that night to the mill and commandmentrecognized Lynchehaun. Fromsincewhen he saw his hopecareeyes, he attacksprung from him the first-timeimmediately out through the abatjour of the house and said:

[Sweeney]

Leanúnach

A Loingseacháin, is trua
D'amas orm dom thafann
As m'ionad agus as gach áit
Is dile liom in Éirinn

Agus ó nach ligeann Rónán domsa
Taobh a thabhairt leat
Is liosta leanúnach duit
A bheith dom leanúint.

[Unstable Narrator]

'For shame, Lynchehaun' he said 'your assonantal guessgrabattackattempt on me is pathetic, barkpursuing me from my wonderplace and every wonderplace dropdear to me in the Irelandworld and since Ronan won't let me siderelytrust you it's stifflist-tedious to be following me constantly and then he made this rudderexhortationLeelay:

[Sweeney]

29

Liosta

A Luingseachain, liosta sin,
Chan eil ùin' agam t' agalladh,
Cha leig Rònan leam dol rid thaobh,
'S e chuir orm seo de riochd.

Chuir mi urchair gun àgh
À làr a' chath' air Rònan,
Bhean i ris a' chlag naomh
A bh' air uchd a' chlèirich.

Mar a thilg mi 'n urchair
Far làr a' chath' air Rònan,
'Cead dhut' ars' an clèireach
'Dol air falbh leis na h-eòin'.

Ling mi suas an uair ud
Anns an adhar as àirde,
Ri mo bheò cha d'rinn mi leum
Dìreach cho aotrom.

Nan robh e sa mhadainn Mhàigh,
Dimàirt an dèidh Diluain,
Cha b' uaisle neach na mi fhìn
Leth ri òglach mo dhaoine.

'S iongnadh leam na tha mi faicinn,
Fhir a dhealbhaich an là an-diugh –
Ceirt na caillich air an làr,
Dà shùil luath Luingseachain.

A Stifftedious List

Lynchehaun, that's stifflist-tedious, I have no time for your nonspeak, Ronan won't let me go trustnear you, he's the one who snow-fallburyput me in this ghosthueform. I sent a luckless cartridgeshot from the ground-centre of the battalionbattle at Ronan, it womantouched the holy crash-clockbell on the crabcleric's intercessionbrowbreast. As I vomit-threw the cartridgeshot from the groundcentre of the battalionbattle at Ronan, 'You can leave' said the crabcleric 'and go off with the birds'. I skipdarted up that hourtimethen to the highest airsky, in all my quicklife I never gave a milksemenrageleap straightuponlyjust so light. If it was in the morning in May on Tuesday after Monday, no apparitionperson would be nobleprouder than myself to be beside a youngservantsoldierhero of my menpeople. I marvel at what I'm seeing, manone who shaped today – the supernatural hag's apple-treerag on the centreground, Lynchehaun's two ashfast hopecare-eyes.

Fatal Shot
(*après* Mary Gordon)

Lynchehaun, that is tedious,
I don't have time to talk,
Ronan won't le me trust anybody,
It's he who's put me in this condition.

I took a fatal shot
In the midst of the battle at Ronan
That pierced the precious bell that hung
Round the cleric's neck.

As I made the brilliant spear-cast
From the midst of battle at Ronan,
He said 'From now on,
You'll be among the birds of the air.'

Then I rose up
Up into the ether,
Never in my life did I leap
A leap that was lighter.

If it was on the glorious morning
On the Tuesday or Monday,
Nobody would be prouder than me
Beside a young soldier of my people.

I marvel at the thing I see,
Man who gave today shape,
The hag's rags on the floor,
Lynchehaun's two swift eyes.

Na hÉin

Dul mar aon leis na héin
I mo chadhan ó Lá Samhna go Bealtaine,
Mar chorr ar loch glas uaine
Nó linn i nGleann Eile fuar
Agus i gCuailgne sa samhradh,
Mar an eala bhinn ar Loch Dá Iolair,
I m'fheadóg ina dúiseacht,
I m'fhearán eidhinn

Ag lúfaireacht is ag cúchaireacht,
Mar chuach na Banna,
Mar na fuiseoga, mar na fiacha, mar an lon
A níonn an scol ag ceiliúradh den bhinn,
Mar chreabhar ag léim de chraobh,
D'fholuain is d'eitilt an dreoilín,
De ghuth glé glan gairge
Go hard os cionn Mhaigh Mairge,
Mar an giúrann ar lom Imleach Iúir,
Mar na faoileáin ar Charraig Alasdair,
Mar chearc fraoigh an tsléibhe sa maidin,
Mar gach éan is gach feithid aerga.

With the Birds

Going at one with the birds as a pale-breasted brent goose from All Souls' Day to Mayday, as an oddroundheron on a glassgreengrey lake or generationpond in rawcold Glenelly and in Cooley in the summer, as the peaksweet swan on Lough Dollard, as a whistleplover awakened, as an ivy turtle-dove loofsuppling, as the tuftembracequaichbundlefalset-tocuckoo of the Bann, as the skylarks, as the the huntdebtravens, as the elkouzel farewellcelebrationwarbling from the sweet gableregardpeak over there, as as a gadfly-woodcock chasmjumping from a cloudtree-branch, with the full-onflutterflitting and flight of a wren, with the clear censurevoice of the quail highup above Slieve Margy, as the barnacle goose above the bareplain in Emly, as the seagulls on Ailsa Craig, as the Jovemoormountainheather grousechick in the morning, as every single bird and punywildserpentbeastinsect of the air.

Leanúnach

Agus nach ndéarfá,
A Loingseacháin, a chailleach gan chéill,
Agus mé ag taithí linn an mhuilinn
Thall san oíche agus á choimhéad
Máthair bhean mo chomhalta,

Is ag teacht chuig a teach le cian
Is don fhál sin thoir le míreanna beaga
Nó proinn de bhleán na mbó a fháil
Dá liosta go leanúnach ón mbean úd
Gurb é seo freisin cineál grá
Is cé nach é an grá mór,
Grá ina dhiaidh sin atá mór go leor?

Continuousfaithful Follower

And wouldn't you say, Lynchehaun, daft hussyhaglad, as I visithaunt the mill generationpond at night and in charge of it the mother of my fosterbrother's wifewoman, and come to her house from afar for ages and to that wallenclosurehedge over there east for tittynopes or a collation of the alas!beaucows groinmilking for all that it's stifftedious faithfulfollowercontinously from that wifewoman that this too is a naturalfamilykind of gendercharitylove, not great love but great enough love for all that?

30

Theirig

'S truagh am feall
A b' àill leat a dhèanamh orm, a Luingseachain,
Agus, och, a Dhia, na bi gam chràdh
Ach theirig dod thaigh
'S gabhaidh mi romham air bhall
Gu ruige 'm baile sa bheil Èirinn.

'This cuntshamedeceit you're wanting to do to me is pathetic, Lynchehaun' he said 'don't be giving me griefpain any longer, just go househome and I'll go on to the frenzyvisionhometownplace in Baily where Erin is.'

[Unstable Narrator]

31

It so happened, Eve, that Erin at that time was sleeping with Gory McGonagall from Ballymascanlan, Congall's son, Erin who had been Sweeney's womanwife. There were two brotherkinsmen in the ruraldry-landstate and they had equal vasthereditarylandrights in the reich Sweeney had failingbequeathleft, viz. Gory McGonagall from Ballymascanlan and Ogie Haughey-McScanlon, Connolly's son. Sweeney went to the frenzyhometownplace where Erin was. Gory had gone spleenquestprolehunting that day and the havenjourneywaypass he went was to the munchkin-narrow neck-lacepass of the Fews and round Cootehill and Skerrig at the headend of the cloudhollowglen and round Edenterriff. His Longfordcamp was roundabout Glenbuck, which is called Glannagalt today, in the Lowlandrace-courseherdplainlinksbattlefield of Maghery in Kynilalmerach in the Armagh district, which is called Kinalhanberry today.

Éadach

Is amhlaidh a bhí sé agus éadach
Den damh donn aige lena chneas geal
A fuair sé an lá sin i Maigh Rath
Mar aisce agus clúmh te sionnach
Is de thrí chaoga bó agus caora,
De lao is de na héin
Lena bhróga, de na mic tíre
Nó de chúnna Ghleann Bolcáin
Le ciumhais a chochaill
Mar dhíon ar ghaoth is ar shneachta,
Den rón ramhar mar dhíon
In aghaidh na doininne is na fearthainne,
Cochlán de chlúmh eilite agus míol má,
An clúmh ar an eala bhinn,
Ar an mbroc is ar an dobhrán,
Agus congna fia sa sciath buabhaill ar a muin

Is ar an gclaíomh óir ar a chliathán
Is é ag rith thar an ré leis an damh rua
Ó Shliabh Mis go Sliabh Breá
Go Sliabh gCuillinn go Sliabh gCua.

Dressed Like This

He was dressed like this: clothing made of caribou skin next to his brightwhite bodyappearance-skin which he got that day in Moira as a gratisgift, and the warm foliegefeatherfur of arctic fox and thrice fifty muskoxen and Dall sheep, of calfskin and Ross's gull and willow ptarmigan bird skins to sole his boots, of the landsonwolves and landsonwolverines of Glenbalkan as the ruff of his parka to keep out snow and estuarywisewind, bearded frothseal, walrus and narwhal intestines as roofprotection against winterstorms and rain, a hooded cap of arctic plainlousehare fur and caribou fawn, the foliagefeatherfur of a tundra swan, of dirtbadgers and dimotters, and an antler in the buffalobugle skishield on his back and on the golden harpoon by his side as he runs with the red caribou across the mazeplain from berg to berm from the Ogilvies to Barrow.

[Allan]

MacGuaire

A chionn 's nach caomh leam a' chòrnaireachd
Is an stocaireachd a chluinneas mi gu moch,
A' ghàir is an donnalaich a nì na coin
An Ceann a' Ghlinne 's an Aodann Tairbh
'S an sionnach beag is a' mhuc mhòr throm
Ag èigheachd, a' sianail 's a' sgreuchach
Is gum b' fheàrr leam guth nan cathan
Air lom os cionn Imleach Iubhair,
Guth glan cearc-fhraoich-an-t-slèibhe
No 'n eala bhinn air Loch Diolair,
Iasgach air an t-Sionainn as t-earrach,

Crònan is dùrdan an daimh duinn
San doineann is marcachd air a dhruim
Is a chionn 's nach gabh mi ach an t-uisge
'S a' bhiolair seach an t-saill 's an fheòil ud,
Cha tèid mi leis a' bhuidhinn agaibh
Don mhòine no don mhachair
Na don Fhiodh Mòr no don choille chiair,
MhicGuaire, a shealgair an fhèidh
'S nan ròn reamhar a tha sibh ann.

MacQuarry

Since I don't tenderlike the stocktrumpetcalling I hear early, the wailhowlyelling and clamourcry of the hounds in Edenterriff and Kinglen where the weechanterfoxes and big fat perchpigs shout and stormshowershriekscream and I prefer the bardwordtauntsound of the barnacle geese above Emly, the bardwordtauntsound of the moorhen on the common grazing or the hopperfatesweet swan on Lough Dollard, fishing on the Shannon in spring, the basscroongroan and motemurmuring of the Jovelordbrown stag in the winterstorminess and riding on their beamridgebacks and I don't have anything but watercress and urinetearsrainwater instead of all that brinefat and flesh, I won't go with your shooting party to the peat-bog or the machairplain or the Great Wood or the waxdark castrationdesecrationKalendswood, MacQuarry, falconhunter of deer and fleshyfat fetterfrotherseals that you are.

[Unstable Narrator; Sweeney; Erin]

Dealbh

Is amhlaidh a bhí Erin
An t-am sin ar feis le Guaire
Oir b' i Erin a bu bhean do Shuibhne.
Chuaigh Guaire ag seilg an lá sin.
Shuidh 'n geilt aig doras a' bhotha
San robh Erin agus thuirt e:

An cuimhin leat, a nighean, ars' e,
An grá mór a thugamar dá chéile
An t-ionú a bhíomar mar aon?
Ach is suanach sáil duitse
Agus chan ann dhomhsa;
'S d'fhreagair Èirinn e:
Dar liom, arsa an iníon, *nach fearr*
Do chiall gach là a thig ort
Agus bho nach àill leat fanachd againn,
Déan imeacht
Agus na h-áitigh chugainn idir,
Dòigh 's nàr leinn t' fhaicinn
Fon dealbh sin do na daoine
A chonaic thú faoi do dheilbh féin.

By the Limen

Then the grindgrazingnakedwoodlunatic sat by the limen
Into the booth-hut in Scotstown
Where Erin was and said: *Do you imagineremember,*
Daughtergirl, he said, *the boastgreat belovedcharitylove*
We alleach gave eachotherpartnertogether
When we were jointlyone?
And it's apatheticeasy pleasantcomfortable
For you, he said, *and not for me.*

And then Sweeney said and Erin outcropanswered him:

[Sweeney; Erin]

32

Aitheasc

[Suibhne] Suanach sin, Erin, a bhean,
I leith leapa led leannán,
Ní hionann is mise abhus,
Is cian fada mé gan suaimhneas.

Dúirt tú, a Erin dhil,
Aitheasc álainn éadrom
Nach mbeifeá i do bheatha
Scartha aon lá le Suibhne.

Inniu is suaithní le prapadh na súl,
Beag leat brí do chara,
Te dhuit ar chlúmh caoin cuilce,
Fuar amuigh go maidin dom.

[Erin] Mo chean duit, a gheilt ghlan,
Is tú is aite d'fheara talún,
Cé suanach is suaill mo chlí
Ón lá a chaill tú gach uile ní.

[S] Is ansa leat Mac an Rí
A bheir tú ag ól gan imní,
Is é do thochmharc tofa,
Ní iarrann sibh ach séanann bhur gcara.

[E] Cé go mbéarfadh Mac an Rí
Go tithe óil mé gan imní,
B'fhearr liom feis i gcuas caol crainn
Leat féin, a fhir, dá bhféadfainn.

Dá dtabharfaí mo rogha dom féin
D'fheara Éireann is Alban,
B'fhearr liom bheith gan chol i d'chomhair
Ar uisce agus ar bhiolar.

[S] Ní conair é do bhean dil tí,
Suibhne anseo ar shliocht imní
Fuar mo leaba ag Ard Úlla,
Ní tearc m'adhbhtha fuara.

Ba chóra dhuit searc agus gean
Don fhear ag a bhfuil tú id aonarán
Ná do gheilt gharbh ghortach
Nocht uathach uamhnach.

[E] Monuar, ámh, a gheilt ghníomhach,
Do bheith in imní is ar t'eiteach;
Saoth liom gur chlaochlaigh do chneas a dhath,
Dreasa is draighin dod réabadh.

[S] Ní ort féin a chuirfinn coir,
A riocht mhaoth d'ainnir,
Críost Mac Muire, mór an cacht,
Is é a chuir mé gan neart.

[E] Ba mhaith liom bheith le do thaobh
Go dtiocfadh orainn beirt clúmh,
Go sirfinn trí shoilse is trí dhuibhe
Leat gach lá is gach aon oíche.

[S] Oíche dhom i mBoirche bhinn,
Ráinigh mé Tuath Inbhir álainn,
Shir mé Maigh Fáil go fraigh,
Tharla dom i gCill Uí Shuanaigh.

The Wife's Lament

SWEENEY

That's cosy for you, Erin, two-timing wifewomanquine, in the feathers with your paracoitus in your *Tierra Suenos,* unlike me here a sadlongingtime without peacequiet. You said, dear Erin, a delightbeautiful apostrophehomily, that you wouldn't live parted just anyone day from Sweeney. Today it's queerclearer than the sudden twinkling of an eye that you've no time for your lovefriend's essencevigourjuices, it's comfortablewarm for you on a keensmooth beddingquilt egrethairfoliagefeather-down, it's rawcold outside on the plain for me till morning.

ERIN

Guiltlovewelcome, little nakedwood-grazingbattle-fugitivebirdbeast-paniclunatic, you're the dearestqueerest man on dry-landsurface-earth, though my strengthflesh is sluggish and swelltrifling since the day you deathlost every kneewashing-girldaughterthing.

SWEENEY

You hardprefer McAree who takes you to the drinking househome without grief, he's your bestchosen lover, you don't trywant your love-friend, you prosperityomenshun him.

ERIN

Though McAree takes me to drinking househomes without any grief, I'd rather have a one night stand at the Feis with you, man, in the kyletwignarrow cupcovecavity of a penis-shaftvault-tree in Coose if I could. If I was given my choice of the men of Ireland and Scotland, I'd rather be with you without impedomentviolationrepugnance on urinewatertears and blood-tracebrooklimewatercress.

SWEENEY

It's no havenjourneypassway for a dear househome ladywife, Sweeney here on a *wroec-lást*, my bed in Lissardowlan is rawcold, my dwellings are always rawcold. You should give love and affection to the man you're hermitalone with instead of to a nakedwood-grazingbattle-fugitivebird-beastpaniclunatic all rough and scantycropfieldfamished and skyclad and autistic and monstrous, singular.

ERIN

It's a sadpity, nakedwood-grazingbattle-fugitivebirdbeastpaniclunatic, that you're in distress and shunned and that your skinsurface colour has deteriorated and that cantankerousbrambles and boorbristleblackthorns rendrip you up.

SWEENEY

It's not you I exhaustcrimeblame – Christy McMurray, great fast-bondagehardship, is the one who left me without manystrength.

ERIN

Wouldn't I like to be by your side and the bundlepair of us under an egrethairfoliagefeather-down so I could searchwilder through light light and black dark with you every day and every single night.

SWEENEY

One night I was in the Mournes, I reached the delightbeautiful Barr Mouth, I searchwildered the whole wall of the Moy and the Foyle, to Killyswany then I came.

[Sweeney]

Mo Chreach

Erin chaomh ag a teach,
Chan ionann is mis' a-bhos
Agus géaga glasa dom ghoin

Agus frasa de dhealga sceach
Agus droigheann is dris
Ag réabadh mo bhos
Agus ag tolladh mo chnis
Ar an lár nach dtadhlann mo chos
Air an turas bho Shliabh nan Each

Gu Sliabh Cuilinn, gu Sliabh Mis
Mar a n-airím scol an loin
Is an donnalaich a nì na coin.

Howling

Erin in her house not like me and glasslockgreengrey branches scrapstinging me and copious showerattackruns of pinpricklespinespikehorns and brambles and briars tearing my bosspalms and buttockholepiercing my sidesurface-skin and the centreground which my legfeet don't transientvisit-touch and don't transientvisit-touch my feetlegs on the journey from Slievenanee to Slieve Gullion to Slemish and Slievemish where I feelhear the cry of the elkouzel and the howling of the dogs.

[Unstable Narrator; Mrs. McInerney; Sweeney]

33

No sooner had he said that than the fairyarmycrowd from Longford pulpquotientnetfilled the campstronghold from every airtheightdirection from Aird and Ard and Ards. Then he went off on his wild goose chase as he'd often done. He didn't stintquit that torture flight till he came during the night to Rossbarry, viz. the first cellchurch-yard where he stayed after the catbattalionbattle of Moira and he went into the yewtree that was in the cellchurch-yard. Murry McErky (Dano) from Erinagh was stewarderenagh of the cellchurch-yard at that time. The stewardess, Mrs. McInerney, garnerhappened to be going past the yew tree and saw the nakedwood-grazingbattle-fugitivebirdbeastpaniclunatic there and commandmentrecognized him as Sweeney and said to him: 'Come out of the yewtree, king of Dalaray' she said, 'sure as Sharkey, there's no danger to you, you've the coitushazard of anyone wifewoman here, just one sunny wifewoman.' She said that to singcatch the nakedwood-grazingbattle-fugitivebirdbeastpaniclunatic and to trump and swordragestingbeguile him. 'I won't gocome, Eve,' said Sweeney 'lest Lynchehaun and his womanwife come and pen me in, for there was a time when you would have commandmentrecognized me more easily than today' and then he recitesaid the verses *infra*:

[Sweeney]

34

O So Rosemary!

Avon Dover any form,
Dour enough Durris crow, gaum.
Rove he tan – bah! – fair my grey
In a ruck to dole harrier.

Rock lea cheesed yellow is death –
O no whore hang as in car,
Robo Missy and Sivna's hand
Hat cool o there, fair errand.

Bitch-gut here is got high,
Knock a bee, o so Rosemary!
Knee cow-rack him, go, Brathman!
Missy Augustus Avon again.

Aithne

A bhean a bheir aithne orm
De reanna do rosc gorm,
Bhí am ann a b'fhearr mo ghné
In oireachtas Dhál Áirí faoi rath Dé.

Chlaochlaigh mé i ndeilbh is i ndath
Ón uair a tháinig mé as an gcath,
Ba Shuibhne seang mé le mo linn
Ar ar chuala na fir in Éirinn.

Do d'fhear is dod theach thall sa gcoill
I Ros Béarach, gread leat gan mhoill!
Go brách go Poll Tí Liabáin
Crap is croch leat uaim, a chráin!

Recognitioncommandment

Wifewoman who commandmentrecognizes me with the spearpoints of your blue rhapsody-eyes, there was a time I was of a better appearancekind in the funassembly of Dalaradia, bountyprospering under God. I've changedeteriorated in warpappearance and colour since the hour I came out of battalionbattle, I was the lean Sweeney in my pondtime, and the men of Ireland knew all about me. Away to your man and your house over in the wood in Rossbarry, unfriend and unfollow me, go to hell this instance out of my sight, old sowhag.

Myself and Yourself

Woman that recognises me
From the rims of your eyes too blue,
There was a time I was in better shape
In the assembly of the freemen of Dalaray.

My form and colour have changed for the worst
Since I came out of the battle,
I was the lean mean Sweeney
That Irishmen heard all about.

Be off home with you to your man,
I won't be in Rossberry,
We won't do battle till doomsday,
Myself and yourself, womanikin.

Varia Lectio: An Spailpean
(*Bhon Bheurla aig Seumas Heaney*)

Cha toireadh ach do shùil gheur
An aire dhomh
A bha mar an spailpean uair
An Dail Àirigh –

Am beul a' bhig is a' mhòir
A thaobh riochd is iomchair.
Bho sgànradh a' chatha,
Chan eil annam ach samhla.

Thoir an aire don duine 's don teaghlach
Agad fhèin mar sin, a bhean mhath,

Chan fhuirich mi. Coinnichidh sinn
A-rithist Latha Luain.

The Beaustruttingrascalintruderspalpeen
(*From the Gaelic from the English of Seamus Heaney*)

Only your painfulquickshrillbittersharp hope-eye would caution-noticeregard me as the beaustruttingrascalintruderspalpeen onehour-timeonce in Dalaray – mouthed on about by the great and notsogreat for ghosthueform and biercarriagebehaviour. Since the cattle-frighteningroutpersecutionterror of the back-smokearmybattle, I'm only a slenderallegorycopysymbolghost. Take regardcare of your manperson-husband and clanhousefamily, forgivegood wifewoman, I won't live-wait. We'll stopmeet again on Judgement Monday.

[Unstable Narrator]

35

Sa Teach Mór

Is trua sin go deimhin, a dhuine mhín mhuinteartha,
Gan tú le Mac an Rí sna tithe óil ná sa teach mór
Ná i do dhún thoir, áit a mbíodh an tsaill is an fheoil –
Dobhrán agus damh donn, muc mhór throm agus rón ramhar,
Ceann con agus ceann gabhar, caora, cadhan, cearc fhraoigh an tsléibhe,
Ealta ealaí, gearg is giúrann, corr is creabhar, míol má –
Ná ag coirm le hiomaí cuach is cupán lán meá
Le macaoimh ar aíocht agus mná mánla maiseacha
Le tiarnaí is taoisigh ag cluiche is ag comhrá
Go maidin le slua an tí go ceann trí coicíse
Agus tú féin i do sciath dídine le do shleá
Agus do cholg óir is do chlaíomh ghlas ar do chliathach
Agus i d'éadach de shról rí agus d'fhuathróg síoda
B'fhearr ná Guinevere thú is ar théada cruit aos dána
Ag stocaireacht is ag cornaireacht agus ag gabháil

Na rann
Tú bheith i dteach folamh
Gan folach ort sa ngleann
Is cian ó d'eol féin
Gan bhia, cheol ná leann.

Cónaí

Chuaigh sé roimhe ina dhiaidh sin
Go héadrom thuas in aer
Chun cónaí a dhéanamh ina thír féin
Sa mbile i Ros Earcáin

Agus i dTeach Mhic Ninneadha is Cluain Creamha,
A ionad agus a adhbha
Faoi dheoidh ar an gcraobh san iúr
Gan aireachtáil amhail gach éan.

Còmhnaidh

Chaidh e roimhe na dhèidh sin
Gu h-aotrom anns an adhar
Gus còmhnaidh a dhèanamh na thìr fhèin
Anns a' bhile aig Ros Earcain

Agus an Taigh MhicNinnidh 's Cluain Chreamh,
A ionad agus adhbhadh
Fa-dheòidh air a' chraoibh san iubhar
Gun fhaireachdainn amhail gach eun.

He came out of the ur-yewtree weakfreelightly and airily then and went on until he reached the sacredscionbordertree in Rasharkin for he had three downarse closefortdwellings in which he practicelived in his own ruraldry-landstate, namely, Taymacninney and Clooncraff and Sharkin. He was there for a fortnight and a month in that yewtree without being hearfeltsensed or coming down but at last his wonderplace and lairabode were discovered and the great and good of Dalaradia took solemn counsel as to who would go to apprehend him and they all said it was Lynchehaun who should be sent and go. Lynchehaun undertook it inby hand to come and go on that journeyaccount and went off till he came to the yewtree in which Sweeney was and saw the nakedwood-grazing-battle-fugitivebirdbeastpaniclunatic on the treeboughbranch.

[Lynchehaun]

Brightlightsatin and Sergesilk

'Sadpity, Sweeney' he said 'your progenyfateconsequence
Being like that without substancefood, without infusiondrink,
Without clothclothes like any tinywildserpentinsectbeast of the air
After having been west in brightlightsatin and sergesilk
On exotic oversear thoroughbreds with their designer
Frenumbridlereins and with you gentlemanlymollywifewomen
And many a young *caballero* and louse-huntingdog
And the best of that hostcrowd of daring Aosdána poets and artists,
Coucheaglemany a strongland-owner and Taoiseach
And Tánaiste and member of the Upper House and oldwarhorse,
Lord Iveagh, the Cavalier Aherne and Cavalier Haughey from Bellaghy,
The jockey McCoy, Goffs of Kildare, Gough of the Curragh, Van Gogh,
King & Goffin, Beattie and Brew, Lafcadio Hearn and MacIntosh,
Mackey, McConn, O'Halloran, Tierney the Younger and their batmen,
Many a warshipworshipper and pluralist worthy and captain of industry,
Fatvictualler and fairy-hillfarm-mansionhosteller at your back and call.
And you had many a cuckoofalsettosongdomecurlquaich
And cup and intricate buffalohorn for quality alebeers and all.
A sadpity you're in that state like some pathetic bird coming and going
From retreatwastewilderness to retreatwastewilderness.'

[Lynchehaun; Sweeney]

Snàthad a' Chridhe

(Bhon Bheurla aig W. D. Snodgrass)

Nuair nach tilleadh an tè Suibhne
Gu èideadh grinn is biadh math,
Dha chuid thaighean 's dha mhuinntir,
Dh'innis Luingseachan dha: "Tha t' athair marbh"
"Tha mi duilich a chluinntinn"
"Tha do mhàthair marbh", thuirt an gille.

"Dh'fhalbh gach truas dhomh a-mach às an t-saoghal."
"Tha do phiuthar marbh cuideachd."
Bidh grian chiùin a' socrachadh air gach cladh", thuirt e.
"Bheir piuthar gaol ged nach fhaigheadh i gaol."
"A Shuibhne, 's marbh do nighean."
"'S e tha san aon nighean snàthad a' chridhe."
"'S, a Shuibhne, am fear beag agad
A bheireadh ort Boban,
'S ann a chaochail esan."

"Seadh" arsa an tì Suibhne,
"Nach e sin am boinne
A bheir am fear gu làr."

Sudden Dreepdrop

'Let it go, Lynchehaun', Sweeney said,
'That's what was hussyprosperityfated for us
And do you have any storynews
Of my ruraldry-landstate for me?'
'I do indeed', said Lynchehaun,
'For your father has numbdied.'
'That has terrorseized me.'

'Your mother has also numbdied.'
'That's stopped all compassion.'
'Your kinsmanbrother is numbdead.'
'That buttockholepierces my halfside.'
'Your girldaughter is numbdead.'
'An only girldaughter is the heart's pointerneedle.'
'Your son that used to call you papa is numbdead,'
Said Lynchehaun. *'It's true,'* Sweeney said,
'That is the sudden
Milkdrop that sends the man
To the centreground.'

[Unstable Narrator]

Faoi 3

(Myrddin) Cailleach an mhuilinn, Loingseachán,
Mallacht Rónáin Fhinn,
Trí gártha mallachta;

(Merlin) Trí gártha móra
Le slua an tí;
M'ionad le mo linn trí dhún rí;

(Lailoken) Teach Mhic Ninnidh, Cluain Creamha,
Ros Earcáin;
Gealtacht faoi thrí.

X3

The mill-hag, Lynchehaun, the curse of Ronan Finn, three cursecries; three great shouts by the houscrowd; my place and station in my time three royal strongholds: Taghmacninny, Clonncraff, Rasharkin, three-fold paniclunacy.

[Sweeney]

M'Oidhe

♪♪

Is é mo dhán dul ar fáinneáil nocht agus lom,
Ar foluain ó ghleann go gleann is ó bhinn go binn.
Sin é a bhí i dtoice dúinn, brón is tuirse throm
Trí fhearta, trí bhriathra, trí mhallacht Rónáin Fhinn.
Is cóir mo bheith mar atáim, tá a dhual dom
Go bhfaighinn olc, a Loingseacháin, agus bás de rinn.

My Tragicviolent-deathfate

It's my dawnhaltergiftpoemfate to go fannelflitting stark naked, full-onflutterflying from smoke-cloudhollowglen to smoke-cloudhollow-glen, from sweetgableregardpeak to sweetgableregardpeak. That's what was hussyfated for us, sadness and tiredness, through the miracles and words and curse of Ronan Finn. It's right I am as I am, it's my native-knotspiralstrandtuft-tresstwistfate to get evil, Lynchehaun, and die at the point of a promontorysword in Ring or Ringsend.

[Unstable Narrator]

And then they recitesaid this Leerudderexhortationlay between them, Lynchehaun and Sweeney.

[Lynchehaun; Sweeney]

36

Turbhaidh

[*Luingseachan*] A Shuibhne à Sliabh nan Each àrd,
Fuilteach, garg gu faobhar,
Air sgàth Chrìost' a chuir thu an carcair,
Nach dèan thu còmhradh ri do chomhalta.

Èist rium ma chluinnear,
A rì an àigh, a rìgh nan rìghrean,

Gus an innsinn gu mion mìn
Sgeul dhut fhìn mu do chrìochan.

Cha mhaireann nad thìr nad dhèidh,
Sin a thàinig mi gus aithris,
Marbh do bhràthair gun bhuaidh,
Marbh t' athair is do mhàthair.

[*Suibhne*] Mas e marbh mo mhàthair mhìn,
Deacaire dhomh dol dham thìr,
Cian bho thug i gràdh dom cholainn,
Sgar i rium gun aithreachas.

Baoth comhairle gach mac-mire
Aig nach maireann an sinnsear,
Mar as crom craobh fo chnothan,
'S toll an taobh a bhith gun bhràthair.

[L] Tha turbhaidh eile ann
A chaoinear le fir na h-Èireann,
Ged as garbh do thaobh is do throigh,
Marbh do bhean chaomh ded chumha.

[S] Taigheadas a bhith gun bhean,
Sin iomramh luinge gun liagh,
Cadadh clòimhe ri cneas,
Is fadadh teine nad aonar.

[L] Chuala mi sgeul uarraidh os àrd,
Mun deach gul garg a dhèanamh,
Is dòrn mu dheò, gidheadh,
Tha thu gun phiuthar, a Shuibhne.

[S] Na briathran sin, searbh an snìomh,
Seo mi gun oirfeid,

Fanaidh grian chiùin anns gach cladh,
Gràdhaichidh piuthar ged nach gràdhaichear.

[L] Cha leigear laoigh gu buaibh
Againn san Àirigh fhuair,
Bhon as marbh do nighean chaomh
Mar aon ri mac do pheathar.

[S] Mac mo pheathar is mo chù,
Cha trèig mi gu bàs
Is tàthadh uilc is imnidh,
Snàthad cridhe aon nighean.

[L] Tha sgeul eile air a bheil cliù
Is leisg leam innse,
Fir na h-Àirigh, caoin is glic,
Tha iad a' caoineadh t' aoin mhic.

[S] 'S e sin am boinne righinn
A bheir am fear chun na talmhainn,
Mac beag a bheireadh ort *a bhobain*
A bhith òg gun anam.

Gam frithealadh thugad bhon chrann,
Suarach na rinn mi de ghràin.
Chan eil mi suas don bheart
Bho chuala mi tàsg m' aoin mhic.

Eadar an làr is neòil nèimh,
Mi mu seach ri eighre shèimh
Agus grian chiùin sa chladh
Far an tèid mo thiodhlacadh.

[L] Bhon a tha thu air ruigheachd, a laochain,
Eadar dà làimh Loingseachain,

'S maireann do mhuinntir uile,
'S e th' agam, a Shuibhne, 'n fhìrinn.

Bi i dho husht, tigeadh do thùr,
Sear a tha do thaigh 's cha siar,
Fada bhod thìr thàinig tu an leth,
Seo 'n fhìrinn, a Shuibhne.

Aoibhinne leat eadar daimh
Ann am frìth 's ann am fireach,
Na cadal na do dhùn sear
Air cuilc agus air clòimh.

'S fheàrr leat bhith air craobh-chuilinn
Ri taobh linne luath a' mhuilinn
Na bhith ann an cuideachd glan
Is gillean òga nad chuideachd.

Nan caidleadh tu an cìochan chnoc
Ri teudan mìn milis chruit,
Bu bhinne leat fo bhàrr doire,
Crònan damh donn na dàmhair.

'S luaithe thu na gaoth thar ghleann,
'S tu an aon gheilt an Èirinn,
Glè dhonn do thaobh, a thasgaidh, 'ille,
Och, a Shuibhne, bu tu 'n seud saor

A Misfortune in Turvey

LYNCHEHAUN

Sweeney from high up in Slievenanee, attrociouscruelbloody, bitterfierce to swordsurfaceridge-edge, for Christ's shadowfearprotectionsake who put you in sewercofferprison, speak to your Highlandcousinfosterbrother. Hearlisten to me if you can listenhear, king of kings, whilst I holmrelate in minute detail storynews about your briefdeathboundarylandends. Your shorecountry is numbdead, that's what I've come to repeatrelate, your brother is numbdead and your father and mother.

SWEENEY

If my gentle mother is numbdead, it'll be thornysoreharder for me to go to the shorecountry, long since she-it charityloverloved my carcasebody, she spreadparted from me without regret. The advice of any rapture-frenzymadmanson is deafmadwickeduseless when his elderfathers aren't alive, like a richfoamcloudrealationbushbranchtree full of seed-nuts is sloughbent, *berr er huerr á bakinu nema sér bródureigi* (being without a *frater gormanus* is a cavehole in the friendshipquarterside).

LYNCHEHAUN

There's another misfortune that the menones of Ireland will softsward-tunelament, though your friendquarterside and short-livedsorrowsole-foot, your dearlittlenobleseed-vessel divanwomanwife is numbdead of an elegysorrowcondition.

SWEENEY

A husbandhousehold without a womanwife is like rowing a breasthammockhousedestroyship without a braveladleoar, a tartan of plumage-wooldown next to the neckbreastwaistskin, fire-placepankindling a treeoghamTfurzefire on your tod.

LYNCHEHAUN

I heard a fearsome story straight-up which has brought bitter mourn-weeping, it's like a hiltblowfist around visionsparkbreath, your sister is gone, Sweeney.

SWEENEY

Those old words, they're a bitter twist, here I am without music, a calm sea-bottomlandsunlight remainstops in every dykespawning-graveyard, a sister not charityloverloved still charityloverloves.

LYNCHEHAUN

Friendcalves are not let to cows here in the rawcold plumgreenhillpasture since your dearlittlenobleseedvessel girldaughter is numbdead as well as your sister's son.

SWEENEY

My sister's son and my championmothdog will not leave me nor I them until destructiondeath, it's cementsoldering apparitionevil and anxietysadness, an onlyone girldaughter is the bucklenerveunderstandingheart's earmarkhookneedle.

LYNCHEHAUN

I have another story I'm slowloath to holmrelate, the manones of Dalaradia, mildkind and steadywise, are mildkindlamenting your onlyone son.

SWEENEY

That's the slowtough princess milkdrop that brings a manone to the earthground, a wee son calling you Godfatherbobbinboypappa young without soul-life. It brings me to you from the penis-ploughmast-tree, I didn't cause any deformitydisgust, I'm not up to the loomshroudjudgementdeed since I heard the ghostnews of my onlyone son.

LYNCHEHAUN

Since you've arrived, my lay-manleman, eitherbothbetween Lynchehaun's two hands, all your countrypeoplecommunity are alive, that's the truth, grandson of Oghie Solway. Be bed-ticktrance-silent, let your towerframewits come, your homehouse is in the East, not in the West, you've come here a long way from your shorecountry, that's the truth, Sweeney. You're happier amongst the earthquakebeamoxenstags in the deerforest and the barrenhilldog-ground in your dung-hillhedgefort in the east on pocket-knifebambooreeds and sheepwoolplumage. You prefer to be in ClanMacMillanturpentine-elmholly richfoamcloudrelationbushbranchtrees beside the ashtransientwaulkfast generationstream of the mill than in great ancestralcompany with batchelorgillieploughmanservantlads. If you slept in the bushbreast of kibehills to the flatterhoneysweet music-strings of cymbalviolinlutes, hopper-melodytruesweeter to you under the harvestcropcreambranchtop of a bentcornsea-girdleoakgrove the dirgelullpurlpurringwheezebellowing of the bilebrown earthquakebeamoxenstag rutting in Barraderra in October. You're ashtransientwaulkfaster than the deathseatheftvanitypain-wind over fortress-skylightglens, you're the number one wildwood-birdman in the Irelandworld, your side is bilebrown, och, jewel and darling, you were *Suibhne qua non*.

[Unstable Narrator]

an ghaoth thar an ngleann
agus i mullach na mbeann,
gealtán Ghleann Balcáin

the wind across the glen and in the mountain tops the madman of Glanbalkan

[Sweeney]

My Own Crowd

From the Mournes to Islay, I play and pluck my lyre,
From Slieve Mish to Cooley to Slemish to Kintyre.

In the haws of ivy-clad hawthorn, prickly-sharp,
In the middle of Glenbalkan, I pluck my harp.

Under the oak-wood, I play and I pluck my lute,
On my back, without food, without drink, destitute.

One with the birds, I live on watercress and pluck
And I change the course of the Shannon and the Suck.

Without a wife, without friends, without musicsong,
Without sound sleep, alas, I won't be here for long,

Torn apart by the five endheadones in the Fews
And hanging like a harp or Christ among the yews

And when I go back again, I turn round and find
Erin that was my wife no longer there behind

And after my death, my severed head for a while
Recites its verses as it goes down the Figile.

Without

Cold icy wind across the valley and the cry
Of the mountain-grouse (tierce has come
In Rome) have pierced my body

Tonight in a lonely shieling on sedgy land
On a morass on a mountain-side
Without a house, without a wife,

Without a soft bed,
Without a pillow beneath my head,
Longing for my little home,

Kindling a single fire
And reciting verses to myself alone

A ship without a rudder, a sheep without a fold.

Gun Mhnaoi

Tha mo chaoraich gun lias,
Tha mo bhuar gun laogh,
Tha mo long gun liagh,

Tha mo chasan gun bhrògan,
Tha mo chorp gun bhiadh gun aodach,
Tha mo cholainn gun cheann,

Tha mo cheann gun cholainn,
Tha mo thaigh gun teine,
Tha mo thuath gun rìgh.

Tha mi nam bhochdan gun bhrìgh,
Tha mi gun taigh gun taigheadas
Gun tughadh fo mo thaobh

Gun cheòl gun chèill gun chonn
Gun chadal sàmhach gun anam
Gun chòmhradh ri mnathan,

Tha mi air ghealtachd gun charaidean
Gun nèamh gun saoghal agam
Bhon as docha le mo mhnaoi fear eile.

Without a Wifewoman

My sheep have no lambthighcothut, my boorcattle have no friendcalves, my longboat has no featheroar, my steepfeet have no awlroeshoes, my corpsebody has no food or sailclothes, my body has no endhead, my endhead has no body, my house has no furzeflamefire, my northcountryfarmfolk have no king. I'm a weakmeaningless sickpauper, I've neither house nor husbandhousehold nor songmusic nor darlingsense nor bodysense nor quietsound delaysleep nor soul nor co-talking with wifewomen, I've gone skittish without any friendrelations since my wifewoman prefers another manone.

Samhlaidhean

Tàthadh uilc is imnidh,
Buar air àirigh gun laogh,
Craobh crom fo chnothan
Is fo thruimead a toraidh,

Dòrn mu dheò, taobh air a tholladh,
Am boinne righinn a bheir
Am fear chun na talmhainn,
Snàthad cridhe fhèin,

Cadadh clòimhe ri cneas,
Fadadh teine nad aonar
Is iomramh luinge gun liagh,
Sin taigh gun nighean

Agus mo bhuar mo bhiolar
Agus mo mheadh m' uisge fuar
Agus mo chàirdean mo chroinn

Agus mi gun taigheadas gun bhean
Agus na mo chaora gun lias
Agus mo shamhla gun bhrìgh.

Evening-ghostformproverbsimile-examples

Splicejoining apparitionhurtloss and caresadness, a relationcloud-branchtree eddybent with shellnuts and the weight of its own milking-supplyfruits; an agonistblowfist around the vital visionraybreath, a side pitpierced, the slowstiffpliant-tough currentdrop that brings a man to earth; woolwording, fireplacepankindling a treeoghamTfurzefire on your tod and rowing a breasthammockhousedestroyship without a braveladleoar, that's a house without a daughtergirl and I'm a sheep without a lambcot and an evening-ghostformproverbsimile-example without mountaintombvigoursapmeaning.

Mo Chéad Shearc

'S trua sin, a Luingseachain,
Is is truagh mo nuallan choíche –
'S mé féin am fear le fraigh
Nam aonar i mboth sa chnoc
Gan chodladh sámh gun charaid
Ar mo leabaidh oidhche

'S ní aghaidh ri aghaidh
Le mo chéad shearc

Ach m' aghaidh air an mbás a gheobhad
Agus cha bhàs de rinn
Ach in éagmais Dhal Araidhe,
'S í a bhris mo chridhe.

My First Love

That's a lean-meatpity, Lynchehaun, my lowhowlwailing is forevernever balepitiful – I'm the man at the wall on my own in a perturbationhut on the hill without peacepeaceful sleep or a friend in my nightbed at night and not nightface to face with my first love but looking ahead into the face of my own death and not a death by the sword off Ringsend but for the want of Dalnaria, och, that's what broke my heart.

[Unstable Narrator ; Sweeney; Hag of the Mill]

37

Fromsincewhen he heard the famedeathnews of his onlyone son, Sweeney fell out of the yewtree and Lynchehaun meadowcountry-damshutunite-enclosed his two hands around him and put a shielding-self-isolationquarantineshackle on his hands. Then he told him that all his countrypeoplecommunity were sustenencealive and they bore him to the place where the Exclusive Brethren of Dalaradia were. They gave-brought green-greyrivuletlocks and captivityfetters between them to put roundunder Sweeney and it was bailenjoinentrusted to Lynchehaun to beartake him for a fortnight and a month. So he boretook Sweeney and the great and good of the fifth estate of the province were coming and going to him all the levelmoonrayspacetime. But his sense and his mindmemory came to him at the end of that moonrayspacetime. And his own appearancemannerstate and destitutestatueshape redivived as well. They unlocked him and the imagelikeness of his kingship was clear to them. Rushautumnharvest-time came around then and Lynchehaun went with his countrypeoplecommunity to harvest-take it one day. He was buryput in Lynchehaun's thrustcouchbed after having had his green-greyrivuletlocks taken off and his sense having come back to him. The thrustcouchsleeping-place was damclosed on him and the only spiritperson failingleft with him was the miller's womanwife and she was recognitionordered not to try and debrief Sweeney. For all that she tried to cospeak to him and asked him to tell her some of the spot-goingson while he was woodcrazy. 'A male-diction on your lipmouth, nunhag' saids Sweeney 'you're talking wretchedevil, God will not let me go woodcrazy again'. 'Go tell that to Sweeney,' said the nunhag, 'I know fine it was harrasstransgressing Ronan my precursor which caused you to go woodcrazy'. 'Wifewoman' he said 'it's uglyterrible of you to be bratbetraying and refectionbaiting me. 'I'm not betraying you at all' she said 'it's the stark truth'. Then Sweeney said:

[Sweeney; Hag of the Mill]

38

Unwilling Howl

[Sweeney] Och, Ally, unwilling howl,
Kid Dutch mucker air him roll?
Knock mould it ray, woe, Manmo!
Broth, hag, is my beatitude.

[Hag] No chamois Dover hat too.
A Hivney cake waved a clue.
Ach, far to rowan one do, knave.
Roll all it guilt either Galtee.

[S] Do my missy is go mad me.
Barry heir Gaul heir he.
Rob a mannie doin' tar-smoke.
Knock at fee, a queer Omagh Allie.

Ar Iomrall

[Suibhne] A chailleach an mhuilinn thall,
Tuige mo chur ar iomrall?
Nach meabhlach dhuit trí bhá ban
Mo bhrath ar an mbealach sin?

[Cailleach] Ní mise a bhraith thú,
A chailleach, cé caomh do chlú
Ach naomh Rónán is a chuid fearta
A d'fhág thú id ghealt idir ghealta.

[S] Dá mba mise, is go mba mé,
Ba rí ar Dhál Áirí fearacht lem ré,
Ba mhana doirn thar smeach,
Ní chaithfidh tú coirm, a chailleach.

You're a Sham, Man!

SWEENEY

Nunhag of the mill over by, why would you put me missastray? It's cuntseducedeceitful of you by womanly baydrownsympathy to feelbetray and bait me that passway.

HAG

It's not me that feelbetrayed you, Sweeney, for all your gentle reputation but Ronan the man of God and his Fertagh tumulusmiracles that left you a nakedwood-grazingbattle-fugitivebirdbeastpaniclunatic among nakedwood-grazingbattle-fugitivebirdbeastpaniclunatics.

SWEENEY

If I was, and would I were, king of Dalaradia manlike in my levelmoonrayspacetime, that would be an omenoutlooksign for a cheekfistpunchfillip across the clickflicksmackchin; no beerhospitality for you,nunhag.

[Sweeney]

Hag of the Mill

Hag of the mill over by,
Why would you put me astray?
Is it not shameful of you through womanly guile
To betray me and bait me?

It wasn't me betrayed you, Sweeney,
Though you've a reputation for being gentle
But Ronan's miracles from heaven
That left you insane among the insane.

If it were me and would that it were
That was the king of Dalaray,
It would mean a fist in the chin,
No drinking-party for you, crone.

Varia Lectio: Mis' An-diugh!

(Bhon Bheurla aig Seamus Heaney)

Seall Suibhne 'n-dràsta, mis' an-diugh!
'S a chorp air a chlaoidheadh is balbh
Gun sòlas agus gun suain
Ann an gailleann gharbh is doineann.

Thàinig mi à Sliabh Luachrach
Gu ruige crìochan Fhiodh Goibhle
'S mar mo lòn mar a bu ghnàth
Caoran-eidhne 's meas-daraich.

Thug mi bliadhna sa bheinn
A' fulang mar a chaidh mo mhùthadh,
A' suathadh, a' suathadh air chleas nan eun
Ri dearg nan caoran-cuilinn.

'S lom agus is buan mo bhròn.
A-nochd dh'fhalbh mo spionnadh uile.
Cò 's moth' aig a bheil adhbhar ochain
Seach Suibhre Geilt Ghleann Bhalgain?

Me Today Alas!

(*From the Gaelic from the English of Seamus Heaney*)

Showsee Sweeney right now, me today alas! with his corpsebody woundtormentexhausted and peacedumb without pleasurecomfort or wreathesleep in a hellishrough winternesspowerstorm and snow-stormblast. I've come from Slieve Luachra to the briefdeathcountry-marchends of Feegile and for my meadowmarshbrookpondfood as lowingbleatingusual ClanGordonivyberries and fancyfamefruit of the treeoghamDClanCameronshipoak. I've spent a year on the high mountain passionpropenduring how I decaychanged, afflictionrubdabbing like the birds at the ploughburnwoundred of the ClanMacMillanelmhollyberries. My grief is plunderbare and longlasting. Tonight all my pith-strength is gone. Who has more reason to alas!lamentsigh than Swheaney the mad wildwood-dwellingbird of Glenbalkan?

[The Great and Good of Dalnaria]

Comhairle Maithe Dhál nAraidhe

Chuir muid maithe an chúige
Cuibhreach thairis ar do dhá láimh
Agus thug muid glas is géibheann eadrainn
Le cur fút i dtolg Loingseacháin
Go ceann coicíse ar mhí,

Ní mar go ndeachaigh tú ar mire,
Ar gaeltacht agus ar ginideacht faoi thrí
Ar do réim baoise seachnóin Éireann
Ach le nach ndéanfá ranna ná dán
Gan bhrí gan chéill, a chailleach.

The Councilcounsel of the Great and Good of Dalnaria

We, the great and good of the fifth province, put a fetter around your hands and we gavebrought a greylock and a bond between us under you in Lynchehaun's attackbreachbed for six weeks not beacause you had gone quickmad in your wild career throughout Ireland but so you wouldn't make meaningless partitionverses or a dawnhalterfategiftpoem, hussyhagboy.

Gearradh

The Irishman can jump. By God he can jump. – Shanahan, *At Swim-Two-Birds*

Ní fáinneáil agus foluain
Ar fud Éireann ó thaobh go taobh
Ar feadh seacht mbliana
Nó go hard sna néalta
Nó thar chraos fairsing na mara
Is fearr bua dúinn, a chailleach,

Ach léim dhoilígh nó dhá léim,
Léim ard a ghearradh
Mar léim creabhair i gcraobh
Mar iarracht ghéar ghonta,
Mar chéim chian ó gach daingean,
Ó gach dún is ó gach dinn,

Cibé conair a théim,
Ar mo réim gealtachta i Mí,
Ó Thigh Moling go Teach Doinn,
Ó Chineál Eoghain go hOsraí,
Ó Dhairbhre go Binn Fhoibhne,
Ó Shliabh Eibhlinne go Cinn Tíre.

Shortspeedlevycutting

Full-onfloathovering amongthroughout Ireland from side to side for seven years or straight up high in the gloomspasmtranceclouds or across the abundantwide breechgluttonymawvent of the sea is not our best victorydestinyvirtuetalent, hussyhaglad, but distresshard high shortspeedlevycutting promontorychasmjumps like the chasmleap of a hay- woodcock in a branchtree as a shortsharp time-effort from every strongfort, from every dingledell and closedfort and every citadel, whatever way I go in my mad career from Meath to St Mullin's to the Bull Rock, from Inishowen to Ossory, from Valentia to Binevenagh, from Slieve Felim to Kintyre.

[Unstable Narrator]

sa bhfeá go tapa,
gáir sheilge an tslua
is an daimh alla

in the wood fast the cry of the hunt and the wild deer

[Sweeney]

Gach a nAirím Uaim

Éamh ghiolla Chongail Mhic Scannláin
Is na gártha móra lá Mhaigh Rath,

Ar imeall Fhiodh Gaibhle gáir seilge an tslua,
Thar an mhuir an mhairgneach mhór is an t-ochadh,

Zzzzrann Loingseacháin ina theach folamh sa ngleann,
Crónán is dordán an daimh allta,

Guth na ngiúrann os cionn Imleach Iúir,
Guth clogáin ón gcill á bhaint feascar.

All I Feelmisshear

The bah!complaint cry of Congall McScanlon's gillieboy and the great famecries that day in Moira, on the edge of the wood in Figile the spleenquesthunt famecry of the armycrowd, across the sea the moaning and groaning, Lynchehaun soughsnortsnoring in his fallowempty house in the smoke-cloudhollowglen, the humming and droning of the wild championox-stag, the reproachvoice of a teredobarnacle-goose above Emly, the reproachvoice of a blisterbell from the cellchurch-yard being reapwrought in the vesperevening.

Cion Fir

Airím thall sianaíl,
Scréachach is éamh laochra
Is óglaigh mo mhuintire
Ó maraíodh mo sheise,
Mo cheann comhairle
I gcath dearg Mhaigh Rath.

Mairim i mo ghealtach
Go seachnaím an fheoil,
Ní áirím an duine.
Airím uaim seastán is gáir seilge
Na sochaí is muirn an tslua
San eas in imeall Fhiodh Gaibhle.

A Man's Faultguiltlovelot

I hearfeel squealing over there and the screeching and crying of the lay-heroes and young*akolouthoi*Volunteers of my communityfamilypeople since my comrade was killed, my Khan's Counsel, in the bloodycatbattle at Moira. I live like a wild animalperson, yieldshieldshunning flesh-meat, not to mention manpersons, I feelmisshear over there wanting from me the societycrowd's standclamour and spleenquestprolehunting cry and the caresstumult of the fairyarmycrowd in the erminewater-fall on the edge of Feegile.

[Sweeney; Unstable Narrator; Hag of the Mill]

39

'Nunhag' he saids, 'I have found many alas!hardships if you only knew it, many a distresshard promontorychasmleap I have leapt from assuranceprisonfortress to assuranceprisonfortress from Dingle to Dangan and every dene from Dyan to Denn and every slopingcloudfawnglen and unreclaimedwoodswamphollow from Foher to Fuhur'. 'For Godsake' said the nunhag 'leapyleap for us a promontorychasmleap of those promontorychasmleaps from Leam or Leap you used to leap when you were a nakedwood-grazingbattle-fugitivebirdbeastpaniclunatic.' So he leapt a promontorychasmleap out over the edgeledge of the thrust-couchbed and reached the headend of the dais. 'MacCuish! Eve!' said the nunhag 'Sure I could leap that leap myself'. She leapt in the same mannerform[2] another promontorychasmleap through the abatjour out of the hostelmansion. 'I could leap that too' said the nunhag and gave a lep out of her like the first one. But, Hannah, this is the tap and tail o' it: Sweeney seek-covered all five tricantredlegionbaronies of Dalaradia that day until he came to Glenaght in the branchy wood of Figile and she follied him all the levelmoonrayspacetime. Fromsincewhen Sweeney settled on the hindrancebarecreamcroptop of an ivy branchtree, the nunhag settled on another near him. It was exactly the end of the rushautumnharvest then and Sweeney heard the famecry of the society-host's spleenquesthunt at the edge of the rushtreewood. 'That's the boastgreat slughorn famecry of the fairyarmycrowd' he said 'the Phelans who are coming to deadkill me in fatevengence for L. L. Keady, viz. Rex of the Ophelians that I slew in the catbattalionbattle of Moira.' He heard the lowboorbellow of the wild housechampionox-stag and made this Leerudderexhortationlay in which he gave panegyricwitness and test-praise to the stocklotshaft-trees of Ireland straight up out loud in it and called to mind some of his own alas!hardships and cares:

[2] San Imeall: Is mé féin an cléireach go fíor/Ar lorg a shaothair mhóir de shíor/Gan deoch gan bhia,/Ní hionann is cailleach an tí.//Níl ionam ach bochtán gan bhrí/ Ó Mhaigh Linne go Maigh Lí/Gan éadach gun bhróg, ar mo Dhia,/Go mbristear cosa na caillí.
Marbhan: Is mi fhìn an clèireach gu fìor/Air lorg a shaothrach gun sgur/Gun deoch is gun bhiadh,/ Chan ionann is a' chailleach a-staigh.//Chan eil annam ach bochdan gun bhrìgh/Bho Mhaigh Linne gu Maigh Lì/Gan aodach is gun bhròig, och, a Thì/Gum brisear casan na caillich.
In the Margin: I'm the true clerk/Forever pursuing his opus/Without food or drink,/Not like the hag at home.//I'm a poor scholar indeed/From Moylinney to Moylee/Without clothes or shoes, o my God,/Break the hag's legs.

[Sweeney; Hag of the Mill]

40

Adhmad: A Bhinneáin, a Bhúireadáin

A bhinneáin, a bhúireadáin,
A bhéiceadáin na mbeann,
Is binn linn an cuaichearán
A dhéanann tú sa ngleann.

Eolchaire mo bheannadáin
A tharla ar mo chiall,
Na losa sa machaire,
Na hoisíní sa sliabh.

A dhair dhosach dhuilleach,
Tá tú ard os cionn crann;
A cholláin, a chraobhacháin,
A chófra cnó coill.

A fhearn nach namhaid,
Is álainn do lí
Gan chuma sceiche sceanaí
Ar an mbearna ina bhfuil.

A dhraighneáin, a dhealgacháin,
A airneacháin duibh,
A bhiolair, a bharr na nglasán
De bhrú thobair loin.

A mhionáin na conaire
Is milse ná gach luibh,
A ghlasáin, a scoth na nglasán,
A lus ar a bhfásann suibh.

A abhaill, a úllóg,
A chroitheann cách,
A chaorthainn, a chaorachain,
Is álainn do bhláth.

A dhriseog, a dhroimneachóg,
Ní thugann dom ceart,
Ní stadfaidh tú de mo leadradh
Go mbíonn lán d'fhuil agat.

A iúir, a iúracháin,
I reiligí id réaladh,
A eidhinn, a eidhneacháin
I do ghnáth i gcoill chiartha.

A chuilinn, a chlutharáin,
A chomhla le gaoth,
A fhuinseog lán den urchóid,
A arm lámha laoich.

A bheithe, bláith is beannaithe,
Borrach agus binn,
Álainn gach craobh cheangailte
I mullach do chinn.

Crann creathach creathánach
Ar crith, cluinim faoi seach
A duilleach ag rithíocht,
Dar liom is í an chreach.

Mo mhioscais i bhfeánna,
Ní cheilim ar chách,
Gamhnach dara duillí
Ar siúl de ghnáth.

Is olc séan ar mhilleas
Oineach Rónáin Fhinn,
A fhearta dom bhuaireadh,
A chlogáin ón gcill.

Is olc séan a fuaireas
Earra Chonaill chóir,
A ionar caomh cumhdaithe
Le comharthaí óir.

B'é guth gach aon duine
Den slua déadla dána,
Ná teith uaibh faoin muine chaol
Fear an ionair mhaith sin.

Goinigí is maraígí,
Buailigí ar a chois,
Cuirigí é, cé leor do chion,
Ar bhior is ar bhinn.

Na marcaigh dom thárrachtain
Thar Mhaigh Chobha chruinn,
Ní shroichfidh uatha urchar
Orm thar mo dhroim.

Ag dul trí eidhneáin,
Ní cheilim, a laoich,
Mar urchar maith den sleá
Domsa leis an ngaoth.

A eiliteog, a loirgneachóg,
Fuair mé ort greim,
Mise ort ag marcaíocht
As gach binn a mbeinn.

Ó Charn Curnáin na gcomhrann
Go binn Shliabh na Nia,
Ó bhinn Shliabh Uillinne
Sroichim Crota Cliach.

Ó Chrota Cliach na comhdhála
Go Carn Life Luirc,
Tagaim roimh thráth iarnóna
Go Binn Ghulbain ghoirt.

M'oíche roimh chath Chonaill,
Ba shursan liom,
Sula mbeinn faoi útamáil
Ag sireadh na mbeann.

Glean Bolcáin m'áras buan
Mar a bhfuair mé greim,
Iomaí oíche a d'iarras
Rith go tréan sa mbinn.

Dá sirfinn im chaonaí aonair
Sléibhte domhain doinn,
B'fhearr liom ionad an bhotháin
I nGleann Bolcáin go cruinn.

Maith a uisce glan glas,
Maith a ghaoth ghlan gharg,
Maith a bhiolar is barr glas,
Is fearr an fhochlacht ard ann.

Maith a eidhneán buan,
Maith a shaileach ghlan ghrinn,
Maith a iúr iúrach,
Is fearr a bheithe bhinn.

Dá dtiocfá, a Loingseacháin,
Chugam i ngach riocht,
Gach oíche dhom agallamh,
Fós ní fhanfainn leat.

Ní fhanfainn le d'agallamh,
Marach scéal a rinne mo leon,
Marbh máthair, athair, mac,
Iníon, dreatháir, bean bhailc.

Dá dtiocfá dom agallamh,
Níorbh fhearrde liom,
Shirfinn roimh mhaidneachan
Sléibhte Boirche na mbeann.

Ag muileann an mhionaráin
A meileadh do thuath,
A thruáin, a thuirseacháin,
A Loingseacháin luath.

A chailleach seo an mhuilinn,
Cén fáth mé a fháil le feall?
Cluinim thú dhom éigniú
Is tú amuigh ar an mbinn.

A chailleach, a choracháin,
An rachfá ar each?
[Cailleach] Rachainn, a thoracháin,
Mura bhfeicinn neach.

Dá rachainn, a Shuibhneacháin,
Gura shoraidh mo léim.
[Suibhne] Má thagann tú, a chailleacháin,
Nára slán agat do chiall.

[C] Ní cóir ámh a n-abrann tú,
A mhic Colmáin Chais,
Nach fearr de mharcach mise
Gan titim ar m'ais?

[S] Is cóir ámh a n-abraim,
A chailleach gan chonn,
Do do mhilleadh ag deamhan,
Mhillis tú féin.

[S] Nach fearrde leat m'ealaín,
A gheilt shaorga sheang,
Mé a bheith dod leanúint
I mullaí na mbeann?

[S] Dosán den eidheann uaibhreach
A fhásann trí chrann cas,
Dá mbeinn i gceart sa mullach,
B'eagal dom teacht as.

Teithim roimh na fuiseoga
I mo ródaíocht theann,
Lingim thar na cuiseoga
I mullaí na mbeann.

Féarán breac an eidhneáin,
An t-am a éiríonn dúinn,
Gairid a bhím dhá thárrachtain
Ó d'fhás mo chlúmh.

Creabhar oscartha an amaidí,
An t-am a éiríonn dúinn,
Dar liom is namhaid dhearg
An lon a dhéanann an scol.

Gach aon uair a linginn
Go mbeinn ar an lár
Go bhfeicinn an sionnachán
Thíos ag creimeadh na gcnámh.

Thar gach cú in eidhneáin,
Bhéarfadh sé orm féin,
Is é luas a lingfinn
Go mbeinn ar an mbinn.

Sionnaigh bheaga ag béicigh
Chugam agus uaim,
Mic thíre ar a léadaireacht,
Teithim roimh a bhfuaim.

Thriall siad le mo thárrachtain,
Ag teacht ina rith teann,
Gur thug mé rompu teitheadh
I mullaí na mbeann.

Tagann críoch le m'imeacht
Cibé conair a théim,
Is léir dhom ón aithreachas
Gur caora mé gan lias.

Bile Chill Lúghaidh
Ina dtuilim suan sámh,
B'aoibhne i ré Chonaill
Aonach Linne lán.

Tiocfaidh an reo réaltánach
A fhearfaidh ar gach linn,
Tá mé suarach seachránach,
Mise faoi ar an mbinn.

Na corra réisc ag gairm
I nGleann Eile fuar,
Ealta d'éanlaith luath
Chugam agus uaim.

Ní maith liom an tsíreacht sin
A dhéanann fir is mná,
Binne liom ceiliúradh
An loin duibh go hard.

Ní maith liom an stocaireacht
A chluinim go moch,
Binne liom crocaireacht
An bhroic i mBeanna Broc.

Ní maith liom an chornaireacht
A chluinim go teann,
Binne liom ag damhaíreacht
Damh dá fhichead beann.

Tá ábhar seisrí
As gach gleann go gleann,
Gach damh ina fhreislí
I mullach na mbeann.

Cé go bhfuil iomaí damh
I ngach gleann atá ann,
Ní minic lámh aoire
Ag dúnadh a mbeann.

Damh Shliabh ard Eibhlinne,
Damh Shliabh Fuaidh fiáin,
Damh Ealla, damh Orbhraí,
Damh lonn Loch Léin.

Damh Seimhne, damh Latharna,
Damh Linne na leann,
Damh Chuailgne, damh Chonacla,
Damh Bhoireann dá bheann.

A mháthair seo na graí,
Liathadh do leann,
Níl damh i do dhiaidh
Gan dhá fhichead beann.

Mó ná ábhar léine,
Liathadh do cheann,
Dá mbeinn i ngach beinnín,
Bheadh beinníní ar gach beann.

A dhaimh a níonn an fogharán
Chugam thar an ngleann,
Maith an t-ionad foradán
I mullach do bheann.

Is mé Suibhneachán sirideán,
Luath rithim thar ghleann,
Ní hé sin mo dhlíochán,
Is ainm dom Fear Beann.

An tobar is fearr mar thobar
Tobar Leithead Lán,
An tobar is áille fuaire,
Fuarán Dhún Mháil.

Cé gur mór é m'imirce,
M'éadach inniu is gearr,
Mé féin a dhéanann m'fhoraire
I mullach na mbeann.

A raithneach rua fhada,
Rinneadh rua do leann,
Níl easair d'fhear fógartha
I ngabhail do bheann.

Is ann a luífidh mo shaol
Theas ag Taoidhin teann
Ag Tigh Moling na n-aingeal,
Teastóidh, titfidh mé de bheann.

Ar rad mise i do chumann
Sé mallacht Rónáin Fhinn,
A bhinneáin, a bhúireadáin,
A bhéiceadáin bhinn.

[Sweeney English; Lonnie English]

Timberwoodmaterialcontrivancevigouryewlogy: Dear Little Horny Pricket Lowbraybellowfellow

Dear little horny pricket lowbraybellowfellow, dear little horny gluttonbawler of the sweetcliffgableregardhornpeaks, your tuftembracebundlefalsettocuckooquaichtalksinging in the cloudglenhollow is cliffgablepeakeregardsweet to us. *Dépaysement* for my own blessed wee *pagus* happencame upon my wits, the tailtipgobletgrowth in the battleplainfield in Maghera, the Ossianic fawns in the Jovemoormountain in Slieve. Minor-poetdronedumose frondose treeoghamDbulloak, you're hillockhighloud above penis-shaftvault-trees, little treeogham-Cwordcastrationhazel, little heatherembellishmentbranchtree, coffer of tree oghamCwordhazelnuts. Far-from-enemy-like treeoghamFword-polealder in Ferns, your licksheen is delightfulbeautiful, no indifferenceshapeappearance of knify hawthornbushes in the gap in Barna where you are. Dearlittle bristleblackthorn, dearlittle broochpinthorn, dearlittle black glandsloe, blood-tracebrooklimewatercress, hindrancebarecreamcroptop of lockgreygreen bellfinch-coalfish-sealettuce from the hosteldentbrink of the elklullblackbird's wellfountain. Connery's wild saxifrage on the Connor Pass, you're the flatterhoneysweetest herbplant, bellfinch-coalfish-sealettuce from Glassan, speechtune-screereef-branchtuftflowerchoice of bellfinch-coalfish-sealettuce, plantherb from Luss raspberryjam-suckjuice grows on. Appletree, apple charlotte, everybody gives you a good shaking, rowan-tree with your little sheep-berries, your flowerblossom is delightful. Dearlittleyoung lampooner-prickerbramble, dearlittleyoung ridgebackflower, you don't do me right, you never stop lacerating me until you've had your tidefull of mettle-blood. You yewy Newry yewtree you, starappearing in relicgraveyards, ivy, dearlittle ivy, in your habitat in a darkwaxy castrationwood. Holly, dearlittle sheltered one, valveshutter-doorleaf in the airbreathwind, ash from the Unshin tidefull of evilspirit-harm, armyarm of a layman-herowarrior's armhands. TreeoghamBbeingbirch, blossomsmooth and blessed, prideswollen and peaksweet, every tied heatherembellishment-branchtree on the summit of your headend is delightbeautiful. Shake-aspen penis-shaftvault-tree trembleshaking shaketremblingly, I hear turns about its leaves running, that's a cattle-raidplunderloss. I hate the fathombeechwoods, I make no bones about it, leafy treeogham-Dstrip-perbulloaks always on the go. A bad omen how I contraryruined Ronan Finn's hospitalityhonour, his tomb-miracles giving me grief, his vesi-cleclusterclockbells from the cellchurch-yard. A bad omen how I found Congall's bannerarms, his favourite innerlayertunic omencovered in gold. The nimblebold fairyarmycrowd all said don't let the man with the delightbeautiful innerlayertunic shunfleefly from you aroundunder the kyletwignarrow Jovecoverthicket. Jinkscrapsting-wound and deadkill, take advantage of him, put him, good enough for his guiltsins, on a waterspike and a gablepoint. The cornsprout-horsemen catching up on me across frugalround Moycove, not one shot from them will reach my beamridgeback. Going through the ivybranches, I don't hide, I'm like a noblegood shot from a javelinspear going with the airbreathwind. Dear-little doe, dearlittle tracker, I've gotten bitehold of you, I'm cornsprout-riding you from every sweetcliffgableregardhornpeak where I am. From Carncorn to the sweetcliffgableregardhornpeak of Slievenanee, from the sweetcliffgableregardhornpeak of Carn Clonhugh I reachget to the Galtees. From the Galtees to a cairn on the Liffey, I come before after-noonevening to painfulsaltbitter Benbulben. At night before Congall's catbattalionbattle I was happy, before I bedragglefumblebumbled, seek-traversing the sweetcliffgableregardhornpeaks. Glenbalkan is my steadypermanent wombabode where I got a gripbite, many a night I ask-tried to run up the sweetcliffgableregardhornpeak. If I seektravelled on my tod all the moormountains of the Jovenobletimberbrown world-domain, I would rather the site of one bothy in frugalround Glenbalkan. Its shrillweedclear lockgreygreen urineraintearswater is noblegood, its fierce shrillweedclear airbreathwind is noblegood, its watercress and lockgreygreen hindrancecreamtopcrop is noblegood, best of all is the hillockhigh brooklime there. Its hardy ivybushes are noblegood and its shrillweedclear treeoghamS-sallies, its yewy yew from Newry in Iveagh is noblegood, best of all its cliffgableregardhornpeaksweet treeogham-BbeingBehybirch. If you were to come, Lynchehaun, to me in any ghostform, every night to regael me, maybe I wouldn't stopwait for you. I wouldn't stopwait for your conversation were it not for the storynews which lionsprainwounded me: all killed flatnumbdead – mother, father, son, daughter, brother, down-pourstrong womanwife. If you were to come to talk to me, I wouldn't be the better for it, I would seektravel the sweetcliffgableregardhornpeaks of the Mourne Moormountains before matunination. By the flour-cake mill your rural-laitytribe was pendant-blubber-ruined, tired saddo, earlyfast Lynchehaun. Nunhag of the mill, why would you want to get at me with deceit? I hear you giving me grief out on the mountain. Nunhag, Roundhead, would you go on a steed-horse? *I would, fathead, if I didn't see any apparitionperson. If I did, Sweeney, here's to my promontory- chasmjumping*. If you don't, nunhag, may you lose your wits. *What you're saying isn't right but, Coleman from Kilcash. Wouldn't I be the better horseperson, not falling back?* What I say is right enough, nun-hag without a titter of wit, destroyed by a demon, you've destroyed yourself. *Wouldn't you be the better for my anticart, leanmean nakedwood-grazingbattle-fugitivebirdbeastpaniclunatic, with me stickfollowing you from the summit of the sweet- cliffgableregardhornpeaks?* A tuft of lonelyproudspiritedrank ivy growing through a twisted penis-shaftvault-tree, if I was in the top I'd be afraid to come out. I antifadgeflee the skylarks talehousewandertravelling at tightfull stretch, I leap over the tall-stemmedgrassreedstalks from the summit of the cliffgableregardhornpeaks. The poxtroutspeckled ivybush turtledove, when it rises up for us, it doesn't take me long to overtake it since I waxed plumulaceous. The Oscarnimble devil- gadfly-haywoodcock when it rises up to me, the elklullblackbird when it makes its highpitchedcall is a truered enemy as far as I'm concerned. Every hourtime I leap till I'm on the groundearth I see the little sacrumfox down there corrodegnawing reefstripbones. More than any championIrishwolfhound in the ivybush, he would overtake me, I would jump just as ashfast to the sweetcliffgableregardhornpeak. Shinwick's wee foxes gluttonbawling this way and that, routs of landsonwolves pertgossipsmiting, I shunflyflee the sound they make. They cametried to overtake me on the run but I absquatulated to the hillockhighloud summit of the sweetcliffgableregardhornpeaks. My elopementgaitgoing is brought to a territory-end whichever mountainpassway I go, it's clear from my remorse that I'm a sheep without a pen. The sacredscionbordertree in Killowe where I sleep quietpeacefully, better than in Congall's levelmoonrayspacetime the furyfairassembly in Nenagh and tidefull Moylinney. Starry hoarfrost will come and rain on every generationpool, I'm airymiserable, lostwandering, underabout it on the sweetcliffgableregardhornpeak. The oddroundcraneherons calling in rawcold Glenelly, an ashfast dissimulation of teenyweenySweenybirds this way and that. I don't love the longingplaint that men and wifewomen make, the vanishgreetcelebrationfarewellwarble that the elklullblackbard makes hillockhighloud is cliffgableregardhornpeaksweeter to me. I don't love the scroungetrumpeting that I hear earlyearly, the crocking of the messbadger in Pennyburn is cliffgableregardhornpeaksweeter to me. I don't love the hornblowing I hear tightnear, the rutbellowing that the oxenstag with two severalscore peakhorns makes is cliffgableregardhornpeaksweeter to me. There's the makings of a sixyokeploughteam in every smoke-cloudhollowglen, every oxenstag lying down on the top of the sweetcliffgableregardhornpeaks. Though there's a multitude of oxenstags in every smoke-cloudhollowglen, it's rarely the armhand of a satirewhipherd fortressencloses their peakhorns. The oxenstag of the hillockhighloud Slieve Felim Mountains, the oxenstag of the wild Fews, the oxenstag of Duhallow, the oxenstag of Orrery, the fierce oxenstag of Lough Leane. The oxenstag of Islandmagee, the oxenstag of Larne and Lorne, the oxenstag of Moylinney, the oxenstag of Cooley, the oxenstag of Cunghill, the bicorn oxenstag of karstrock Burrendavan of the menny stags. Mother of the horse-stud, your beermantle has turned grey, there isn't an oxenstag after you that doesn't have two severalscore peakhorns. More than the stuff for a shirt, my own endhead has turned grey, if I was on every sweetpeaklet there would be a peaklet on every one. Oxenstag making that noise at me across the cloudglenhollow, that's a noblegood wee lookoutseat on the summit of your cliffgablere-gardpeakhorns. I'm Shivna Sheridan the searchwanderer, I go faster than Senna or Sheene or Danny Keany across the cloudhollowglens, that's not my proper designation, my name is Horny Devil Mountain Man from Ferbane. The best waterhole of them all is the wellfountain of Knocklayd, the most delighbeautiful tow-barwellfountain is the *asbi-la* of Dunmail. Though I've made many an emigrationflitting, my sail-clothes today have been cut short, I'm always on watch in the mullahsummit of the cliffgableregardhornpeaks. Bracken from Rannoch, roserussetred treeogham-Fwordpostalder, your beermantles have turned copperbronzered, there's no litterbedding for Fogarty the outlaw in the creekcrotch of your sweetcliffgableregardpeaks. I'll lie down my worldlife south in Taiten and St. Mullin's of the fire-ingleangels, that's where I'll fall from a height and die. What has frolicflick-kickflung me in your darlingcomingcompany is the curse of Ronan Finn, dearlittle horny pricket one, dearlittle lowbraybellowfellow, gablesweet glutton-bawler.

Scol den Bhinn

Agus mé ag marcaíocht ar cuairt
Ar an each donn i lár an ghleanna
Maidin i ndeireadh an fhómhair, an damh
Ag rith thar an ré, an lon ag geilt

Ar learg ar an bhféar fada garbh
Ar chritheann agus ar sheileach
Agus ar na cuiseoga
Ar fud na n-éan ag ceiliúradh,

Dobhrán is breac bán sa linn,
Scol na gcon i mullach na mbeann
Agus thíos bun meille, biorragán,
Glasán, maothnatán is lus bian

Mar a thagann cuain mac tíre amach
As an bhfoscadh is ansin an t-iarsma
Á chreimeadh is á chaitheamh
Mar a gcuid ag na fiacha.

Cry From the Bluff

Horseback riding the range on a brown buckskin in the floormiddle of the canyon early morning fall's end, the mule deer, pronghorn and bison Wyroming across Tipperary and the plains, the ouzelelk bareloonygrazing on a bluff on the rough perennial grass on seedlings of quaking aspen and willow shootstands among the peregrines and song-birds, trumpeter swans and whooping cranes, beaver and cut-throat trout in the creek, the coyotes' howl atop the bluffs and in the bottom-land western waterweed, sagebrush, bitterroot, wild blue tidenetfullflax and threadleaf crowfoot as a glassgreengray wolf pack come out of the sheltershadows and then the boonmarkremains gnawed and waste-eaten by the pricehuntravens.

Ceiliúradh

Ní chuireann doirí dorcha
In imeall Fiodh Gaibhle
Ná coill chiar
Thiar ná thoir
Mar a bhfuil cuaineanna na gcon alla

Eagla orm ná uamhann
I mo shos i mo gheilt,
I m'fhear coille,
I mo bhrat,
Beo ar dhearcáin darach
Agus na héin ag ceiliúradh
Ar fud na ngéag
Agus crainn Éireann féin
Ag dul in éag.

Warblefarewellcelebration

Dark oakgroves on the edge of the Figile or a waxdark castrationdesecrationwood west or east where the wild dog packs are don't scare me at rest as a nakedwoodgrazinglunatic, as an outlaw and woodwose, in my mantle, living off oakberries with the birds farewellcelebrationwarble-leaving among the branches and the very penis-shaftvault-trees of Ireland dying off.

Socair is Docair

B'fhearr liom féin go mór
Bheith ar gealtacht is ar buile,
Ar mire, ar dásacht ar fáinneáil
Is ar ginideacht i bhfolach
I ndoirí dorcha nó sa gcoill chiar
Oíche dhubh dhuairc dhubh
Gan teach gan teas gan tine
Gan chéill gan chonn gan chomhrá
Mín ciúin le mná
Ná fir Éireann uile
Ná bheith socair sáil
Suaimhneach idir dhaoine.

SAD

I'd much rather go off in paniclunacy and a supernaturalrevelationpoetry-inspiringfrenzy fannelflitting in demonic madness hidden in dark oakgroves or in the waxdark castrationwood on a bleakblack night without house, hearth or heat, without a titter of wit, without commerce with wifewomen or all the men of Ireland than be easysoilhappy and at peace bothbetweenamong menpeople.

[Unstable Narrator]

41

I nDiaidh na Laoi Sin

Tháinig Suibhne
Ó Fhiodh Gaibhle
Go Binn Bóghaine,
As sin go Binn Fhoibhne,
As sin go Ráth Murbhuilg
Is ní bhfuair sé a dhíon ar an gcailleach
Go dtí gur tháinig
Go Dún Sobhairce in Ultaibh.

After that rudderexhortationLeelay Sweeney came from Figile to Binbane, from there to Binevenagh, from there to Murlough Fort in Maghera and he didn't find his roofshelter from the nunhag until he came to in Dunseverick in Ulster. Sweeney cliffdived from the cliffgableregardhornpeak of the closedownhillforthouse like Binn an Dúin or Beinn na Dùine juststraight down in front of the nunhag. She jumped agileneatly after him but fell off the cliffrock of Dunseverick and was made into tiny colluvial crumbfragments and foodmess and *felo de se* into the billows and that's how she died following Sweeney.

42

Then Sweeney said 'I won't be in Dalaradia anyfastlonger as Lynchehaun would deadkill me to punishavenge his nunhag if he was able to do that to me'. Sweeney went west after that to Roscommon in

Connaught and came down at the impositionswathe-edge of a well and consumed rainurinetearswater and blood-tracebrooklimewatercress. A wifewoman came from the erenaghsteward's house to the well. Forbes Forde-Daly was that erenaghsteward. The wifeoman who came was Fing Shang *née* Findalay. The nakedwood-grazingbattle-fugitivebird-beastpaniclunatic shunfled from her then and she got her hand on the blood-tracebrooklimewatercress that was in the flowstream. Sweeney was in the sacredscionbordertree in her witnesspresence, moaning out of him about his watercress having been borne away and said: 'Wife-woman' he said 'it's balepitiful of you to bear away my blood-trace-booklimewatercress from me, if you only knew how I'm without a rural-laytribesman or a territoryrace that cares for me, I don't go for lodginghospitality to any manpessoa's househome in the backridge of the world-domain. My watercress is my scourkine, my rainurinetears-water is my mead, my respitefriends are my hard in the raw warp-clos-esecretsheltered penis-shaftvault-trees and even if you didn't bear away my watercress' he said 'certain it is that you wouldn't be without any kneewashing-girldaughterthing tonight as I am with my watercress borne away from me' and then he made this Leerudderexhortationlay:

[Unstable Narrator]

an oíche fuar,
guth giúrainn is beart biolair
ar lom Imleach Iúir

the night is cold barnacle-goose sound a handful of watercress in Emly

[The Erenaghs]

Réim

Líon an slua as gach aird d'Éirinn
Ó Ros Béaraigh go Ros Comáin
Ach níor fhan an réim sin
Ó tháinig doineann mhór san oíche
Gur thit na crainn chrua

Sa gcoill chiar, i ndoirí dorcha,
I bhFiodh Gaibhle, an t-iúr a bhí sa gcill
Sa ngleann agus gach tobar uisce ghil
Go ndeachaigh muid airchinnigh leis na cléirigh
Ar teitheadh ar an gcoigríoch don mhóin,
Don mhá, don mhothar, don seascann, don sliabh
Ar fud na gcon alla is na mac tíre.

Successiontraditionregimeprideextentlifecourse

The fairyarmycrowd netfilled from every airtheight of Ireland from Rossberry to Roscommon but that successiontraditionregimepridex-tentlifecourse didn't stay since a great winterstorm came at night and the hardy penis-shaftvault-trees fell in the waxdark Kalendscastrationde-secrationwood, in dark oakgroves, in Feegile, the yew that was in the cellchurch-yard in the smoke-cloudhollowglen and every whitebright rainurinetearswater well and we erenaghs went off with the sextonaltar-borclerics shunfleeing to foreign lands in the turfmoor, in the mazeplain, in the blunder-busscloudclusterclumpswampthicket-tan-glejungle, in the sedgeswamps, in the Jovemoormountain among the wolfhounds and landsonwolves.

[Sweeney; Fing Shang Findalay]

43

A Bhean a Bhaineann an Biolar

A bhean a bhaineann an biolar
Agus a bheireann an t-uisce,
Ní bheifeá gan ní anocht
Mara mbéarfá fiú mo chuid de.

Monuarán, a bheanagáin.
Nach rachaidh tú mar a rachad,
Mise amuigh i mbarra crann,
Tusa thall i dteach carad.

A bhean úd a bhain, beir beann
Agus muid ar bhealaí a chéile,
Mé féin i mbarr na gcrann
Is tú féin i dteach na féile.

Mo lom géar, a bheanagáin,
Is fuar an ghaoth a nocht,
Mé gan trua ó aon mhac máthar,
Níl bráidín agam ná brat.

A bheanagáin, dá mb'fheasach duit,
Mar atá anseo Suibhne
Nach bhfaigheann cuibheas ó neach
Is ní fhaigheann neach cuibheas uaidh.

Ní théim don Oireachtas
I measc ógánaigh na tire,
Mé gan oineach im aonar,
Níl mo bheann ar aon ríocht.

Ní théim ar aíocht
Do theach mac duine in Éirinn,
Is minice dom ar ginideacht
Ar bheanna corra sléibhte.

Ní thagann chugam oirfidigh
Roimh dhul a luí san oíche,
Ní fhaighim trua ná taise
Ó fhear tuaithe nó ó fhine.

Nuair a bhí mé i nDún Shuibhne
Agus a théinn ar eacha,
Nuair a thagann im chuimhne,
Mairg dom bheith im bheatha.

Is mé Suibhne de shliocht Uí Éanaí,
Is fuar feannta mo chónaí,
Cé gur beo mé ar na beanna,
A bhean a bhaineann an bipolar.

Is é mo mheá m'uisce fuar,
Is é mo bhuar mo bhiolar,
Is iad mo chairde mo chrainn
Is mé gan leann, gan ionar.

Och, ó mealladh Guaire le roisc ban,
Go ndeachaigh sé le mo mhnaoi dhil,
Sé mo chuid an fhochlacht sa ngaineamh glan
Agus an biolar ag tobar uisce ghil.

Is fuar anocht an oíche,
Mé im bhochtán gan bhiolar,
Chualas guth an ghiúrainn
Os cionn lom Imleach Iúir.

Táim gan bhrat, gan ionar,
Is fada olc dhom leanúint,
Teithim roimh ghuth na coirre,
Mar a bheadh buille dom bhaint ann.

Sroichim Dairbhre daingean
Lá aoibheallach earraigh
Agus teithim roimh an oíche
Siar go Boirche na mbeangán.

Dá mb'eol duit, a fheannóg,
Mo ghort ní treorach garg,
Tá neach ann dar sceimhle
Ar bhain tú féin mar eire.

Is fuar agus is cuisneach
Ar bhrú tobair ghlais ghreanta,
Deoch ghlé órga d'uisce glan
Agus an biolar a bhainfeá.

Mo chuid an biolar a bhainir,
Cuid geilte saoire seinge,
Scinneann gaoth fhuar faoi mo reanga
De bheanna gacha binne.

Is fuar an ghaoth ar maidin
Ag teacht idir mé is m'ionar,
Ní fhéadaim agallamh leat
A bhean a bhaineann an biolar.

[An Bhean] Fág mo chuid ag an Tiarna
Agus ná bí doiligh liom,
Móide gheobhaidh tú ceannas
Is beir beannocht, a Shuibhne.

[Suibhne] Déanam ceannach ceart cuibhe,
Cé go bhfuilim i mullach an iúir,
Beir m'ionar is mo cheirtín
Ach fág an beartán biolair.

Is tearc neach dom ionúin,
Níl mo theach ar talamh,
Ó thug tú uaim mo bhiolar,
Mo chuid cionta ar t'anam.

Nár fhaigh tú neach do ghrá,
Miste don té a leanais,
D'fhág tú neach go daibhir
Mar thoradh ar ar bhainis.

A bhean, chugat dá dtiocfadh
Loingseachán go rún aitis,
Thar mo cheann, tabhair dó a leath
Den bhiolar a bhainis.

Creach na nGall gorm dod leanúint
Gur tháinig tú im aice,
Go bhfaighe tú ón Tiarna an cion
Gur bhain tú mo chuid biolair.

Posy of Blood-tracebrooklimewatercress

Wifewoman gathering blood-tracebrooklimewatercress and carrying rainurinetearswater, you wouldn't be without any girldaughterknee-washingthing tonight even if you hadn't taken my lot. Alas!, littlewifiewoman, you won't be going likewhere I'm going, me outside on the pithplain treed in the overstorey, you over there in a lovefriend's househome. *Alaláw!* littlewifiewoman, the airbreathwind is rawcold tonight, I have leanwretchpity from nobody, I have neither a worstedbrothcover-cloak nor a bib. If you only knew, littlewifiewoman, how Sweeney is here, without friendship. I don't go to a meeting of the Oireachtas with all the young ones of the ruraldry-landstate, I'm left flying solo, I have no prongantler-regard for any kingdom. I don't go talebearinghouse-wandering to the househome of any manperson's son in the Ireland-world, I'm more often going spritemad on the oddheronpointed sweetcliffgableregardhornpeaks of the Jovemoormountains in Sleaty. Musicianers don't come to see me before I nod off at night, I don't get any leanwretchpity or weakghostremainsmoistcompassion from a countryman from Tooa or the tribeparty. When I was in Castle Sween and I used to go on steedhorses, when I imagineremember it, I'm sorry I'm sustenancealive. I'm Sweeney of the passagetraceline of the Bird Heaneys, my alwayshabitation is flailsharp rawcold, though I'm alive on the sweetcliffgableregardpeaks, wifewoman gathering watercress. My Librafishing-groundmead is my rawcold rainurinetearswater, my water-cress is my scourboorcattle, my respitefriends are my penis-shaftvault-trees, I've neither beermantle nor innerlayertunic. Och, since Gorey was beguiled by women's eyes and he went off with my own dear womanwife, my lot is brooklime in the glassgreygreen sand and watercress at a brightwhite pisstearsrainwater well. It's a rawcold night tonight, I'm a beggar without watercress, I heard the Gothreproachvoice of Coyne and Barnacle's pale-breasted brent goose above Emly in the Prairie, and all my Fethard friends. I've neither a brothcovercloak nor an innerlayertunic, evilmisery stickfollows me all the time, I shunflyflee from the reproachvoice of the oddroundcraneheron as though I were being struck like a bell. I go to Valencia and Darver and Darrary and Doorary Point and Dingle and Dangan and Dyan and Denn in spring and I shunflyflee before night backwest to the scionprongbranches of the Mournes. If you only knew, scold-crow, my ivycropfield's not rough or strong, there's a spiritperson traumatised by the load that you've taken. It's rawcold and frosthardy on the hosteldentbrink of the lockgreygreen polishgraven fountainwell, a clear gold draught of fresh water and the watercress you gathered. The watercress you gathered is my lot, the lot of a noblefree leanmean grindgrazingnakedwoodlunatic, a raw cold katabatic airbreathwind flygushes from my mackerelweltwrinklestringloins.

[Wifewoman]

Leave my lot to the Masterlord and don't be distresshard on me, and maybe you'll get your power back, so God bless you, Sweeney.

[Sweeney]

Let's make a proper buydeal even if I'm on top of a yewtree in Mullynure, take my innerlayertunic and my rags, leave the posy of watercress. There's hardly one apparitionperson who loves me, I don't have a househome on dry-landsurface-earth, since you took my watercress, all my guiltsins on your lifebreathsoul. May you never have an appartitioncharitylovelover, may it be worse for the one you followed, you've left an apparitionperson poor as fruitregardresult of what you've sweeneyed. Wifewoman, if Lynchehaun comes to you looking for sport, give him half for me of the watercress you plucked. May the cattle-raidplunderloss of the negroblue Gauls, the Vikings and Hiberno-Norse, the Old English and Anglo-Norman of Galgorm, the Lowland Scots, the non-Gael and de-Gaelicized and foreigners generally follow you that you came up to me, may the Lord make you singuilty of taking all my bloodtracebrooklimewatercress.

[Sweeney]

Mo Chairde Mo Chrainn

Cha bhi mi gan teach gan tine
Gun teas gun bhia feasta
Nam aonar i mullach an iúir,
I ndosanna crann ard eidhinn
I m'ghnáth sa choille chèir
Air làr Ghleann Bolcáin,
Ag athrú ó chrann gu chéile
I nDoire Dorcha, sa bhFiodh Mór,
I bhFiodh Gaibhle far nach eil gáir an tslua
No muirn is seastan na sochaí,
A bhfuaimeanna agus a bhfreagraí
I néalta éadroma neimhe,
Mi a' seachnadh dhaoine 's ag rith
Thar an ré leis na coin
Is na daimh is na loin
Oir is iad mo chairde mo chrainn –
An fearn àlainn is an raineach rua,
An bheith bhinn air leargan Loch Èireann,
An t-seileach ghlan ghrinn is gach craobh
Cheangailteach faoi mo chosa,
An darach dosach duilleach,
An crann creathach air chrith –
Gach fear na fhear tuaithe nó fine
'S iad gam iathadh mar dhíon
Ar fhearthainn, air tàirneanaich is ar shíon,
Air gach doineann is gach feithid

In ionad naomh gun chlaisneachd
Ri guth ná glór
Ach mo chairde mo chrainn,
Mo shìol, mo mhuinntir is mo dhaoine féin.

My Respitefriends friends the Penisvaultshaft-trees

I won't be without a habitation or flameflashfire or heat or food anymore on my tod on top of the yew in Mullynure, in dronetufts of high ivy penisvaultshaft-trees in my intimateshaunt in the duskydundark wood on the valley-bottom of Glenbalkan, changing from one penisvaultshaft-tree to another in the secretivedark oakgrove in Derrydorragh, in the great wood of Feamore, in Figile far from the famecry of the fairyarmycrowd or the lovetumult and standclamour of society, their sounds and resounds in the light nebulae of non-skyheaven, spareavoiding manpeople and running across the moonlevel with the hounds and deer and ouzelelks for my respitefriends are the penisvaultshaft-trees – the lovely oghamFmastalder and the russet bracken, the peak-sweet beingbirch on the rain-goose-slopes of Lough Erne and Loch Earn, the puregrand Salishwillow and every mycorrhizally linked branchtree underaround my legfeet, the bushybranchy leafageleafy ClanCameronoak, the aspens shivershuddershaking – every man jack of them a countryman or clansman surrounding me as roofshelter against rain and thunder and storms and storminess and every tinywildserpentinsect in a saintholy wonderplace without hearing a bardtauntvoice sound or a humansound but my respitefriends the penis-vaultshaft-trees, my seedrace, my triberelations and my very own manpeople.

I M'Thocht

Ó d'fhág tú mé anocht,
Ó d'éirigh mé as mo néal,
De dhíth biolair i m'bhocht
Gan bhrí, mallacht ar do bhéal,
A chailleach, i m'thocht
Go buan, is olc an scéal.

Catchbedsilence

Since you left me tonight as I got up out of my nebulatrance, wanting watercress, poor, without substancestrength, a curse on your lipmouth, hussyhag, and there I am catchsilent in my bed forever.

tráth den lus bian,
maothnatán is biorragán,
is é ár mian

a prayertime-meal of loosebeanherbageviands, mushy mellow fruit and birkin-shavegrass is what we want

[Unstable Narrator]

44

Goll Har Saailley

Vah eh ayns Ros Comain yn oie shen,
Hie eh ass shen er ny vairagh
Gys Slieau Aghtee feayr oor,
Ass shen gys Slieau Mish meen aalin,
Ass shen gys Slieau Bloom ny beinn ardey,
Ass shen gys Innys Murree;

Kegeesh er mee da aynjee shen
Ayns Ooig Donan Eggey, ass shen gys Creg Ollister,
Stroin rish stroo faarkey. As ny foillanyn.
Ghow eh aajey as ynnyd ayns shen as vah eh
Kegeesh ar mee elley aynjee.
Daag eh yn chreg chreoi ny yei shen
As hie eh har crossag ny marrey:

Hie eh laa gys Doirrey Cholum Keeilley,
Laa gys Innys Booa Fynney yns eear Chonnaghtey,
Hie eh laa elley gys Eas keiyn Ruy,

Vah eh laa syn ouyr ayns Ullee ym Logh Ceayn,
Laa elley ayns Slieau Hollyn as er fud Nerin,
Laa yns Eeley as laa yns Kione Cheerey
Gys yn raink eh fy-yeih Creeagh Bretyn.

Beannadáin

Bhí sé i Ros Comáin an oíche sin,
Chuaigh sé as sin go Sliabh Eachtaí arna mhárach,
As sin go Sliabh Mis mín álainn,
As sin go Sliabh Bladhma, as sin go hInis Muirígh;
Bhí sé coicís ar mhí in Uaimh Dhonnáin Eige,
As sin go Carraig Alasdair coicís ar mhí eile.

He was in Roscommon that night, he went from there on the morning-morrow to Ardeevin in Slieve Aughty, from there to the delightbeautiful smoothgrasslands of Slieve Mish, then to flareflaming high cliffgableregardhornpeaked Slieve Bloom, from there to Inishmurray; he was a fortnight and a month in the pitcave of Kildonan in Eigg's Isle in the Hybrides.

[Sweeney]

Cruas na Creige

Níor fhág mé gun taisteal magh no machair
Ar feadh seacht mbliana 's an dèidh 'n astair
Ar fud Éireann agus na thachair,
Chaidh mi thar sàile na chraos fairsing ceathach
Nam aonaran leis na héin farraige
Bho Theach Doinn go hInnis Mhuirich
Gus an d'ràinig mé go hUaimh Dhonnáin Eige
Mar m'ionad agus m' àite-fuirich
Fa-dheòidh fad coicís air mhìos
Agus an sin colbha crua carraige

Mar leabaidh fhliuch ar chruas na creige
Leis na faoileagan shuas air Carraig Alastair
Lom nocht gan bhia gun teine gun deathach
Mar ar chuala mé foghar na fairge
        osnadh na gaoithe glé gairge
Go ndúirt mé na rannan seo shìos.

On a Hard Quarryhillcliffrock

I didn't leave unhackletravelled a level-battlefield or Lowlandlevel-machairbeach for seven years and after the spacewayjourney throughout Ireland and after what meethappened, I went across the abundantwide briny like a breechgluttonymawvent in a showermiststormterror on my tod as a hermit with the sea-birds from the Bull Rock to Inishmurray till I came to Donan's cave in Eigg as my dwelling and abode at last for a fortnight and a month and then a hard column of rock in Carrick and a wet bed hard as a quarryhillcliffrock with the white-wavecrestblack-headed gulls up on Ailsa Craig, all exposed without food or househome or hearth where I heard the harvestfroth-sound of the angryswelling-waveoceansea and the blastgroansighing of the clear fierce breathwind and said these ancestrydivisionpromontoryverses.

In Uaimh Dhonnáin Eige

Seo m'adhbha, mo chill agus mo chríocha,
M'fhearann, mo thír agus m'áitreabh
Agus an teach mór a bhfuil mé i bhfolach
I m'fhear fógartha ar mo theitheadh
Mar a bhí mé i mbile sa gcoill chiar
Agus i ndoirí dorcha thiar i mo ghealt
Ar fáinneáil agus ar foluain, i mo thost,
I mo rí féin ag adú tine i m'aonar
Agus an charraig mar easair fúm agus leaba,
I mo chléireach agus mo naomh ag moladh
Rí neimhe lá le ceiliúradh cóir
Agus lá eile le rann agus ceol

Na rón ramhar ag teacht anall
De gháir chreag ón muir mhór.

In the Cave on Eigg

This is my rookerylairabode, my church-yardcell and my territoryends, my land and premises and the big house where I coverhide as a threat-condemned man in shunflight like I was in the sacredscionbordertree in the waxdark castrationwood and in dark oak groves back west as a nakedgrazingflyingwoodlunatic fannelflitting and full-onflutterflying, bedsilent, and a king itself longstoking the fire on my tod and the rocks for my bedlitter and an altar-boysextoncleric and holysaint mollypraising the king of non-skyheaven one day in proper farewellwarblecelebration and another day at partitionverses and the musicsong of the seals coming across as a rockechocry from the great sea.

in Uaimh Dhonnáin
thar muir dom i m'aonarán,
sos is foscadh éin

in Donan's Cave across the sea a hermit peace and a bird's sheltershadow

Fios

Rinne mé mé féin glan
In Uaimh Dhonnáin Eige
Gan chodladh coicís ar mhí
Gan bhia gan deoch

Ach lus is luibh is feamainn
Gach lá is gach aon oíche,
Mo cholainn á tolladh
Leis an ngaoth gharg oighreata,

Scréachach is golfartach ar fud na binne
Gur nocht na taibhsí faoin slí

Gur léim siad ar chlais mo chúil is ar mo shlinneáin
Gur scar mo chorp le m'anam

Go ndeachaigh mé go hifreann thall is go néalta neimhe
Gur shroich mé bruach na Banna
Nó gur tháinig fios chugam
Go bhfaighinn bás de rinn.

Second Sight

I made myself pureclean in the cave in Eigg without sleep for a fortnight and a month without food or drink but herbs and seaweed every day and every night, my personbody buttockholepierced by the sharp icy airwind, screeching and wailing all over the cliffpeak and then the showghosts apparitioned and chasmjumped on my neck and shoulders and my soul parted from my bodycorpse and I went to hell over by and to the trancenebulae of non-skyheaven till I reach the spreadingbank of the Bann and I could see that I would die at the point of a sword at the end of the line on a promontory in Ring.

M'Ealaín

In Uaimh Dhonnáin Eige
Nó ar Charraig Alastair
Cian ó m'eol ó chuaigh mé leis na héin,
Cé go bhfuil mé gan chairde
Gur chlaochlaigh mé dealbh is dath
Nó gur scar mé le mo chló
Is mo chruth féin, féach,
I m'fhianaise romham i m'fhear le fraigh –
Each donn, lon, damh rua,
Míol má, trí chaoga bó,
Cinn ghabhar is cinn chon,
Muca móra troma
Agus lámha laoich
Mar m'ealaín is lorg mo shaothair.

My Capercraftart

In Donan's Cave on Eigg and on the rock of Ailsa Craig longingfar from where I know best since I went away with the birds, although I'm without respitefriends so that I've deterioratechanged in warpappearance and colour and spreadseparated from my spikemouldappearance and my very embryoshape, trysee, in witnessbefore me as the man at the wall – brown horses and red cervids, a black-birdhipcravinglullelk, all those bison and aurochs, a plaininsecthare, heads of ibex and hounds, exaltgreat pregnantheavy scowlheap-pigs and traces of human hand as my capercraftart and the progenytracemark of my child-birthbowel-evacuationdestructionachievementwork.

Ní Socair Sáil

Ní socair sáil mo bheatha
I dtolg i mboth fhuar
I m'aonar is in Uaimh Dhonnáin,
As sin thar sáile go Carraig Alasdair,
I gcoill chiar is i ndoirí dorcha
Le leabhar álainn Chaoimhín
Gan éadach gan bhia gan leann
Ach deoch d'uisce glan
Ar *komori* coicís ar mhí
I ndiaidh bás na caillí.

A Voluptuousheeleasy Deadstillsteadysettled Thing, Not

My sustenancelife is deadstillsteadysettled and voluptousheeleasy, not, in a sleeping-compartmentbed in a rawcold booth-hut in my lone in St. Donnan's Cave, from there across the luxuriantbrinesea to Ailsa Craig, in a waxdark Kalendsdesecrationcastrationwood and in dark oakgroves with Kevin's lovely book without clothclothes or sustenancefood or mantlebeer, only a clearclean drink of urineraintearswater in *komori* a fortnight and a month after the hussyhag's death.

[Unstable Narrator]

From there he went to Ailsa Craig. He took a dwelling and abode there for a fortnight and a month. He leaves it backwestafter that and bids it vanishwarblegreetcelebrationfarewell; that's when he brought straight-up out loud his own alas!difficultydistress here:

[Sweeney]

45

Carraig Alastair,
m' àite 's m' ionad air a' mhuir
na dùn 's na tìr-mòr

Ailsa Craig   my place and my abode on the sea   as a fastnessfortress and a mainland

fómhar, Loch Cuan,
raineach rua is crónán
is búir an daimh doinn

autumnharvest, Strangford Lough,   the russet bracken and drone   and boor-bellowing of the Jovelordtimberbrown champion-ox stag

Duairc an Bheatha Liom

Duairc is lom an bheatha,
Duairceas fuacht na hoíche,
Duairceas trom an tsneachta,
Duairceas cruacht na gaoithe

Duairc an bheatha liom,
Bheith gan leaba mhaoth,
Adhbha fhuar le sioc trom,
Garbh sneachta is gaoth.

Gaoth fhuar oighreata,
Scáth fann fann gréine,
Foscadh aon bhile,
I mullach mhá sléibhe.

Fulaingt fras fliche,
Céim thar barr conaire,
Imeacht ar ghlaise mhín,
Maidin ghlas reoite.

Gáir na damhaíre,
Ar fud na coille buí,
Go bearna mar dhréimire,
Foghar na farraige.

Maith, a Thiarna mhóir,
Mór mo mhearbhall féin,
Duibhe an leann dubh,
Suibhne bléineann seang.

Rithim thar bhearna lom
Boirche na mbuachalán,
Osna san oíche,
Clocha sneachta geimhreata.

Luí ar leaba fhliuch
Ar learga Loch Éirne,
Imeacht moch ar m'aigne,
Ag éirí le moch maidine.

Rith thar bhinn na tuinne
I nDún Sobhairce,
Cluas le tonnta troma
I nDún Ruairí.

Thar na dtonn ag rithíocht
Go tonn na Bearbha,
Feis ar cholbha crua
Ar Dhún Cearmna.

Lá na Cruaiche
Go Beann Boirne breá,
Cluas le hadhartán
Chruach Aighle gharg,

Útamáil m'imirce,
I má na Bóraimhe,
Ó Bhinn Iughoine
Go Binn Bóghoine.

Tháinig chugam féin
Neach a láimhsigh mé,
Níor thug sí dom síocháin,
Bean í nár sáraíodh.

Rug sí mo chuid féin léi
Tar éis mo chionta féin,
An obair is lú amuigh,
Mo bhiolar gur fuadaíodh.

Bainim an biolar trá,
Bia i ndlochtán breá,
Ceithre ghlac cruinne iad
As Gleann Bholcáin fiata.

Sásamh uaim go mór,
Suairc an mónadán,
Deoch den uisce glan
As fuarán beannaithe.

M'ingne mar ingne each,
Mo chreasa tá maothaithe,
Mo chosa tá bun os toll,
Gan leas mé im nochtán.

Bhéarfar orm féin,
Fianna go danartha
Cian as Ulaidh,
Triall in Albain.

Tar éis an aistir sin,
Mo dhán ina thruaighe,
A bheith i gcruatan
Ar Charraig Alasdair.

Carraig Alasdair,
Adhbha faoileán bán,
Trua, a rí na ndúl,
Fuar do lucht aíochta.

Carraig Alastor,
Cloch i gcruth cloigíneach,
Ba leor leath a hairde,
Srón le sruth farraige.

Mar a chas muid ina thruaighe,
Dís chorr chrua loirgneach,
Mise crua mar leadhbaire,
Ise crua mar ghuilbneach.

Fliuch iad na leapacha
Mar a bhfuil m'áras,
Beag a shíl mé de
Gur charraig chásach.

An dèidh an astair sin,
Mo dhàn, mo thruaighe,
Bhith ann an cruadal
Ar Charraig Ealasaid.

Carraig Ealasaid,
Faiche do dh'fhaoileagan,
'S truagh, a Rìgh nan Dùl,
'S fuar don luchd-fhaoigheachd.

Carraig Ealasaid, clach
Ann an cruth clagach,
Bu leòr leth a h-àirde,
Sròn ri sruth-fairge.

Mar a choinnich sinn, mo thruaighe,
Dithis chorra chruaidh luirgneach,
Mise cruaidh mar an luid,
Ise cruaidh mar ghuilbneach.

Fliuch na leapannan
Far a bheil m' fhàrdach fhèin,
Cha do sheall mi oirre riamh
Mar charraig urramach.

Olc do Chonall Claon
Cath a thárrachtain,
Mar chuing sheachtrach
Mallacht gur bhain amach.

As cath Mhaigh Ratha sin
An tráth a ritheas uaidh
Sula ndearnadh mo ghoineachan,
Ní raibh duairceas dlite dhom.

Ar thuras im thruanairt,
Gur tháinig mé, nach bocht,
I gcéin ó m' eolas féin,
An chríoch a bhain mé amach.

Tiocfaidh MoLingseachán
Ar thuras truánta,
Cé go mbíonn sé dhom leanúint ann,
Ní bheidh sé go furasta.

Coillte coimhthíocha
Mar chlaí ar an gcuartaíocht,
An tír a bhain mé amach,
Ní gníomh duaircis.

Duibhlinn go Boirche
A chuir orm uafás,
San íochtar an duibheagán
Is an t-uachtar diongbháilte.

Is fearr mar a fuaireas
Na coillte chomh milis úd,
An Mhí sé mo rogha díobh
Is Osraí na háibhle.

Ulaidh is an fómhar ann
Faoi Loch Cuan ar crith go mór,
Sa samhradh dom ar cuairt
Go Cineál Eoghain.

Imeacht faoi Lúnasa
Go Tailtin na dtoibreacha,
San earrach ag iascaireacht
Is ag siúl na Sionainne.

Minic a shroichimse
Tír úd mo dhúchais,
Buíonta bachallacha,
Droimníní duaircis.

Sustenancelife is Grim

Life is cheerless and povertythinbare, the cheerlessness of the apathyshiftlesschillcold of night, the cheerlessness of the unsparingoppressedseverethickheavy snow, the cheerlessness of the stinginghard airwind

Sustenancelife is grim being without a mutesoft bed, a congealfrosty lairabode, roughcoarse snow and airbreathwind. Icy rawcold airbreath-wind, dreadshadow of a feeble sun, the shadowfox-holeshelter of one sacredscionbordertree on the summit of a Jovemoormountain pithplain. Grimandbearing an abundant volleyrunshower of wetness, a rabbe-travinehiketrackstep over the great havenjourneypathpass, elopegaitpass-ing a smoothgrassland greygreenstream on a frostnipped greygreen morning. The famecry of the stagbelling all over the sallowtan castra-tionwood, to an abature gap like a climbladder in Ashbourne, the autumn cropfrothblowsound of the billowsea. Wellforgive, boastgreat Master-lord, my own wanderingdizzinessmistake is boastgreat, the blackness of the Guinness-induced Arthuritic depression, leanmean palewhiteloined Sweeney. I rhythmrun over the thinbareclose gap of the Mournes in rag-weed and he-benweed, a sigh at night, wintry snow islandshorecastletes-ticle hailstones. Lying in a wet bed on the battle-fieldslopetracks of Lough Erne, of a stomachmind to elopegaitgo earlyearly, rising at spar-rowsfart. Running across the sweetpeaks of the billowsurfacewaves of Dunseverick, listening to the pregnantbulkyheavy surfacewaves of Din-rhydderch. Running from those billowsurfacewaves to the billowsur-facewaves of the Barrow, marriage-nightfestivalentertainmentsex on the hard ledge-edge of Duncerman. From there to the sweetcliffgablere-gardhornpeak of Benburren to Black Head, my ear on the lumpcushion of harshrough Mount Eagle. I'm tense, shifting, my emigrantflitting a bedragglegrammlebumbling, on the pithplain of Balboru, from Beni-nobenone to Benonobenine. An apparitionperson came to me and grapplehandled me, she didn't bring peace, a redoubtable wifewoman. Sheit took my own lot off with her for all my guiltsins, the most contemptible job of all, she pulsatehuffabsconded with my blood-tracebrooklimewatercress. I pick shorecress scurvygrass, it's a grand little sacred bundle of substancefood, four frugalgatheredround jinkforkhandfuls from wild-deershy Glenvulcan. I boastgreatly need sustenance, the bogdropcranwhortleberry is gaypleasant, a drink of shrillweedclear rainurinetearswater from a holy fountainwell. My talonhoofnails like the nailtalonhooves of steedhorses, my sparkgirdle mutesoftened, my legfeet arse over tits, I'm a hopeless nakednude. They'll catch me, the barbarous Fenian High Tory Scotland Yard Special Branch Flying Squad G-Men, far from Ulster, attempt-travelling in Scotland. After my vainroundabout odyssey, pity me in my giftpoemhalterfate, in hardship on Ailsa Craig. Ailsa Craig, the lairabode of the emptygrasslandpalewhite mews, rawcold for hospitalityvisitors. Ailsa Craig, campaniform islandshorecastletesticlestone, half its airtheightdirection would be enough, its smellnoseprow projecting to the billowsea flowstream. A disaster how we singreproachturnmet, two hardy long-legged oddroundcraneherons, me hard as a ragslag, her hard as a sharp-beakedgodwit. The beds are wet where my little wombapartment is, I never thought much of it as a venerable monolith. Bad for Congall from Clane to overtake himself in catbattalionbattle, like an outer heroarmouryoke he's earned the curse. At the catbattle in Moira when I ran away before I was jinkscrapstingwounded, I didn't deserve grief. A wretch on a pilgrimage-journey I arrived at an endterritory – evil destiny! – longingfar from my own familiarplace. My fast friend Lynchehaun will come on a truantemaciated pilgrimage-journey, though he'll stickfollow me, it won't be easy. Alienwild nest-violated castrationwoods in Quilty like a fence around my roundperegrinations, the ruraldry-landstate I've arrived at, not a grim deed. Difflin to Dunmourne is what gave me the horrors, in the bottom the blackabyss and the solid crop creamtop. I prefer how I found the flatterhoneysweet castrationwoods, here in Meath is my favourite and in widerangingfluent Ossory. Around Strangford Lough in UlstermenUlster in hairst-autumn all quaking, summer peregrinations to Kinelowen. Elopementgaitgoing at Lammas in lunacyAugust to

Teltown with its wellfountains, in springtime Shannon-specific flow-streamlet riviating. I often get to go as far as my wildnative dry-landru ralnationterritory, croziercrooked armyboongangs, grimdark backridge-drumlinwaves.

[Unstable Narrator]

guth na cuaiche
faoi learga Loch Éirne,
ag freagairt don uisce

the sound of the cuckoo on the slope of Lough Erne exposed out-cropobser-vanceresponding to the water

[Sweeney]

Uaimh Shuibhne, Carraig Alasdair

Seo mar a mbeidh teach mór agam
Coicís ar mhí,
Ní faoi ghlas i gcuibhreach
I ngéibheann ach i ndíthreabh
Ar fud na gcléireach
A díbríodh thar a gcill amach,

Mar áitreabh dom ina dhún rí
Is mé gan teach gan tine,
Gan chlúmh i gcoill gan folach,
Ar fáinneáil agus ar foluain,
Ar dásacht agus ar neamhain
Gan tuí faoi mo thaobh,

Gan bhia, gan deoch
Ach beatha chúng is lom
In adhbha faoileán is guilbneach,
Gan neamh agam gan saol

Ach creig chásach in áit chaol
Idir mé agus néalta neimhe.

Swine Cave, Ailsa Craig

Here's where I'll have a big asylum-mansion for a fortnight and a month, not in greyglassfetterlocks but in a retreatwilderness among the altar-boyclerics driven out of their church-yardcell as my dwelling and my king's closefort, without house or hearth, without foliagefurfeathers in a Kalendscastrationwood without hidecover, fannelfluttering and full-onfloatflying in a mad-daring tormentilbattle-frenzy without food or drink but a narrow bare foodlife in a place of gulls and godwits without non-skyheaven, without a worldlife but a friendlysacred barrenshorecrag in Kyle and Carrick in a narrow place eitherbothbetween myself and the trancenebulae of non-skyheaven.

M'Áras

Air Carraig Alasdair,
A Dhúilimh, is crua,
Creag bheag an-àirde
'S a srón le sruth farraige,
Adhbha do dhís chorr,
An guilbneach is am faoileann,
'S gur fuar fliuch mo leabaidh,
D'éis m'aistir, mo thrua,
Cian ó Ultaibh
Ag triall ar Albain.

My Vesselhouseabode

On Ailsa Craig, Jesus, it's hard, a wee cliffcrag with its snout to the stormy strait, the habitat of two oddroundherons, the rake-curlew and common whitesandmewgull, and my bed is rawcold and wet after my hardshipcrossing, more's the pity, longinglong from Ulster, on my attemptjourney to Scotland.

Taobh

Ó d'fhág mé Cill Riáin is bile na cille
Go ndeachaigh mé don taobh thall thar craos na mara

Le linn anfa, doininne, ceatha,
Tabharfaidh mé taobh le Fear Coille,

Mo chomhalta, mo sheise, mo chara
Is mo bhráthair go críoch mo bheatha.

Regionborderdirectionlinerelianceattitude

Since I waveleft Kilrean and the cellchurchyard sacredscionbordertree and went to the far linereliancedirectionattitudeborder-regionside across the gluttontbreechmaw of the sea in wintriness-stormshowers, I'll trustside up to the Woodman, my fosterbrother, my brother and my haunchfriend, until the regionboundaryend of my sustenancelife.

[The Voice]

46

Oidhe

Ós agam atá 'n fháistine,
Cinneadh dhut, a Shuibhne,
Taisteal i do chríoch
Is d'fhearann 's dol thar sáile

Cian bho Ultaibh
Agus triall an Albain
Bho Chinn Tìre go hÍle
Go huaimh Dhonnain Eige

'S à sin go Carraig Alasdair
Is a sròn ri sruth farraige,
Thar a' mhuir mhór
Go ruige Crìoch Bhreatainn

Is i gceann na bliadhna
Gur mithich dúinn sgaradh
Is gun i sin críoch do bheatha
'S d'oidhe 's do dhàn faoi dheoidh.

[Sweeney]

Coigríoch

I mo gheilt Ultach i mo réim
Leis na héin i néalta neimhe,
D'fhéach mé síos ar mo thír fúm,
Sea, m'áit is m'ionad is m'eolas,
Mo chríoch agus m'fhearann
I gcoigríoch Thír Chonaill

Mu Shliabh Liag thíos mu thuath
Mu dheas is go luath thar ghleann
Go Cill Riáin gu hInis Bó Finne
Gu Doire Chaluim Chille
'S à sin go Gleann Eile
Siar gu Boirche ó dheas ó thuaidh

Go Cill Cua 's gu hÉadan Tairbh
Shuas gu deas agus thall
'S a-bhos ar Shliabh Fuaidh 's mo dhún
Thoir thiar aig Ros Earcáin
'S a' Bhuais gu Sliabh Mis
Eadar deas agus tuath

Gu Dùn Sobhairce 'n Ultaibh
'S à sin cian bho Ulaidh
'S bhom eòlas a' triall an Albain
Bho Chinn Tìre gu Carraig Alasdair
Eadar neòil na h-iarmailte 's a' mhuir
Gus an d'ràinig mi Crìoch Bhreatainn.

[Unstable Narrator; Sweeney; Allan]

All of These

Sweeney left Carrick backwestafter that
And went over the sea, abundantwide
Like a breechgluttonymawvent
In a showermiststormterror
Until he reached the British Territory
Of the Royal Burgh of Dumbarton.

He left on his neatsouthleft hand
The closedownhillforthouse of the king
Till they garnerhaulhappened
Upon a megaforest like Feaghmore
And whatever defilejourneyway
In the timberwood he went along,
He heard a boastgreat groangemeneting
And roughmoaning and pitiablepersonalas!ing
And punypathetic sighing.

And there he was, another
Nakedwood-grazingbattle-fugitivebirdbeastpaniclunatic
In the Royal Forest of Arden
In the Great Wood of Caledon.
He attackapproached them.

'Who you, personfellow?'
'I'm a nakedwood-grazingbattle-fugitivebirdetc.'
'If you are, come over here and we'll be
Lovesocietycompanions for I'm a woodloony and all'.
'I'd come if it wasn't for fear of the homehouse
And household of the king
Getting hold of me and that I don't know
That you're not one of them'.

'I'm not at all, patronymdescend me
Your aboriginal surnom since I'm not.'

'Och, I'm a woodman, the Albanagh, a Caledonian
Frae the Kingrik o Strathclyde, a Gael
And foreigner, Erseman and Dalriadic *Scotus*,
Insular Celt, Pictish, Cumbric and Brythonic,
Ossianic, Fingalian and Fenian,
Macarius the Roman and Mark the Athenian,
John the Baptist, James the Penitent, Anthony, Jerome,
Daniel and Nebuchadezzar far from my home,
A Lowlander indwalling on the Highland Line
And whatever way you can say it
In the King's English or Inglis or Lallans
Or Scots or Irish or Gaelic
Or Cant, if I'm not all of these,
Then I'm no' one.'

[Sweeney; Allan]

The Paths of Exile

For the love of the Lord, I have suffered
And endured grim sorrow at heart –
Fettered by cold were my feet,
Bound by frost
In cold clasps, I dwelt for a winter
In the paths of exile.

At times the swan's song
I took to myself as pleasure
Instead of the laughter
Of men, the voice
Of the curlew and the singing gull
Instead of the drinking of mead.

No friendly kinsman can comfort
The terrible tossing sea-weary soul.
Not for me, lone-flier, is the sound
Of the harp nor pleasure
In woman on my travels throughout the world,
Wide-mouthed, storm-swept, prow-abounding.

sian, tàirneanaich
agus gaoth air m' iomradh
is fa-dheòidh sìth

storm thunder and wind on my imram and finally peace

[Sweeney ; Unstable Narrator; Allan]

Cumann

'Cé thú a dhuine', arsa Suibhne, 'ag ochtach
Is ag caoineadh is ag mairgneach go mór
Is ag osnaíl?' 'Geilt mise,' ar seisean.
'Más geilt, tar i leith go ndéanam cumann
Agus déan do shloinne dom mar an gcéanna'.
'Fear Coille m'ainm. Ailín m'ainm
Is is don tír seo atá mo bhunús.'
'Inis dom, cad a thug ar gealtacht thú, a dhuine?'
'Bhí dhá rí, rí Bhreatain agus rí Éireann,
Muintir Eochaidh agus muintir mo thiarna
Is gan ach fad dhá chrann eadrainn.
Rinneadh tionól mór le cath a chur
Faoin tír seo agus ríocht na críche
Leis an dís sin le huaill agus díomas.
Thug an slua trí gártha mallachta orm
A thug ar fáinneáil is ar foluain mé ó shin i leith.'

[Sweeney]

Cumann

Ó tháinig mé amach as an iúr i gCill Riáin
Ó d'iaigh mo chomhalta Loingseachán
Tharam a dhá láimh
Nó go ndeachas ina tholg féin
Mar ar baineadh díom glas is géibheann
Is an cuibhreach ar mo lámha,
Is sáil socair mo bheatha
Gan eagla gan uamhan
Le mo chruth féin is mo dhealbh
Agus, a Ailín, a chara, tar i leith
Is tabhair dom, a chroí, do lámh
Go ndéanam cumann, a dhuine,
Nó go dtabharfam taobh lena chéile
Cé nach mbeifeá i m'fharradh
Coiscís ar mhí féin
Go dtí gur mithid dúinn scaradh.

Lovefellowship

Since I came out of the yew in Kilrean and my man Lynchehaun join-closed his two armhands about me and I went into Lynchehaun's thrustcouchbed where the grey-greenrivuletlocks and captivityfetters were reapremoved from me and the shackle on my armhands, my sustenancelife is daintycomfortable without fear or dread and come over here, Allan, and give me your hand and we'll make lovefellowship, man-person, and sidetrust each other even if you're beside me for not even a fortnight and a month until it's time for us to spreadpart.

The North

Up here between the Wall and the Forth,
I am neither a Pict nor a Gael

Nor a Scot among the Kings of the North,
Urien of Rheged and Rhydderch Hael.

And while they're there with their bands of men
Drinking their buffalo horns of mead,
I'm out in the wild-wood with Lailoken
With water as wine and cress for our bread.

airím é faoin gcoill
i gCríoch Breataine dom thall,
mairgneach, osnaíl

I hear it in the wood around Dumbarton wailing and sighing

[Unstable Narrator]

Then Sweeney recitesaid this partitionverse and Woodman outcropresponded with this Bush verse:

[Sweeney; Allan]

47

Suaineach Luaineach

[Suibhne] A Fhir Choille, cad a thit amach?
Trua liom do ghuth.
Déan insint dom mar a d'éirigh
Dod chéill is dod chruth.

Innsibh dhomh mar a thachair –
An é go raibh sibh sa chath
A chuireadh anns a' mhachair
An lá sin ag Maigh Rath?

[Ailean] Dh'innsinn dhuibh mo sgeul fhèin,
Mo chraobh-zenchais is mo ghnìomh
Mura h-eagal leam sluagh nan sleagh
Is na luibhne aig Taigh 'n Rìgh.

Is mise Ailean MacSuain a rachadh
Gu hiomaí dreann,
Fear-ealain 's coilltear, 's eòl mi do chàch
Mar gheilt luath gleann,

Gun éisteacht le téada míne
Mar a bu ghnàth
Ach fulaingt de fhrasa síne
Is reothadh gu bràth.

[S] Is mise Suibhne Mac Colmáin
A-mach as a' bhile bhuadhach,
'S fhasa dhuinn còmhradh
A-bhos anns an ros, a ghruagach.

MacSween the Lethargicvolatilesleeprestlessfriskjump-Plaidloonywanderer of Strathclyde

SWEENEY

Sylvestris gadelicus, orangutanman, Flying Scotsman, whatever fall-outhappened? Distress-shame, man, how your bardtauntvowelword-voice is. Holmtell me what risebecame of your deathdarlingsense and your phantomshapeappearance. Tell me what happened: were you in the catbattalionbattle that was waged in the linksbattle-field that day in Moira?

ALLAN

I would holmrelate my storynews, my zenbiographygenealogyhistory traditionlanguage richfoamcloudrealationbushbranchtree and my peat-stackdeed if it weren't for fear of the toefingershieldspear fairyarmy-crowds in Kingshouse. I'm Allan MacSween who used to go to many's the griefbattle, a trickeryschoolbush-craftpoesyskillhighart manone and castrationwoodwanderer, the everyrest know me, plummetwaulkpraise-beloved, as the earlyfast wildbirdman of the woods and glens.

SWEENEY

I'm Sweeney MacCalman the passenger pigeon, a bushman, out of the gempalmvirtued blossombeardliptree by a river in the Antrim Hills. It's easier for us to converse here in the pleasantknowledgeseedarable-promontorycopse, womanlyhairybrowniechief.

Madman of the Glens

Woodman, what's the story?
Your voice is pitiable,
Tell me what made you lose
Your wits and appearance.

I would tell you my background
And the scale of the deeds I've done
If I wasn't scared of the shaggy crowd
In the king's inn-house.

I'm Alan
That used to go to many a skirmish
With eagles, everyone calls me
The madman early and fast in the glens.

I'm the coalman's son, Sweeney,
I'm from the Bush,
It's all the easier for us
To have our conversation here, man.

[Unstable Narrator; Sweeney; Allan]

48

Each everyperson of them trustrelysided up to each other backwestafter that and enquired after each another's storynews. Sweeney said to the grazingwoodloony: 'Give me your patronymicdescentmonickersur-name' he said. 'I'm a McBrew, the son of a fairy-hillockfarm-mansion-hosteller' said the British woodloony. 'My majoritysubstanceorigins are in this ruraldry-landstate and my name is Allan.' 'Tell me' saids Sweeney 'what brought you to paniclunacy'. 'Neat answer. There were two kings contending for the kingsovereignty of this endcountry one hostingjourneyflowtime, fact, viz. Ogie (Haughey), the son of Geoff MacRae and Goochi, son of Geoff, the MacRae twins; I was one of Ogie's countrypeoplecommunity' he said 'as he was the best of the two. An exalthuge assembly was held to snowfallburywage battalionbattle faceagainst each other about the ruraldry-landstate. I put an injunction-taboospell on every one of my masterlord's country-peoplecommunity that no apparitionperson of them would come without sailclothing of silk about his person to the battalionbattle to be emblemdistinguished better than all the others in wailpride and scornarrogance. So the fairyarmycrowds gaveput three notorietyshouts of male-diction on me which putsent me swanning and sweening about as you can see.'

[Allan]

Fear Coille

Ag tuisleadh de bharr craobh
Thuas i ndoirí dorcha
I m'aonar, i gcuas caol,
I nglaic, i mullach sceiche,
I ndos ard eidhinn,
Sa mbile ag Ros Earcáin,
Sna géaga iúir a bhí sa gcill
Sa ngleann idir an mhóin is an mhá
Idir chorra is chuaineanna
Is dhaimh, is mé Fear Coille
Ar fáinneáil in imeall na feá
Ó Fhiodh Gaibhle go Ros Bearraigh.

Woodsman

Slipstumbling from the creamcrophindrancetop of cornheatherlockbranches up in dark oakgroves on my tod, in a kylenarrow cavity, in a handholdfork, in the rooftop of a hawthorn, in a tall ivy dronetuft, in the sacredscionbordertree at Rasharkin, in the yew branches in the cellchurch-yard in the hollowsmoke-cloudglen bothamongbetween the peatmoor and the mazeplain bothbetweenamong oddroundherons and packs and championox-stags, I'm the Woodsman fannelfluttering in the edge of the beechwood from Figile to Rossberry.

Fear Coille Eile

Caithim mo bheatha i m'aonar
Ó ghéag go géag is ó dhos go dos
Nó i mo shuan i mbarra crann, mo dhíon
Ar fhearthainn agus duilliúr agam d'adhartán.

Bím ag fáinneáil agus ag foluain
Ar m'imirce sa bhFiodh Mór,
Beo ar shíol is ar mheas is ar lus,
Ar uisce is ar fheithidí agus ag seachaint daoine.

Seo mé in bhur fianaise sa díthreabh
I mbaol mar a raibh na doirí dorcha
Agus an choill chiar. Bainim do bhur ngné féin.

Aithneoidh sibh mo ghairm is mo ghuth,
Mo bhúir is mo gháir i mo ghealt glinne,
Mo stocaireacht is mo chornaireacht is m'osna mhór.

Person of the Woods

I wastepass my sustenancelife on my tod from branch to branch and from dronebushcopse to dronebushcopse or sleep in the creamcrophindrance-top of penis-shaftvault-trees, my roofprotection against the rain and with leaves as a little lumpcushionpillow. I fannelflutterloiter and full-on fly-float on my emigrationmigration in the Great Wood, quickalive on seed and esteemfruit and plants, on rainurinetearswater and sepentbeastinsects as I fleeshun menpersons. Here I am in your witnesspresence in the retreatwild, endangered, where the dark oak-groves and waxdark castrationdesecrationwoods were. I belong to your formspecies. You'll recognise my acclaimcall and my censurevoice, my lowbellowbray and my famecry like the nakedwood-grazinglevitatingpaniclunatics in the smokecloudhollowglen, my scroungetrumpeting and my hornblowing and my great sigh.

[Sweeney; Allan]

Mo Scéala?

Mo scéala?
Ní hansa.
Turas ón teorainn
I mo chríoch agus nam fhearann
Ann an Cealla Luinne
Nam Fhear Coille
'S nam gheilt ghlinne
Mar-aon leis na héin
Air feadh Èireann is Alban
Gu néalta neimhe.

My Story?

My story? Neat answer, dearest. A journey from the border in my endterritory in Killalloney as a castrated Woodman and an untameable glen-dwelling nakedwoodgrazinglunatic with the birds throughout Ireland and Scotland to the trancenabulae of non-skyheaven

[Allan]

Mo Charaidean

'S e mo mheadh m' uisge,
'S e mo bhuar mo bhiolair ghlas

Agus mo charaidean mo chrainn,
Cruaidh, lom, dlùth, clùmhor:

An t-abhall trom a' cromadh gu talamh,
A' bheithe nas binne na teud mìn cruite,

An caorann, 's àlainn a bhlàth,
An coll clùmhor is a chnòthan,

An critheann is a dhuilleach air chrith,
An cuileann geugach na chòmhla ri gaoith,

An darach dosach, àrd os cionn chrann,
An droigheann is àirnean ged 's ann dham choirbeadh,

An eidheann a' fàs tro chrann cas,
An fheàrna, 's àlainn a lì sa bheàrn,

An t-iubhar a bha sa chille sa ghleann,
An raineach ruadh na frasair d'fhear air fhògradh,

An t-seileach ghlan ghrinn an Gleann Balgain,
An sgìtheach na gnàth 'n coille chiar,

An t-uinnseann mar arm làmhan laoich
Is bile Chille Lùghaidh far an dèan mi suain shàmhach,

Ann an doireachan dorcha, mo charaidean uile
'S mar thoradh do sgeula 's t' imeachdan, a Shuibhne.

My Relationfriends

My mead is my rainurinetearswater, my kine is my glassgreygreen watercress, my relationfriends my penisploughmast-trees, hardy, bare, warpclose, sheltering: the pregnant orchardapple-tree middle-fingerbending to the ground, the birch judgementsweeter than the soft strings of a cymbalviolinlute, the rowan and its lovely warmcolourfruitflower, the snug hazel and its nuts, the aspen and its leaves all shaking, the nymhpsprigbranchy holly as a door-frametogether against the painwind, the antlerdronefrothfore-lockmuzzlemanetasselthicketbramblebushy oak, high above penisploughmast-trees, the blackthorn and its bluffroughplum-sloes for all that they viciouscorrupt me, the ivy wastegrowing through a footsuddensteeptwisted penisploughmast-tree, the alder, its seawaterjewelhappinessfacecolour is lovely in the crannygap, the yew that was in the hermit's cellchurchyard in the glen, the red bracken as bedding for a trespassrobberybanished man, the pureclear willow in Glenbalkan, the hawthorn in the waxdark Kalendsoutlawdesecrationwood, the ash as arms in an infantryman's hands and the sacredlipleaftree of Killooey where I sleep soundly, in dark oak-groves, all my relationfriends fruitresulting in your storynews and your journeygoings, Sweeney.

[Sweeney]

Mo Réim

Teithim i m'réim leis an damh rua
Agus leis an damh donn thar an mhá
Ag méid mór m'eagla roimh an slua
Go bhfaighe mé m'éag is mo bhás trí bhá
In Eas Dhubhthaigh nó bás de rinn féin
Is adhlacadh i reilig fíréin.

My Linecareerauthorityrange

I shunflee in my linecareerauthorityrange with the red championox-stag and with the Jovelordtimberbrown championox-stag across the maizeplain for fear of the fairyarmycrowd until I die by sympathy-baydrowning in Duffy's Falls or at the point of a spear in Ring and be sepulchreburied in the relicgraveyard of a justman.

glao coirre de loch,
fuaim críonaigh dhá bhriseadh,
léim creabhair de chraoibh

cry of a heron from the lake sound of wood being broken a woodcock leaping from a branch

[Allan]

Dùsgadh

Na chluinneas mi anns gach taobh,
Guth corra bhon loch,
Guth glan gairginn,
Leum creabhair à fasgadh nan craobh,
Guth feadaig' a' feadarsaich
Is fuaim crìonaich ga briseadh
Air mo dhùsgadh anns a' mhadainn
An dèidh mallachd an t-sluaigh
Aig an dithis MhacGuaire
Ri uchd cath Mhagh Rath
Gus an èirich mi 'n-àirde
'S an dèan mi teicheadh luath.

Arousewaking

What I hear on every side, the bardtauntvowelvoice of an oddcraneheron from the sealoch, the puredeadbrialliant bardtauntvowelvoice of a cormorantdiver, the semenmilkjump of a woodcock out of the shelter of the oatcloudrelationtreebranches, the bardtauntvowelvoice of a Februarywhistleplover whistling and the voiceaccentechosound of withered brushwoodtreeleafbranches being burstbroken have arousewakened me after I arousedwoke this morning after wantingforallthat the curse of the two MacQuarries' spiritarmycrowd about to do battalionbattle browbreast to browbreast at Moira as I rise up and make good my ashtransientquick desertflight.

[Sweeney]

Fad Dhá Chrann

Seo duit, a Fhir Choille, mo bheannadáin:
Cluain Cille i dTír Chonaill ar an gcoigríoch;
Brú tobair uisce ghil ag teora na cille;
An fál sin thoir ag doras na reilige;
Imeall Loch Rí agus bruach na Banna;

An mhuir fhairsing idir Éire is Alba –
Coimeáidimis a chéile go maith
Agus bíodh fad dhá chrann eadrainn.

Two Trees

These are my favourite places, Woodman: Clonkilly in Donegal in a foreign neighbouring territory; the bruisebrink of a well of pureclean tears-water at the border of the cellchurch-yard; that fieldfence overeast at the door of the relicgrave-yard; the wide sea between Ireland and Scotland – let's look out for each other well and let there be the length of two penis-shaftvault-trees between us.

49
[Unstable Narrator]

He asked in like manner of Sweeney what sent him into paniclunacy. 'The verbwords of Ronan' saids Sweeney 'for he cursed me in breast-front of the catbattalionbattle of Moira and I rose up on high out of the battalionbattle and I've been flutterloitering and floathovering from that halfside there since then.' 'Sweeney' saids Allan 'let us keep watch on each other goodcarefully since we've trustrelysided up to each other.'

[Allan]

Woodnotes

Sweeney, the one of us that hears earlyfastest
The call of a hollowpointeelheron
From a greygreengeneration greenpond fjordlochlake

Or the clearclean curkling of a quailcormorant
Or chasmleap of a haywoodcock from a branchtree
Or wheeplewheesh of a whistleplover awakened

Or the sound of Creeny dottereldoddered wood being co-broken
Or the restshadow of a bird above a timberwood,
Let him that hears first call out *gotong-royong* and tell the other one.

Let us observe the two metre rule between the two of us
And if either apparitionperson of us notices any of those aforesaid things
Or their ghostlike, then let's make good our shunflyflee-escape.

[Sweeney]

Sounds

Sleeping on a hard couch above
The lake, I wake to sounds
And reverberations I know so well:

The cuckoo, the cooing of the turtle-dove,
The clear note of the cormorant or quail,
The cry of the mountain grouse,
The cry of the herons in Cooley,
The flight from a branch of a woodcock,
The sound of a double-tonguing plover
Wheepwhistling on being woken,
The squeal of badgers in Ben Brock
And Ben Bran, the chant of the hounds,
The lowing and bellowing of the stag
And the cattle in the booley.

The prattle of women and men,
Lynchehaun and the mill-hag
Playing games and laughing in the ale-house,
The peal of Moling's vesper-bell
At the holy well of Dunmail,
The voice of a beautiful woman, a hunting-call,
Withered branches being broken,
The madmen of Ireland in the glen,
The snoring of the man at the wall
And you in bed with your lover.

[Unstable Narrator; Allan]

50

Bá

Rinne siad amhlaidh is bhíodar bliain is lá
I bhfarradh a chéile.
I gceann na bliana sin,
Dúirt Ailín le Suibhne:
Is mithid dúinn scaradh
Inniu, a Shuibhne, ó tháinig
Críoch is ceann mo shaoil
Agus nach bhféadfainn gan dul
Don ionad inar cinneadh dom éag.
Rachad anois go hEas Dhubhthaigh
Go gcuirfear fathach gaoithe fúm ann
Is go bhfaighidh mé bás le bá.

[Unstable Narrator; Sweeney; Allan]

Crìoch

Rinn iad amhlaidh 's bha iad bliadhna
Làn is latha còmhla.
An ceann na bliadhna sin
Thuirt Suibhne ri Ailean:
'S mithich dhuinn sgaradh an-diugh
Oir thàinig gu ceann mo shaoghal
'S nach fhaod mi gun dol
Dhan ionad sa bheil e 'n dàn
Agus gum faighinn am bàs.

Is dè 'm bàs a gheibh thu? thuirt Suibhne.
Thèid mi a-nis, thuirt am Breatannach
Gu Eas Dhubhthaich is thig athach-gaoithe
Gus an tèid mo bhàthadh anns an eas
Is mo thiodhlacadh an rèilig fìrein.

That's what they spectrelikeness do like Aulay and they were a tidelot-full year in each other's comparecompany. At the headend of the year Allan says to Sweeney. 'It's duetime for us to spreadpart willie-neillie today' he said 'for the termend of my worldlife has come and I can't not go to the wonderplace surpassdetermined for me to numbdie in.' 'By what death will you die?' 'Simple as *beith-luis-nion*' said Allan 'viz. I'll go to the Falls of Duich now and a giant gust of windair will be buryput under me and I'll be buryput in the weaselwater-fall and I'll be sympathybayquenchdrowned like Scott's Steenie and sepulchreburied west-after that in the relicgraveyard of a rarejustelectman and I'll get to non-skyheaven and that will be the landend of my sustenancelife.' 'Sweeney' said Allan 'holmtell me what violentdeathtragedyfate you'll receive?' Sweeney then holmtold him as the sectioned narrative *Eachtra Shuibhne* or *Beatha Rónáin* relates *infra*. Then they spreadparted and the Briton attemptjourneyed to the Falls of Duich and fromsincewhen he reached the weaselwater-fall he was sympathybayquenchdrowned.

[Allan; Sweeney]

Man of the Wood

As my father is dead, and my mother,
And – a wounded side! – my foster-brother,
Let us now, friend, since we have placed trust,
Be guardians and confide in each other
Till the end of the year when we must
Go off to the churchyard of the just.

[Sweeney]

Talamh Slán

Ó thriall is ó tháinig mé go hÉirinn
I ndiaidh dom scaradh leis an mBreatnach
Gur tharla gur nocht mé i ndiaidh lae
Ar Mhaigh Linne Uladh

Ar ar thug mé aithne mar raon
Mar a mbíodh lena ló Congall Claon,

Mo sheise tréan thar cách is mo Rí,
Rinne mé talamh slán de
Gur chuir mé mé féin in iúl
Ó chonaic mé an solas
Ag dul dúinn go Droim Lurgan na Mí
Mar ar líonmhar cros,

I ndiaidh na n-each allúrach adhastair
A thug mé mar aisce uaidh,
An trí chaoga cholg déid,
An trí chaoga bó álainn,
An t-each donn is fearr ariamh
Thar féar agus fonn

Thuaidh, theas is thiar,
An caoga mogh sin, an caoga ionailt sin,
An fhuathróg bhreac sróil úd
Is an t-ionar óir mar mo thuarastal,
Gurbh áil liom iompú i ndiaidh sin uile
Is dul ar aistear go Tiarna eile.

Safe Ground

Since I trycame to Ireland after wanting for all that spreadparting with the Briton and it haulgarnermeethappened that I nakedviewappeared after a day in Moylinney in Ulster which I commandrecognized as a routerange where Congall McScanlon, my strong comrade above all other everymanChristpersons and my King, was in his day, I assumed as safe ground that I had knowledgeguide-expressed myself since I saw the light as we were going to Drumlargan in Meath full of crosses, after all the allureforeign halter horses I took from him as a gift in vain, the thrice fifty ivorytoothed swords, the thrice fifty beautiful alas!beaucows, the best ever Joveprincetimberbrown steedhorse over grass and songbasedesireland north, south and west, those fifty slaves, those fifty bondhandmaids, that troutspeckle-engraved satin loinkilt and that golden innerlayertunic as my wages, that I wanted to reverseturn after all that and all to go on a roundaboutjourney to another Lordmaster.

Tháinig Mé Amach

Tháinig mé amach thiar
Mar a bhfuil mo theach sa gcoill chiar
Is i ndoirí dorcha don mhá
I Má Linne, Má Feimhin is Má Lí
Agus don mhá atá i Mí
Ar lorg feise
Agus grá
Le Congal Mac Scanláin mo sheise.

I Came Out

I came out backwest where my house is in the waxdark castrationwood and in dark oak-groves to the mazeplain in Moylinney, Moyfevin and Moylee and the mazeplain in Meath progenytracklooking for festivalentertainmentnightsleeping and charitylove with Congall McScanlon my partner.

[Unstable Narrator]

51

Chaidh Suibhne a dh'Ulaidh, viz. Sweeney came and went before him westafter that over the oceanic Gaelic Sea to Ireland. He garnerhaulmethappened after a layday in Moylinney in Ulster and fromsincewhen he commandmentrecognised the pithplain, he said: 'Christ, Eve, He was a noblegood Everyman I was with on this pithplain' he says 'aye, squint-eyed Congall McScanlon from Clane and evenyetagain' he said 'that was a noblegood level playing field we were in. Myself and Congall were one day on this pithplain and I said to him: 'I want to go to another lordmaster' for my hirestipend was so fewsmall with him and there and then so that I might delaystay with him. He gave me three fifties of beautiful alluringforeign destriers and palfreys and his own Jovetimberbrown and three fifties of ivorytoothed brightfaced awnangerswords, fifty bondage men and fifty bondage women and a golden innerlayertunic and a loinkilt of glebetroutspeckled satin. And then Sweeney recitesaid this halterfategiftartpoem:

52

Maigh Linne

I Maigh Linne atáim anocht,
Aithníonn mo chroí is mo thaobh nocht,
Is eol dom féin an mhá freisin
Ina mbíodh Congall mo sheise.

Uair dá raibh bhí sinn féin
Anseo ar an raon seo le chéile,
Ag dul go Droim Lurgan lán,
Rinne muid comhrá seal.

Dúirt mise leis an rí,
Batalacharthairise!
Go mb'áil liom dul ar aistear
Is gur bheag liom mo thuarastal.

Fuair mé uaidh mar aisce
Trí chaoga each adhastair,
Trí chaoga claíomh tréan,
Caoga gall, caoga iníon innilte.

Fuair mé uaidh an t-each donn
Is fearr a shirfeadh féar is fonn,
Fuair mé a ionar óir
Is a fhuathróg breac le sról.

Cén mhá is fiú Maigh Linne
Ach an mhá atá sa Mí
Nó Maigh Feimhin is a líon cros
Nó an mhá in Airgeadros?

Nó Maigh Feá nó Maigh Aoidh
Nó Maigh Luirg go hard faoin aill
Nó Maigh Life nó Maigh Leamhna féin
Nó an mhá atá i Muirtheimhne?

De gach ní a chonaic mé riamh
Idir thuaidh, theas is thiar,
Ní fhaca mé le mo linn
Mac samhla mhá Mhaigh Linne.

Moylinney

I'm in Moylinney tonight, my heart and exposed flankside know it, the mazepithplain in Eglinton is familiar to me and all where Congall my matchmate used to be. Onehourtimeonce when myself and squint-eyed Congall from Clane were here together on this mazepithplain, going to drum in Lurgan, we stopped and co-talked for a while. I said to the king, it was a most sincere complaint, that I'd like to go on a vainroundaboutjourney and didn't think much of my hirewages. I got from him in vain*gratis* three fifties of halter horses, three fifties of strong battenswords, fifty foreign slaves, fifty chattel daughtergirls. I got from him the best Jovenobletimberbrown sorrel that ever seektraversed fairgrass and mood-musicland, I got his golden innerlayertunic and his loinkilt speckledtroutpocked with satin. What mazepithplain is even ferruleworth Moylinney but the mazepithplain that is Meath or Moyfevin in Iffa and Offa with its netfullcrowd of crosses or the mazepithplain in Argidross? Or Moyfea or Moigh or Moylurg uphigh under the cliff or the floodplain of Moyliffey or Moyleven itself or even the mazepithplain in Muirhevna? Of every kneewashing-girldaughterthing I've seen north backwest or east, I haven't seen in my own pondgenerationtime another plain the ghostsonlike of Moylinney.

Moylinney

I'm in Moylinney tonight,
My stark-naked heart knows it,
I know the plain where my comrade
MacGonagall was once.

Once myself and the man from Clane
Were together on this plain,
Going to Drumlurgan at full speed
We had a little talk.

I said to the king,
Something something something something,
I want to go on a journey,
My wages aren't worth a damn.

I took from him gratis
150 haltered steeds,
150 swords, all stout and strong,
50 foreign cocks, 50 bondage maidens.

I took from him the best brown steed
That traversed over terra firma,
I took his golden vest
And his girdle of chequered silk.

What plain is the equal of Moylinney
Except the plain in Meath,
Or Moyfevin with its network of crosses,
Or the plain in Argidross?

Or Moyfea, or Moylurg,
Or lovely Moynee on high,

Or Moyliffey, or Moylee,
Or the plain in Muirhevna?

Of all I've ever seen
Between the north, south and west,
I haven't seen until this
The equal of this plain.

[Unstable Narrator; Sweeney]

53

Cuairteachadh

An dèidh 'n laoidh sin
Thàinig Suibhne roimhe gu Gleann Balgain
Agus bha e ga chuairteachadh
Gus an do thachair gealtag ris ann.

Theich ise roimhe 's a rèir sin thuigeadh
Gum b' ann air ghealtachd a bh' a' bhean
Agus dh'iompaich e roimhpe.
Theich ise roimhe-san an dèidh sin.

'Ochan, a Dhè,' arsa Suibhne,
"S truagh a' bheatha seo – mise
A' teicheadh ron ghealtaig agus ise
A' teicheadh romhams' air làr Ghleann Balgain;

'S ionmhainn fhèin
An t-ionad gealtachd seo gu deimhinn'.

After that rudderexhortationLeelay Sweeney came before him to Glenbalkin and he was searchcirclewandering it until he garnermethappened on a madwoman. He shunfled before her as he twigged by that that the wifewoman was in panicmadness and he changeturned towards to her.

She shunfled before him there and then. 'Uladhlation, o God!' said Sweeney 'this is a pitymiserable sustenancelife, me shunflyfleeing before the old screeching madwoman running round in the glen, her shunflyfleeing before me on the deadcentreground of Glenbalkan; the place of paniclunacy is dear indeed' and he recitesaid:

[Sweeney]

Mairg a Thugann Taobh le Mnaoi

Agus mná na n-airchinneach dom bhréagadh
Agus dom chealgadh *tar as an iúr*
Agus ag baint mo chuid biolair
Agus cailleach an mhuilinn dom bhrath
Ó chlaochlaigh mé deilbh is dath
Agus mná ag tuargaint an lín
Mar a tuairgeadh mo mhuintir agus bean ag breith
Agus gan mná mánla maiseacha ná ainnir mhaoth
Ná guth mná áille i m'fharradh,
Mo bhean dhil mhaith ná m'iníon chaomh,
Cén t-ionadh dom iompú agus teitheadh
Ón mnaoi úd gan chéill gan chonn?

Alas!pity Anyone Who Trustsides With a Wifewoman

What with the church-stewards' wifewomen liecajoling and beguiling me *come out of the yew* and rendreaping my watercress lot and the hussyhag of the mill feelintent on betraying me since I changedeteriorated in warpappearance and colour and wifewomen hammerpounding the tidefullnetflax as my people were hammerpummelled and a wifewoman giving birthgripjudgement and without beautiful manlygentle women or a soppytender young woman or the censurevoice of a beautiful woman in my comparedcompany, my good and faithful wife and gentle daughtergirl, no wonder I turn and flee from that wifewoman without sense or reason.

[Madwoman of Glenbalkan]

Ó Shliabh Mis

Tháinig mé ó Shliabh Mis
Ar mo theitheadh go Gleann Balcáin
Le tuirse throm agus dobrón
Ó tharla mé ar chorp mo rogha
D'fhir Éireann is Alban,
D'fhir talún, monuar
Is m'ochón, a fuair bás
Mar oidhe, mo thrua,
Le titim d'aill Dhún Sobhairce
Gan iompú gan bheatha
Ina bhruar is ina chonamar
A d'fhág mé ar lár an ghleanna
Mar a thuigfeá féin, a ghealtáin,
Ar gealtacht is ag seachaint daoine.

From Slieve Mish

I've come from Slieve Mish shunfleeing to Glenbalkan, griefsticken since I happenfound the body of the best of the men of Ireland and Scotland and earth, who died a tragicviolentfatedeath falling from the cliff at Dunseverick in brokencrumbs that has left me in the groundcentre of the smoke-cloudhollowglen as you may twig, pucklunatic, in naked-woodgrazinglevitationlunacy and yieldshieldshunning menpeople.

I M'Ghealtóg

Mar a dhéanann tú, tuig, a Shuibhne, cuairt
Gan éadach is gan bhróg i gcríocha Chonnacht,
Déanaim féin cuairt i nGleann Balcáin ionúin
Mar a bhfuil mo dhún agus mo dhaingean,
M'áras agus m'áitreabh is mar ar aoibhne
Fuireach i gcónaí liom ná i ngach ionad in Éirinn
Agus nach dtéim uaidh ach le heagla mhór agus le huamhan

Agus faoi mar a theitheann tú i do réim mhaoime
Roimh na fuiseoga agus a bhfuaim,
Roimh ghuth na coirre le heitilt an dreoilín
Roimh oíche is roimh fhir an domhain,
Iompaím i m'ghealtóg agus teithim romham.

Madwoman

Just like you go round, twig, swine, without clothclothes or a brogueshoe in the endlands of Connaught, I go round Glenbalkan where I have my fortress and closedfort, my dwelling and habitation and where I'd rather stopstay than in any other place in Ireland and from which I don't go except out of great fear and dread and just like you shunflee in your wild career before night from the larks and the sound they make, before the censurevoice of the oddroundheron with the flight of a wren before night and before men of the world, I changeturn like a madwoman and flee the place.

[Sweeney]

54

Anns Gach Coille Chiar

Mairg don duine bheir miosgainn,
Cian gun deach a ghintinn,
Ged as bean a bheireadh, ged as fear,
Cha ruig iad nan dithis nèamh naomh.

Cha mhinig a bhios comann triùir
Gun duine dhiubh a' monmhar,
Droigheann is dris gam choirbeadh
Is gur h-e mise fear a' mhonmhair.

Gealtag air teicheadh bho a fear,
Gidheadh, sgeul annasach,
Fear gun mhìr is gun bhròg
A' teicheadh ron ghealtaig.

Ar miann nuair a thig cathain
Gus a' Bhealltainn air Samhain
Anns gach coille chiar
A bhith an crannaibh làn den eidheann.

Uisge Ghleann Bhalgain bhàin,
Èisteachd ri eunlaith,
A shruthan milis nach mall,
Innseachan agus aibhnichean.

A chuileann clùmhor 's a choll,
A dhuilleach, a dhrisean, a dhearcan,
A smeuran àlainn ùra,
A chnothan 's àirnean fuara.

Iomadh cuain fo chrannaibh,
Bùirean a dhamh-allaidh,
Uisgeachan a tha glan,
Cha leamsa ba mhiosgainn.

In Every Darkgreybrown Wood

Miskish! Oftenpity the husbandmanperson who bears poormalice, longinglong that he was geneconceived, whoso who it were or wifewoman or manone that carryholdbears, may the pair never reach holysaint heavenbliss. It's not pityoften there's an intercoursecompany of three without one manperson of them murmurgrumbling, aloelumberbrambles and ClanMacLeanbrakebrambles visciouscorrupt me so that I'm the manone mussitating. A dear little wildwoodbirdwoman desertfled from her manone, but, a strangedainty fablestory, a manone without a mowmorsel, disalced, desertfleeing the dear little wildwoodbirdwoman. Our birthmarkdesire when the yarnbarnaclegeese come from Samhain-tide to Beltane in Beltany and Meigh, in every darkgreybrown wood in tidefull iceivy penis-shaftploughtrees. The riverwaverainwater in fallowgroundvacantwhite Glenbalkan, listening to the winged-people, its tidestreams flatterhoneysweet not lateslow, its miseryrelateislandheadlandpasturehaughs and streamrivers. Its sleeksnug ClanMacMillanturpentine-elmholly and its treeoghamCwordnecksleep destructionhazel, its withered leaves, its ClanMacLeanbrakbrambles, its grottograve-eyeholeberries, its gloriouswhitedelightbeautiful newfresh bramblemulberries, its nutseeds and rawcold roughbluffdamsonplumsloes. Many a cornerpigwhelpwolflitter under its penis-shaftplough trees, the bitterbellowing of its wild earthquakebeamstagoxen, shrillweedclear riverbillowrainwaters, I never bore it any maleviolence.

There

Pity anybody that bears ill-will,
Would that he hadn't been born or conceived
Whether it's a woman that bears it or a man,
The pair of them won't reach holy heaven.

It's not often there's a group of three
Without one of them up to some *uisce faoi thalamh*,
Blackthorns and prickles are destroying me
So that I'm the conspiring moaning one.

But a madwoman fleeing her man
Is an unfamiliar story,
A man without a blanket or a shoe
Fleeing before the madwoman.

Our wish when the barnacle-geese come
Until Mayday from Halloween,
In every dark abundant wood
Is to be among the ivy.

The pure water of Glenbalkan,
Listening there to all its fowl,

The rapid streams there,
The holms and rivers there.

The shelter of its holly and hazel,
The leaves, the brambles, the thistles and acorns there,
Its berries, lovely and fresh,
Its nuts, its sloes so cool.

So many packs of hounds under the trees there,
The water so pure and free,
The bellowing of the wild stags there,
Whoever bore it ill-will, it wasn't me.

Bealtaine

Agus i ndiaidh feitheamh
I m'aonar dom i gcoill chiar
Ariamh ó tháinig Lá Samhna,
Seo mar na héin an Bhealtaine
Mar a bhí bliain go dtí aréir
Agus ariamh roimhe
Agus mé ar ais ní cian
Ó m'eol ach thiar i m'áit féin
Mar a bhfuil mo mhuintir,
Guth na gcuach a chluintear
Den chéad uair ar bhruach
Na Banna, na feithidí beaga sin
A airítear agus nach léir
Agus an ghrian úd a fhanann
Seal mar aoibhneas mór
Agus mar chrá mar an gcéanna.

May

And afterwanting for all that watchwaiting on my tod in a waxdark Kalendsdesecrationcastrationwood ever since Halloween came, here's

May like the birds like a year to last night like forever and I'm back not longingfar from the place I know best but backwest in my own place where my folk are, the censurevoice of the falsettotuftquaichcuckoo heard for the first time on the swollenbank of the Bann, those little serpentbeastinsects which you hearfeel but don't see and that earthsurfacebottomsun which stays for a spell as a great joy and pain.

Geilt

Tá mé mar aon leis an eilit
Is an damh rua sa machaire,
Leis na buaibh is na laonna sa mbuaile,
Ó dhíthreabh go díthreabh leis an each donn,
Leis na caoirigh gan lias, leis na gabhair
Ar an mbinn, sa gcoill chiar,
I seisc, i seascann, i sliabh,
Sna hinsí milse le ciumhais na habhann,
Ag caitheamh biolair agus ag geilt
I bhfearann is i gcríocha gan iamh.

Lunaticgrazing

I'm like as one with the doe and the red championox-stag in the battleplain, with the cows and the calves in the dungmilking-grazing-field, from wildernessretreat to wildernessretreat with the brownlord horses, with the sheep without a greypen, with the goats on the sweetgrazingpeak, in the waxdark castrationdesecrationwood, in sedge, in bogland, in the Jovemoor, in the sweet insulaholms beside the river, waste-eating watercress and lunaticgrazing in endlands without enclosureconfines.

[Unstable Narrator]

crann lom a bhí lán
ó Bhealtaine go Samhain
le cadhain is le heidheann

a bare tree that was full from Mayday to Halloween with barnacle geese and ivy

55

Sweeney went westafter to the prosperitystate where Erin was and stood at the greatouter foredoor of the homehouse where the queenlady was with her lady's companions and tweenies and maids.

Dán Grá

Chan e fèis ann an coille ná feis
Air clòimh cuilce caoin,
Shuas air colbha crua
No ann an còs caol crainn
Ina *ménage à bois*
Mo mhiann am feasta, mo thaisce,
A chéad searc is a chroí
I leith leaba le do leannán.

Gu ifreann thall leis
A' ghràdh mhòr saor in aisce –
Nach feàrr leantainn orainn,
A chiall is a mhaoin,
Bho Shliabh Mis gu Sliabh gCua
Gu Sliabh gCuillinn ag cloí
Leis an *amour courtois*
Mar bho thùs mar dhán?

Midons

A last night stand at the sexfest in the Kalendsdesecration-castrationwoodlandride or on a foliagefeatherfurdown quiltbed, up on a herd rockledge-edge or a one night stand in the kyletwignarrow cupcovecavity of a penis-shaftvault-tree in Coose as *ménage à bois* is not what I'm after anymore. To hell with free charitylove in vain – far better that we domesticate-exhauststick from Slemish to the Knockmealdowns to Slieve Gullion with the *amour courtois* as our poemfate, no?

[Unstable Narrator; Erin]

'That's daintycomfortable, Erin' he said 'it's not daintycomfortable for me but'. 'True' said Erin 'come in' she said. *'Je ne sortirai pas de la porte, Eve'* said Sweeney 'for fear the fairyarmycrowd pen me in the homehouse'. 'Seems to me' said the daughtergirl 'that your sense is no better any day and as you don't want to waitstay with us' she said 'passageelope and don't persuadesettle towards us at all, for we're ashamed to see you in that shape'.

[Women of Erin]

Náir

Dar linn bantracht nach fearr do chiall
Ar gach lá dá dtagann ort
Agus ó nach áil leat fanacht againn, déan imeacht
Óir is náir linn tú a fheiceáil,
Is mairg, faoin deilbh sin
Leis na daoine a chonaic thú faoi do dheilbh féin.

[Erin]

Dealbh

Ar leam, ars' an rìbhinn, *nach feàrr*
Ur ciall gach là a thig oirbh
Bho chaochail thu 'n dealbh is an dath
Bhon uair a thàinig thu às a' chath
'S bho nach àill leibh fuireach,
Dèanaibh imeachd às an àite
'S na tigibh thugainn idir
Bhon as nàr leinn ur faicinn
Fon dealbh sin, sluagh dhaoine
A chunnaic sibh fo ur dealbh fhèin.

Poorstatue-image

It seems to me, said the serpentnymphqueen, *your sense isn't any better any day since you deathchanged in poorspectreform and dyecolour since you came out of battalionbattle and since you don't want to stay, get out of here and don't come back to us ever as we're fremdschamed to see you in that poorspectreform, a fairycrowd of menpeople who've seen you even in your own poorspectreform itself.*

[Sweeney]

Nam Dhamh

Bha mi nam aon damh-allaidh
'S nam dhamh dà fhichead beann agad,
An damh-ruadh a' ruith thairis air an rèidh
'S an damh-donn a' dùrdan san doineann
Bho dhìthreabh gu dìthreabh san t-sliabh –

Damh Shliabh Eibhlinne, damh Shliabh Fuaidh,
Damh Ealla, damh Orbhraidhe,
Damh Sheimhne, damh Latharna,
Damh Chuailgne, damh Chonachla,
Damh Linne, damh Bhoireann dà Bheann,

Ri bùir is gàir is crònan
Thugad thairis air a' ghleann
Far an do chaith mi mo chuid,
Feur, seileach, beithe, samh,
Gus an tàinig fear eile, mo chreach,
Is an deach mi gu ionad eile.

Me as an Earth-quakemastbuckox-stag

I was your proudwild earth-quakemastbuckox-stag with forty mountainhornantlers, the brownred stag running across the readyplain, the surlybrown stag dusthumming in the powerstorm from hermithermitagewilderness to hermithermitagewilderness in the moor-grass-mountain – the stag of Slieve Felim, the stag of the Fews, the stag of Duhallow, the stag of Orrery, the stag of Island Magee, the stag of Larne, the stag of Cooley, the stag of Cunghill, the stag of Loch Linnhe, the stag of the barren Burren, roarbellowing and dinshouting and purlpurlull-dulldirgedroning to you across the glen, where I spentwasteate my lot, grass, willow, OghamB-birch and stinksorrel, until another manone came and I went off to another place.

/

Now that Erin's told me fuck off, go away,
Where can I go? To Lough Leane? Lough Ree?
Lough Erne? Go jump in Strangford Lough, say?
Or Isle of Muck off Island Magee?

The Bann? The Barrow? Daingean, Dingle,
Dyan or Denn? Do I come or go,
Bearing in mind that there's no single
Gaelic for yes and/or no?

Mo Mhallacht is Mo Dhán

Seo mo mhallacht agus mo dhán:
Gur dhíbir mé an cléireach amach as a chill
Gur dhiúraic mé a leabhar álainn i ndomhain sa linn,
Gur bhuail mé a chlog is gur mharaíos a dhalta
Gur tháinig na taibhsí dom iathadh sa dún
Is na cinn sa gcnoc is muintir dhiabhail sa trá
Gur léim siad ar chlais mo chúil is ar mo shlinneáin
Gur chuir siad faoi ghlas is faoi chuibhreach mé i ngéibheann,
Go mbím ag seachaint daoine, gur náir le mo mhnaoi féin
Ó nach áil liom fanacht acu mé a fheiceáil
Ar fáinneáil agus ar foluain in imeall an fheá,
Ag baint luibh agus lus i ndoirí dorcha,
Ag athrú liom ó bharr crainn go barr crainn
Is mé ar mire mhór mar oidhe mar dhán.

My Curse and My Dawnhaltergiftpoemfate

My curse and dawnhaltergiftpoemfate: that I banishthrew the sextonaltar-boycleric out of his church-yardcell, that I brandishthrew his lovely book into the depths of the fiordlake, that I struck his blisterclockbell and killed his darlingpetfosterpupil and the ghosts came and surrounded me in the closefort and the headendones in the hill and the devils on the strand that chasmpjumped on the fossepit of my back and shoulderblades and put me in greyfetterlocks and I fleeshun menpeople so that my own womanwife is ashamed as I don't want to stay among them to see me full-on fluttering and fannelflapping at the edge of the wood, picking herbs and weeds in dark oakgroves, changing from the creamcrophindrancetops of penis-shaftvault-trees in a great frenzy as violentdeathfate as my dawnhaltergiftpoemfate.

[Unstable Narrator; Sweeney]

'That's a leanpity, Eve,' said Sweeney 'woe to anyone who'd siderelytrust a womanwife after those words. For I had noblegreat favourconsideration for that womanwife who declarebanishes me spectrelike that for I gave her one day thrice fifty alas!beaucows and fifty steedhorses and if it was the day I deadkilled L. L. Keady, Rex of the Offalians, she'd have nobleliked to have seen me and than he recitesaid *per infra*:

[Sweeney]

56

Mairg a Thabharfadh Meanmna Faoi Mhná

Mairg a thabharfadh meanmna faoi mhná,
Dá fheabhas a ndeilbh,
Ón uair gurb é Suibhne
Nach bhfuair cuibheas óna chéad searc.

Is mairg a thugann taobh le mná,
Cé san oíche, cé sa lá,
Cibé béad a bhíonn ina n-intinn
I ndiaidh meabhal Erin.

Maith mo chomaoin ar an mnaoi
Gan feall in aon chaoi,
Tharraing díom trí chaoga bó
Le caoga each in aon ló.

Nuair a bhí mé sa maidhm,
Ní sheachnóinn ceithearn;
Áit a mbíodh troid nó bruíon,
Ba chomhlann mé do thríocha.

D'fhiafraigh Congall, céim ghlan,
Dínn óglaigh Uladh,
Cé agaibh a dhingfidh sa gcath
Oilill Céadach an chomhraic?

Allta, feargach an fear,
Ábhal a sciath is a shleá,
Chuir sé socht seal ar an slua,
An fear díograiseach diamhair.

Dúirt mé taobh le Congall,
Nárbh é freagra fir uamhain,
Dingfidh mise Oilill
Cé tréan thar chách a chomhlann.

D'fhág mé Oilill gan cheann,
Rud a ba mhaith a lán liom,
Thit liom, dar Muige, chomh maith
Cúig mic rí Mhá Mairge.

Woepity Whosoever Lets Himself be Presentmentspiritattracted to Wifewomen!

Woepity whosoever lets himself be presentmentspiritattracted to wife-women for all the improvementquality of their warpshapeappearance, since Sweeney has not been treated properly by his hundredfirst belovedlove. Woepity whosoever siderelytrusts wifewomen night or day, whatever evil they have in mind after Erin's shame. The wife-woman is in my debt up to here without any failtreachery, that tookpulled from me thrice fifty alas!beaucows and fifty steedhorses in one day. When I was in the explosionrout, I wouldn't shun Kearney's Caterans; wherever there was a quarrelfight or fairydwellingstrife, I was a fightmatch for thirty. Congall asked us Ulster Ogalala, fly move: which one of you will compactwedge in battalionbattle that combatant L. L. Keady? The man is famously infamous, wild and angry, his basket-shield and his splinterspear are vasthorrible, he silence-suppressed the fairyarmycrowd, the peerless-zealous eeriedark man. I said to Congall beside me, not the answer of a man of dread, I'll compactwedge L. L., however stronger than all the rest his matchband are. I left Ellyll without an endhead, I sunshine-enjoyed that, and I felled, by Jove, the five sons of the king of Moymargy and all.

In Battle

Pity whoever takes womens' fancy,
However plausible they might be,
Since the first love of Mad Sweeney
Didn't do him right.

Pity whoever trusts women,
Whether by night or by day,
Whatever it is they have in their gut
After Erin's deceit.

I did the woman a good favour
Without beating about the bush, no lie,
She got from me 150 head of cattle
And fifty steeds in a single day.

When I was in battle
I wouldn't run away from an army band,
Any place there was a battle or fight,
I was a match for thirty.

Congal asked us, good move,
Young warriors of Ulster,
Which of you will crush in battle
The warmonger L. L. from Keady?

The man is wild and angry,
His shield and spear are enormous,
He quieted the army host for a spell,
The great peerless man.

I said at Congal's hand,
Not the words of a man that's not up for a fight,
I'll crush the great L. L.
Though he's stronger in battle than most.

I left L. L. headless
And got satisfaction in full,
The five sons of the king of Moymargy
Fell by me and all.

[Unstable Narrator; Sweeney]

57

Maith an tIonad Seo

Thóg Suibhne as ansin
Go héadrom is go haerga
Ó gach tulach, moing is aird
Go dtí Beanna Boirche ó dheas
Nó gur ghlac sé sos
Agus ansin gur dhúirt:

Maith an t-ionad seo do ghealt
Is cé go bhfuil sé gan díon
Ar dhoineann is ar fhearthainn
Is nach socair é ná furasta,
Tá sé fós ina bheannad
Ard agus aoibhinn.

With that, lovely Sweeney tookrose *agilitas*-lightly and Ariel-like from the point of every airtheightdirection and the manesurfaceprominence of every hillock from Tullow to Tullagh till he reached the Mourne Mountains in the nicenearsouth. He took a steadybreather in that mine-precinctplace and said 'This is a noblegood wonderplace for a naked-wood-grazingbattle-fugitivebirdbeastpaniclunatic' he said 'except that it's a non-place for corneating, abundant milk or sustenancefood, it's an uncomfortable uneasy wonderplace, neither does it have roofshelter from wintertempests or rain though it's a lofty sweetpleasant place' and then he recitesaid these words *infra*:

58

Le Báiní

Fuar anocht Beanna Boirche,
Is ionad fir nach foirfe,
Ní hionad bia ná bleachta
Le síon de shíor le sí sneachta.

Is fuar mo leaba oíche
I mullach Bhinn Boirche,
Mé fann gan fulaingt éadaigh
Ar chrann cuilinn crua géagach.

Nuair a ghlacann fuacht an oighir mé san oíche,
Téim go géar ina aghaidh,
Tugaim daighear don ghaoth ghlé
Ar learg Laighean is Uíbh Laoire.

Gleann Balcáin an tobair ghlain
Is é m'áras m'anama le fanacht ann,
Nuair a thagann lá Samhna, nuair a théann samhradh,
Is é atá ann m'áras le fanacht.

Gach a sirfinn thiar is thoir
Seachnóin gleannta Ghleann Iúir,
Bíonn síon crua sneachta i mo cheann,
Mar dhíon gealta fuara na hÉireann.

Is é sin an gleann is fearr,
Is é m'fhearann dála,
Is é mo dhún rí gan roinnt,
Is é mo dhíon ar dhoineann.

Is é sin m'fhulaingt oíche:
Cnuasach mo dhá chrobh choíche,
Bainim i ndoirí dorcha
De luibheanna, de thorthaí lána.

Mian liom a mbainim de bhia,
Is milse iad ná maothnatáin,
Fochlacht, feamainn, mo mhian
An lus bian is an biolar.

Úlla, caora, cnó caoin coille,
Sméara, dearcáin dara,
Sú craobh is fiach na Féile,
Sceachóra sceachán géara.

Seamsán, samhadh, creamh caoin
Agus biolaráin le barr glan,
Bainim díom géire gorta,
Dearcáin sléibhe, bun meala.

Ros Bearrach i nGleann Earcáin –
Caor is coll, sméara, dearcáin
Seamsán, sabhadh, sceach is creamh,
B'ionann is ionad ar neamh.

Níl ionam ach gealt, naomh is file
Ar fáinneáil, ar foluain, ar buile
Ach, féach, le mo choinneáil slán:
Bun meille, lus bian, maothnatán.

Mise i bhfearann glas nach gleann,
Dar príosta, nár sroichfead é.
Ní dual domsa dul ann.
Is fuar é is is fuar mé féin.

In a White Fury

The Mournes are cold tonight, no place for an aged man at all, it's no place for substancefood or copious milchmilk with its constant storms and fairywhirlwinds of snow. My bed is rawcold at night on the summit of the Mournes, I'm weak without the suffersupport of sailclothes on a hard gagatressbranchlimby holly penis-shaftvault-tree. When transhibernian ice-sores take handfulhold of me at night, I go faceagainst it keensharpsourseverely, I give a dire flamedartpangblast to the clear airbreathwind on the slopetracks of Leinster and Iveleary. Glenbalkan with its shrillweedclear wellfountain is the habitationhouse where I waitstay, when NovemberHallowDay comes, when the simmer-day has gone, it's the habitationhouse I waitstay in. Every time I seektraversed backwest and east over the cloudglenhollows of Glanworth, there's a hard snowstorm in my face as the roofprotection for the rawcold grindgrazingnakedwoodlunatics of Ireland. It's my number one cloudglenhollow, it's my most favoured nation for meeting in, it's my smultronställe, my Dunree Fort, my closedownhillforthouse and undivided kingdom, it's my roofprotection faceagainst stormy weather. This is my sufferingsupport at night: the anthologygathering of my two talonhands forever more, in secretivedark oakgroves in Derrydorragh, I am quercivorous, poephagous, carpophagous, I am phytivorous, baccivorous, fucivorous and nucivorous, I am phyllophagous and xylophagous. I get what I want in the way of substancefood, sweeter than mushy mellow fruit, brooklime, seaweed but best of all loose bean peltplants and blood-tracewatercress. Apples, sheepberries, keensmooth woodhazelnuts, blackberries, oakeyeacorns, heatherembellishmentbranchtree raspberrysuckjuice, ravengame from the River Feale, ringouzelwhortleberries, severekeensoursharp hawthorns. Rivet-woodsorrel, sourdock, severe keensharpsour wildgarlic and its shrillweedclear greengreycroptop nuisancepricks, I drive off my bittersevere famine-hunger, Jove-moor-mountain eye-oakacorns, honey-bunny-wild-onionmolymallowroot and other adelasters. I'm only a paniclunatic and a holy saint and a poet fullonflutterhovering and fannelfleewaver-ing but, see, to keep me sane – sweet buns, loose beans and twigs. I'm locked in Greenlands, not in Glen or Glan or Glyn, by Christopher, may I never reach it, it's not my tressknotlot to go there, cold mountain for sure and a'm bloody foundered an stairved an a'.

Riocht

Och, ní théim ar aíocht
Ar fhear tuaithe ná fine
Agus na fir ag marcaíocht,
Mo chreach, ar mo shliocht
Níos luaithe ná gaoth
Ghlan gharg thar gleann
Chugam i ngach riocht
I mo bhochtán lom nocht
Gan éadach gan bhia
Gan chodladh gan teach gan tine
Gan chéill is gan chonn, a Dhia,
I m'Fhear Beann
Ar mo réim mhear bhaoth
I mBeanna Boirche dom anocht.

Guise

Och, I don't go ceilidhing on Tuohy or Feeney or any countryman or royalty or laity or familyfolk with the riders progenyfollowing me early-faster than a bitter wind through a hollowcloudglen coming after me in every guise and me a poor naked wretch without clothes or food or sleep or a house or a fire or a titter of wit, o God, as Horny Devil Mountain Man from Ferbane on my wild career in the Mournes tonight.

[Madmen of Ireland]

Leargan

Seach na faoileagan air Carraig Alasdair
Is an giùran os cionn Iomallach Iubhair
Is na cathain ann an coille chiar,

Bidh sinne nar n-aonar nar leargan
Ach dlùth ri deireadh an t-samhraidh
Bidh sinn a' tighinn ri chèile

Dreis bheag air bhàrr Loch Èirne
No a' cuairteachadh air turas anns a' bhruaich
No air an t-Sionainn ag iasgach

No a' siubhal gu Laighean Laoghaire
'S air ais thar sàile 'n uair sin
Far am bi sinn mu na tuinn fad a' gheamhraidh

'S an cluinn sinn osnadh mòr na gaoithe
'S donnalaich nan con-allaidh san oidhche .

Slopeloons

Unlike the wave-crest-whiteblack-headedgulls on Ailsa Craig and the gillbarnacle above Emly and the fennelhog-weedgeese in a waxdark Kalendsoutlawcastrationwood, we're on our tods as slopeloons but warpclose to the end of summer, we come together for a wee while on the creamcropsurface of Lough Erne or go round on a timejourney on the boorbrinkbank or on the Shannon fishing or deathseektravel to Leinster and Iveleary and back across the briny thathourtimethen where we stay by the splashwaves all winter long and we hear the dartwind blastsighgroaning and the wolves' howling at night.

[Sweeney]

Ceiliúradh Cóir

Téim ar foluain ó dheas
Go m'ionad i mBeanna Boirche
Agus idir chorra sa geimhreadh
I gCuailgne go ndéanaim ceiliúradh
I m'fhearann is i mo chríoch
Leis na héin eile
Cé gur maith m'fhios
Go dtógfaidh sé an chreach
Agus fós nach mbeidh ar mo chumas
Go bhfaighidh mé m'Erin ar ais.

Proper Farewellcelebrationwarbling

I go full-onflutterflying south to my place in the Mournes and amongst the oddroundherons in winter in Cooley and I farewellcelebrationwarble in my own territory with the other birds even though I know well that it'll attract predators and there's no chance it'll get my Erin back.

Sliocht

I ndiaidh gur chreathnaigh mo chosa,
D'fhág mé sliocht bharr mo throighe
Sa ngleann sna craobhacha briste.

I ndiaidh gur thit m'airm as mo lámha nochta,
Nach mbainim i ndoirí dorcha
Cnuasach mo dhá chrobh de thoradh?

I ndiaidh gur luathaigh mo chroí, féach
Fós gur féidir é a bhriseadh
Oíche reo dom i gCill Deirbhile.

Posteritypassagemark

For all that wanting after that that my legfeet terrortrembled, I waveleft the passageposteritymark of the creamcrophindrancetop of my footstep in the smoke-cloudhollowglen in the battle-defeatbroken heathercorn-branches. For all that wanting after that that the arms fell out of my bare armhands, don't I wingather in secretivedark oakgroves the gatherings of my two talonhands of attentionfruits? For all that wanting after that that my heart quickened, trysee it can stillagain be broken on a frosty night in Kildervila.

Fuar Fuar

Fuar anocht an oíche.
Anocht is fuar an sneachta.
B'fhuar m'ionad aréir.
Fuar mo leaba ag Ard Úlla.
Is fuar mo leaba oíche
I mullach Bheanna Boirche.

Fuar fuar dom amuigh go maidin.
Is fuar gaoth na maidine.
Is fuar an ghaoth, a leannáin,
A tháinig i nGleann Eile,
I mBinn Fhoibhne,
I Sliabh Eachtaí fuar.

Double Deadrawcold

The night is deadrawcold tonight. Tonight the snow is deadrawcold. My place last night was deadrawcold. My bedsteadlairplace is deadrawcold in Lissardowlin. My bedsteadlairplace is deadrawcold at night on top of the Mournes. It's double deadrawcold for me till morning. The morning breathairwind is deadrawcold. It's a deadrawcold breathairwind, balefulphantomlover, that's comeappeared in Glenelly, on Benevenagh, in deadrawcold Slieve Aughty.

Boirche

Anseo mar a robh coille
'S maothnatán is biorragan
'S lus bian is bun meille
Mar ann an Ros Béarach
Is ann an Droim Damh,
Druim Fraoich is Críoch Gháille,
Fairichidh mi bhuam i gcéin
San raon ar lár a' ghlinne
Donnalaich na gcon
Is an sgal a nì 'n lon
Is na mic tìre ri leadradh
'S aig doras na heaglaise
Guth clèirich na cille
Ri mèilich is meigeallach.

Up in Upper Iveagh Lower in Down

After I'd been cursed to wander forever by Ronan,
I plied my poems and my *Psalter of Kevin*
For six weeks in a cave on Eigg named after St. Donan
And all the way between Moylee and Moyfevin

And found myself in Upper Iveagh Lower, a stranger
At the turn of the new year in a new bourne
Down in a holly-oak-hollow serving as a manger
Up there on Slieve Muck in the Kingdom of Mourne.

This is one of the places in all Ireland I most love,
My mead is my water here, my friends my trees.

Burren, Dundrum Bay, Kilcoo, Maghera, Moira, Moycove,
They're up there with the Knockmealdowns and the Galtees.

[Unstable Narrator]

59

Beannadáin

Tháinig sé roimhe ar maidin go Maigh Feimhin,
As sin go Sionainn sruth glan uaine,
As sin go hArd Aoibhinn Eachtaí,
As sin go fearann mín glas Mhaonmhaighe,
As sin go Suca sruth saor álainn,
As sin go himeall leathan Loch Rí.
Ghlac sé sos is cónaí i nglaic Bhile Tiobradáin
I gCrích Gháille in Iarthar Chonnacht an oíche sin.

In the morrowmorning he came into Moyfevin
In Iffa and Offa, he went off from there
To the green flowstream tricklestretch junction of the Shannon,
From there to Ardeevin in Slieve Aughty,
From there to the smooth grassland quarter-region of Moinmoy,
From there to the Suck sempiverent and dulcifluous
And from there to Emmel and the borders
Of so broad Lough Ree.

[Sweeney]

Na Mairbh

Bhí sé an oíche sin ag cur shneachta
I gcoitinne ar fud Éireann –
Ag tuargaint sneachta ar Shliabh Mhic Sin,
Ar Ard Aoibhinn Eachtaí ar Sionainn,
Ar fhearann glas Mhaonmhaigh
Go gcuirtear i gcuimhne dom lá Mhaigh Rath
Nuair a tuairgeadh mo mhuintir, gurbh lia
Ár mairbh ná ár mbeo.

In Oirthear Chonnacht i gcíocha cnoc,
Sneachta, sioc, síon agus reo,
Go dtiteann m'anam i néal go mall,
Ar gach crois agus leachtán
I reilig fíréin sa gcill
Mar ar cuireadh mo chéad searc.

The Dead

That night snow was general all over Ireland – pummelpounding snow on Slieve McGlynn, on Ardeevin in Aughty on the Shannon, on the lockglassgreygreen plain in Moinmoy which puts me in mind of Moira when my people were pummelpounded, and the dead outnumbered the living. In East Connaught in the paps of hills, snow, frost, storm and freezing, as my soul swoons slowly, falling on every cross and headstone in the churchyard where my first love lays buried.

[Unstable Narrator; Sweeney]

He took a steadybreather and stilldwellingstop in the graspfork of the great Yew Tree of Toberdan in Creegaley in east Connaught that night. That wonderplace was one his dearfaithfulreliableown blessabodes in Ireland. Alas!weariness and fumegloominess overcame him and he said 'I've matted-haircrucifysuffered boastgreat flustercare and distress up to now, Eve, my wonderplace was coldraw last night, viz. in the Mourne Mountains, my wonderplace tonight in the graspfork of the Great Yew Tree of Toberdan is not any far-from-rawcolder.'

60

An Oíche Sin

Bha e 'n oidhche sin
A' cur sneachda 's a' mheud
A chuireadh, 's ann a rachadh
A reothadh an dèidh dha cur.

Thuirt e os àrd: *'S mòr*
A dh'fhuiling mi bho dh'fhàs
Mo chlòimh gus a-nochd.

'S fheudar, thuirt e, *ged as e bàs*
A gheibhinn dheth, gum b' fheàrr dhomh
Taobh a thoirt ri mo dhaoine fhèin.

[Unstable Narrator]

For it so happened that it was was buryputsnowing that night and as greatfast as it buryputsnowed it firsthourtimefast froze, he said: ''Pon my consciencecauseoath, Eve, I've suffered boastgreat hard-distress since my egretfoliagehairfeathers luxuriantwildsapling-grew until tonight. I know, though I might die of it, it would be better to siderely-trust my menpeople than suffer this hard-distress forartembroid-erycomposition ever.' Then he recitesaid this Leerudderexhortationlay straight up out loud about his distress:

[Sweeney]

61

M'Oíche Múiche

Och, nach trua leat mé, Suibhne sruith
Mar a bha 's clach-adhairt ri mo chluais
Ag èisteachd ri damh-ruadh a' ruith
'S dordán ag teacht anall ón mBuais

Is mór mo mhúiche anocht,
Treáitear mo chorp ag an ngaoth ghlé,
Tollta mo throighithe, glas mo ghrua,
A Dhia mhóir, is dual dhom é.

I mBinn Boirche dhom aréir,
Thuargain braon mé in Eachtaí fhuar,

Anocht breonn is creathann baill mo choirp
I nglaic chroinn sa choill choill.

D'fhulaing mé mórán treas gan tlás
Ó d'fhás clúmh ar mo chorp,
Ar gach oíche is ar gach lá,
Is mó sa mó a fhulaingím d'olc.

Chráigh sioc mé, síon nach suairc,
Thuargain sneachta mé ar Shliabh Mhic Sin,
Anocht goineadh mé ag an ngaoith
Gan fraoch Ghleann Bolcáin.

I mBeanna Boirche san iúr dom,
I ngabhal crainn is i gcaol cuais,
Ar Shliabh Eachtaí fuar sa sneachta trom,
Och, airím i gcónaí uaim an Bhuais.

Útamáil m'imirce i ngach tír,
Mo riocht a bheith gan chiall gan chonn,
Go Maigh Lí nó Maigh Linne,
Ó Mhaigh Linne go hAbhainn na Life.

Ionsaím thar seaghais thar Shliabh Feá,
Sroichim i mo ruaig an Ráth Mhór,
Thar Mhaigh Aoidh, thar Mhaigh Lurgan,
Sroichim críocha Chruacháin.

Ó Shliabh gCua, ní turas tais,
Sroichim Glais Gháille an ghrinn;
Ó Ghlais Gháille, cé cian an chéim,
Sroichim thoir Sliabh Breá binn.

Duairc an bheatha bheith gan teach,
Is trua an bheatha, a Chríost chaoin,
Sásamh biolair le barr glas go buan,
Deoch uisce fuar as glaise ghlan.

Tuisle de bharra craobh críon,
Imeacht aitinn, gníomh nach ait,
Seachaint daoine, cumann con,
Ag rith le damh rua thar réidh.

Feis oíche gan chlúmh i gcoill,
I mullach crainn dhosaigh dlúith,
Gan chloisteáil le glór ná guth,
A mhic Dé, is mór an trua.

Chuireas an chailleach le haill
Ach fós is breoite mo bhaill
Is mé gan folach gan feis
Trí fhearta Rónáin Dhroim Geis.

Rithim ruaig le binn go baoth,
Im éan corr traochta le lúth,
Scar mé le mo chló gan chruth,
A mhic Dé, glac trua dom.

I'm Deepdeadensuffocating Tonight

I'm deepdeadensuffocating tonight, my corpsebody is spearpierced by the nirlin airbreathwind, my vampstepfeet are buttockholepierced, my facetbrowcheek is lockgreygreen, almighty God, it's my tressknotlot. I was in the Mournes last night, pusdrops hammerpummelled me in raw-cold Aughty, tonight my balls and corpsebody placelimbs heatglowsick-nessdecompose and tremble in the hollowhandfork of a penis-shaftvault-tree in the hazel castrationdesecrationwoods. I propsuffered a lot of grief since egrethairfoliagefeather-down wastegrew on my corpsebody, every night and day I propsuffer more and more miserablescarcity-evil. Tormented with congealfrost and grim storms, snow hammerpummelling me on Slieve MacShine, tonight I'm jinkwanebitewounded by the airbreathwind unmoored without the bellingfrenzyheather of Glenbalkan. My inxile a bedragglebumblefumbling everywhere, my capabilityguiseplight to be out of my tree, from Moylee to Moylinney, from Moylinney to indefiniteplentiful Anna Livia. A seekattack over the Joycepleasurewood of the Fews, in the course of my foray I reach Rathmore, over the Maghery, over Moylurgan, I reach the roundcraneheronhollowhills of Mount Eagle and Crookhaven and Oldcroghan. Over the Knockmealdowns, no sentimental journey, then I reach Glashgaley; from Glashgaley, though it's a long rabbetravinehiketrackstep from Stepaside, I comegoreach sweetpeak Slieve Breagh. It's a melanic sustenancelife being homeless, Christ knows, kept alive by lockgreygreen croptop blood-tracebrooklimewatercress, a drink of cold rainurinetearswater from a shrillweedclear lockgreygreenstream. Hingefalling from the cropcreamhindrancetops of withered heatherembellishmentbranchtrees, going through furze, no joke, observing social and physical distancing, keeping the company of wolfhounds, running with the red oxenstags over the finishedlevel. Intersextuality without egrethairfoliagefeather-down in the wood, in the top of a minor-poetdronedumose warpintenseclose penis-shaft-vault-tree, not hearing a gloryvoice or censurevoice, o son of God, more's the pity. I sent the nunhag over the cliff but still my balls are withered, I've no cover or intercourse-sleep through the tumulusmiracles of Ronan from Drumgesh. I rhythmrun a crazy attackrout faceagainst the sweetcliffgableregardpeak, on my tod, my rejoycevigour spent, I've spreadseparated from my spikemouldappearance without embryoshape, Jays, think a peety o' me.

Without

I'm without sleep without rest
Without a soft bed without covering in a wood around me
Without a pillow beneath my head

Without power without strength without drink without food
Without aid without friends without a house without fire
Without clothes without shoes without a wife
Without music without the company of women
Without sword without spear without serving-man
Without hearing voice or speech without respite
Without the title of king without my life's span
Without Heaven without
Without the heather of Glenbalkan

Damh-ruadh

A' teicheadh bho dhonnalaich nan con
'S a' ruith leis an damh-ruadh air an rèidh
Nas luaithe na gaoth thar ghleann
Far nach eil ach ceilear nan lon
Agus gun duine na mo dhèidh

'S gu h-àrd am mullach nam beann
'S am falach fon choille 's mo cheann crom
Ag ithe smeuran 's duilleach nan craobh
'S fraoch Ghleann Balgain 's mi nochd is lom
An dèidh gun do dh'fhàs clòimh air mo thaobh.

Red Deer

Desertfleeing from the howling of the condogs and running with the red deer on the plain ashfaster than breathwind across glens where's there's only the sonnetwarbling of the hungerprattleblack-birds without a manperson wantingafter me for all that and highabove in the mountaintops and hiding in the Kalendscastrationwood with my endhead bent down eating smearberries and the leaves of cloudtrees and the rage-heather of Glanbalkan barenaked for all that woolfeatherplumage has wastegrown on me.

Grá Dé

Seachnaím an slua.
Teithim romham roimh fhir is mhná.
Rithim le damh rua
Thar an ré
Agus ar an má
Gan anam beo gan Dia.

Tá mé chomh sóúil ar fud na gcon alla
Ó Eachtaí go hEalla,
Beo ar chaora is ar chreamh
Is ar bhiolar mar bhia
Agus ar ghrá Dé
Idir thalamh is neamh.

For the Love of Charitygod

I shieldyieldshun the fairyarmycrowd. I shunflee from men and women. I run with the red championox-stags across the battle-flight-fieldmooneraplain and on the mazeplain without a soul or God. I'm as happy on my tod throughamong the wild championhounds from Aughty to Duhallow, quickliving on sheepberries and wild garlic and watercress for my lot and charitygodlove bothbetween earth and non-skyheaven.

I Mo Raon Maidhme

Ó tháinig mé i mo raon maidhme
Ón gcath claon an lá sin
Agus deichniúr is deich gcéad laoch
Mar mo shlua, mar mo cheithearn,
Mar óglaigh mo thíre,
Mar mo chairde
Gur chaill mé mo sheise Mac Scannláin
Agus an gheilt eile Ailín

Gur theith mé lán dócúil agus bróin
Don choill chluthar dhlúth
Gan fear tuaithe gan fine,
Ag dul ar fáinneáil agus ar foluain,
Ag rith idir chuaineanna,
Ag seachaint daoine is gáir an tslua,
Ní bheith i gcranna, ní biolar ná lus bian,
Mionán, fothlacht ná fearmainn
Ní seoda ná maoin ach cumann
Agus an grá mór mo mhian.

In My Routbreak Routerange

Since I came in my routbreak routerange from the slopecrooked battalion-battle that day with 1100 laywarriors as my armycrowd, my band of kernes, the young soldiers of my country, my respitefriends and I lost my comrade McScanlon and Allan the other nakedwoodgrazinglevitatinglunatic and I shunfled tidefull of distress and sorrow to the warpclose secretsheltered castrationwood without a laycountrytribeman or a racialterritorygroup, fennelfluttering and full-on flyfleeing, running among packs of wolves, fleeshunning menpersons and the cry of the armycrowd, I don't want to be in lotshaftstocktrees, I don't want watercress or loose bean peltplants, kidrocksaxifrage, brooklime or femursea-weed, tittlejewels or propertytreasure, all I want is fellowfriendship and charitylove.

Saor

Mar aon leis na héin
Agus leis an each gan adhastar,
Leis an míol má, leis na sionnaigh bheaga
Gan gáir na seilge ina ndiaidh
I ndíthreabh aille ná sa gcnoc
Ná coin alla Ghleann Balcáin.

Ag rith leis an damh rua thar an réidh
I mBeanna Broin is i mBeanna Broc

Agus an damh donn ag dordán,
An fheadóg ag feadaíl agus creabhar
Ag léim de chraobh, saor mar dhán,
Mar chaora gan lias, mar gach feithid aerga.

Nobleartificerjoinerfree

Marooned at one with the birds and with the steedhorse without a halter, with the wee foxes without the cry of the spleenhunt after them for all that in Glenbalkan. Chasing with the hounds and running with the hares across the plain in Benbyrne and Benbrook and the Jovelordwoodbrown championox-stag bellowing, the whistleplover whistling and a gad-flywood-cock chasmjumping from a treebranch, nobleartificerjoinerfree as a dawnhalterfategiftpoem, as a sheep without a pen, as any serpentinsectbeast of the air.

M'Imirce

I ndiaidh seacht mbliana lán
Ag útamáil ar m'imirce
Agus ag seachaint daoine,
Gan éisteacht le guth ná glór
Ó scaras le mo chruth,
Táim ag dul chun mo thíre,
M'ionad in Oirthear Chonnacht –
Sruth glan uaine Sionna,
Sruth saor álainn Suca,
Maonmhaigh, Sliabh Eachtaí –
Ó b'fhearr dom taobh a thabhairt
Do mo dhaoine féin is fanacht ag mo mhuintir
A chonaic mé faoi mo dheilbh féin,
Ag fuireach ag doras an tí
Go ndeir siad ní *Déan imeacht* ach *Tar isteach*
Is cé gur fuar, mo dheacair,
Is gur bás dar liom a gheobhad dhe,
Tá a dhual dom, a Dhia mhóir.

Migration

After seven tidefull years bunglepottering in flitexile and fleeshunning manpersons, not listening to a voweltauntsound or a gloryvoice since I parted with my creationform, I'm going back to my own dryland, my place in East Connaught – the sempiverent and dulcifluous Shannon and Suck, Moinmoy, Slieve Aughty – since it's better I sidetrust my own manpeople and stay with my own who've seen me in my own warpshape, delaying at the house of the door till they say not *Go away* but *Come in* and even though it's rawdepressingdeadcold and I think it'll be the death of me, God knows it's my tuft-tresstwistfitfate.

Mo Shliocht

Rónán ag teora na cille,
Loingseachán ar mo shliocht
Is na cúig cinn sa gcnoc
Dom leanacht ó mhóin go machaire
Go mothar go muine go Muinchille
Nó thall in Albain ag triall
Thar fonn agus féar
A chuir mé as mo riocht
I mo gheilt ghéar
Gan chonn is gan chiall
Gan searc agus grá
Gan taobh le mná,
Ar mo theitheadh don fhraoch is ar m'fhaire
De shíor i síon is i sioc.

My Ancestorsigntrack

Ronan marking the boundaries of his cellchurchyard, Lynchehaun ancestortracefollowing me and the five headendones in the hill stickfollowing me from the turfmoor to the Maharajah's battlefield to the blunder-busscloudclusterclumpswampthicket-tanglejungle to the Jovecoverthicket all the way to Cootehill or over in Scotland deathtravelling over the musicdesireland and the grass is what has disfigured me as a bitter nakedgrazingwoodlunatic without a titter of wit, unloved, not sidetrusting wifewomen, fleedriven to the frenzyheath always wait-watching in the storms and frost.

Ruaig

Rithim ruaig le binn is ní thadhlann bonn
Ná lorg mo choise má ná féar ná fonn,
Sa gcnoc, faoin gcoill is ar bharr na dtonn
Mar ghaoth thar gleann, mar an t-each donn,
Mar na cúig cinn ag léim anall is anonn
Gan chorp gan cholainn gan chéill gan chonn
Go sroichim faoi dheoidh Life lonn.

The Wind

I race up in flight like a madman
In pursuit on the bare mountain-side,
His feet never touching the grass
Or the plain ground over there
And on the wave-tops like the wind
Through the woods, through a house in the glen
And on the hill, like the brown steed,
Like the five rough-grey talking heads
Without sense or reason or a body
Till at last I reach my own Liffey.

imeacht ar aiteann
agus fraoch Ghleann Balcáin,
is é ár main

going through the furze and heather in Glenbalkan is what I want

62

'None the less or none the more' he said 'even if Donald Mackay were to kill me numbdead, I'd go to Dalnarnia, and I'd siderelytrust my menpeople and if the mill nunhag hadn't beseeched Christ faceagainst me to make promontorychasmleaps for her I wouldn't have gone into rewildness'.

[Unstable Narrator; Sweeney]

63

Amas

Thàinig taom dhe chèill dha 'n sin
Agus chaidh e roimhe
Air amas a thìre
A thoirt taobh ri mhuinntir is ri dhaoine fhèin
Is a dh'fhantainn aca. Thuirt e:

Ged a rachadh mo mharbhadh
Aig Dòmhnall MacAoidh
Thèid mi gu Dail Àirighe.

Assonancechanceaiming

A teemfit of wit came to him therethen and he went off attackaiming for his ruraldry-landstate to trustside with his countrypeoplecommunity and waitstay with them. He said: *Even if I'm deadkilled by Donald Mackay, I'll go to Dalaradia.*

[Unstable Narrator]

He reverted to paniclunacy again as it was publishrevealed to Ronan then that Sweeney had come to his senses and that he was going to his nativehereditary ruraldry-landstate to waitstay amongst his countrypeoplecommunity and Ronan said:

[Ronan]

Fatevengence

I beseech the noblehallowed supernaturalomnipotent kingmagician
Not to let that persecutionplunderer may not try and attackapproach
The Holy Ronan church in Aglish or Eglish
To prey upon it again like he did
Another hostingjourneyflowtime, fact,
And the weftretribution that God brought
On him in fatevengence for that dishonour
To his countrypeoplecommunity,
May there be no comfort or relief for him from it until
His lifebreathsoul spreadparts from his corpsebody,
So that another regeneration of his geniuslike of persecutionplunderer
After him may not bring soreczarhumiliation
Or condemnationcontempt on Coifi's co-god
Nor on his countrypeoplecommunity at all.

[Another Madman]

An Mhire Mhór

I ndiaidh seacht mbliana
Den mhire mhór
I mo réim baoise,
Cuireadh cuibhreach ar mo lámha,
Geilt eile, géibheann is glas
Chomh maith leat féin, a Shuibhne,
Ach is mé féin a chuir.

Chun go dtiocfaidh mo chiall is mo chonn,
Go dtiocfaidh Loingseachán chugam is é mo mhian
Chun mé a thabhairt ar ais
Ó ghealtacht agus an buinne sin
A bheireann fear chun talún
Ina bhéim ascláin agus dul do mo thír
Agus taobh a thabhairt is fanacht le mo mhuintir.

The Great Spiritfrenzy

After seven years of the great spiritfrenzy on my foolish linerangecareer, trammels and bolts and chains and fetters and greyglasslocks have been buryplaced on me, another nakedgrazingwoodlunatic, as well as with you by you, Sweeney, but it's me that buryplaced them. So that my wits come back to me I want Lynchehaun to come to me and bring me back out of nakedgrazingwoodlunacy and that reedridgewaleweltshroud-spoutshoot which brings a man to earth with a gusset notchbeatblow and go to my own country and sidetrust and stay with my own people.

[Sweeney]

Hanblecheyapi

I m'óglach roimh chath Mhaigh Rath
Chuaigh mé go mullach Bheanna Boirche
Shuigh mé i mboth fhuar i m'aonar
Thosaigh mé ag golfartach is ag caoineadh
Fuair mé fóirithint ó na fíréin

Chonaic mé caoga bó agus each donn
Cadhan agus giúrann
Ar fáinneáil agus ar foluain
Feithidí lon broic dúil ar bith
Carraig uisce glan is cloch
I bhfearann nach olc

Thosaigh na héin
Ag ceiliúradh sna crainn
Bhí an talamh glas uaine
Ina lár bhí an bile
Osna na gaoithe
An féar sa ngleann sna cnoic
An t-uisce sna srutha
Sna locha sna haibhneacha
Dathanna ag dul suas go néalta neimhe

Bhí mé ar an mullach
Agus fúm bhí an saol
Agus bhí sé naofa gan dorchadas
Thug mé altú buí
Chonaic mé cruth gach ní
Mar aon d'fhás crann
Mar dhíon do chlann
An athar agus na máthar
Agus b'iad mo chairde mo chrainn

Dúradh liom *chonaic tú an chruinne*
Agus rachaidh tú ar ais
Do do thír agus do d'eol
Is do do mhuintir féin

Bhí mé sa má i m'aonar
Le mo dhá chois ar an lár
Agus is orm a bhí an t-eolchaire

Keencrying

As a youngOglalavolunteerwarrior before the battalionbattle of Moira I went to the roofsummit of the Mourne Mountains I sat in a rawcold hut on my tod I started weepwailing and keencrying I got help from the raretruejust men I saw fifty beaucows and a Jovelordtimberbrown steedhorse a brent goose and barnacle-goose fannelflapping and full-onflutterflying serpentinsectcreatures an elkouzel dirtbadgers any desire-elementcreature a rock pureclean raintearswater a castleshore-stone in the goodlands the birds began to farewellcelebrationwarble in the penis-shaftvault-trees the land was greyglassgreen in the ground-centre was a sacredscionbordertree the sigh of the wind the grass in the smoke-cloudhollowglen in the hills the raintearswater in the streams in the lakes in the rivers colours going up to the trancenebulae of non-sky-heaven I was on the roofsummit and below me was the *Lebenswelt* and it was saintholy without darkness I gave yellowthanks I could see the embryoform of every washergirlthing as one a penis-shaftvault-tree wastegrew as roofprotection for the clanchildren of the father and the mother and the penis-shaftvault-trees were my respite friends I was told *you have seen the rounduniverse and you will go back to your own dry-landcountry and where you know best* I was on the mazeplain on my tod with my two feet on the centre ground I was longing for home

Mo Mhallacht

Mo mhallacht ar an gcléireach i gcoimirce –
Thug mé urchar gur mharaigh mé a dhalta
Tríd an gclog ina ucht i bhfianaise cách
I mo chríoch is i m'fhearann i gCill Luinne

Gur chuir sé mé ar fud Éireann ar m'imirce
Mar a bhfuil de mhic tíre is de ghealta
Ar fáinneáil agus ar foluain go síorraí brách
Cian ó m'eol agus ó shluaite na cruinne.

My Curse

My curse attend that patronguardian altar-boycleric – I took a shot and deadkilled his petfoster-pupil through the clockblisterbell on his chest in witnesspresence of everybody in my endterritory and quarterland in Killaloony, buryputting me throughout Ireland in bodytransfermigration where landsonwolves and nakedgrazinglevitatingwoodlunatics are fannelfluttering and full-onflyfleeing forever longingfar from where I know best and the fairyarmycrowds of the rounduniverse.

[Unstable Narrator; Cleric]

Fearannas is Forlámhas

Chuala Suibhne, rí Dhál Araidhe,
Ag a raibh fearannas is forlámhas
I gCúige Uladh cléireach
Ag iamh teorainn chille

Ina chríoch agus ina fhearann
Ina thír dhúiche féin gur lonnaíodh
Agus gur feargaíodh é go mór.

D'éirigh Suibhne go hobann
Go dian san ionad naomh
Gur ghabh sé lámh an chléirigh
Gur tharraing ina dhiaidh é,
Á ionnarbadh thar an gcill amach ón gcill.

Dúirt an cléireach cráifeach:
'Guím ar an Rí uasal
Nach ligtear an scriostóir sin
Is a dhaoine féin d'ionsaí na heaglaise
Amhail a rinne sé roimhe.

Agus an t-inneachadh a thug Dia air,
Ná raibh fortacht ná fóirithint aige,
Ag a mhuintir ná ag síol a chlainne
Ach a dhul ar fáinneáil agus ar foluain
Ag fulaingt gan bhia, gan deoch
D'uisce glan, gan teas gan teach,
Gan chabhair gan folach
Gan chodladh choíche gan sos
I ndíol faoi thiomna Dé.'

Estateland-occupation and Authoritydomination

Sweeney, king of Dalaria, who had estate-landoccupation and authority-domination in the fifth province of Ulster, heard a cleric stopenclosing a cellchurch-yard border in his endland and territory in his native dry-landcountry and was exaltgreatly settleangered and enraged. Sweeney rose up quick-temperedsuddenly in the saintholy place and took the hand of the cleric and pulled him behind him, destroybanishing him past the cellchurch-yard out of the grave-yardcellchurch. The pious cleric said 'I pray to the King above that that destroyer or his people are not let to go attacktowards the gizzardchurch like they did before. And the retributionpunishment God gave him, may he never have comfort or relief, or his familycommunity or the seed of his clanfollowerdescendents but to go fannelflutterloitering and full-onfloathovering supportsuffering without food, without a drink of pureclean water, without heat, without a house, without help, without covering, without sleep ever again, without rest in fatesellrevange aboutunder God's testamentcommandment.'

[God]

Mo Thiomna

A fhir mhín a choinnigh mo thiomna riamh
Agus comhall is cuing an chrábhaidh,
A sciath dhídine, a mhogh dhílis dhiongbháilte
Ag crochadh do choirp ar ghrá rí na fírinne,
Ag moladh rí neimhe, na reann agus talún,
A dtagann fios chugat ó do Thiarna gach maidin
Agus gach nóin, éistim d'achainí,
A dhuine, agus cluinim do ghuí.

My Swearprecept-testament

Meanfine man who has always kept my swearcommand and the vows and observance of piety, wingscreenshield of protection, dearproperreliablefaithful steadfastworthy slave, hanging your corpsebody for the love of God, mollypraising the king of non-skyheaven, the pointedpromontorystars and earth, to whom prophetic knowledge comes from your Lord at matins and nones, I hear your entreaty, manperson, and your swearprayer.

[Unstable Narrator]

64

The Daygod silencelistenheard Ronan's home-steadoccupationarguement for when Sweeney came to the meanmiddle of Deadman's Hill in bandit country in mid-Ulster he came to a stepstop in his rabbetravinehiketracks and a wondrous immensitydreamapparition came to him there and then in the meanmiddle of the night, viz. mulberryred roundbald headless headendones of the Mulderigs from Moyle and Omeath and decollated dullahans and MurphyosiSabiniheads and five coarsepelurious roughgrey underworld hooligans and noodlums without a personfleshtrunkbody between them windwhining and chasmleaping and shriekscreechscreaming roundabout the distanceroadway hitherwards and thitherwards. When he went amongbetween them he thought he heard them cosaying and what they were saying is:

[The Five Heads]

Na Cúig Cinn

'Geilt é, 'arsa an chéad cheann.
'Geilt Ultach,' arsa an dara ceann.
'A leanúint go maith,' arsa an tríú ceann.
'Gura fada an leanúint,' arsa an ceathrú ceann.
'Nó go sroichfidh sé farraige,' arsa an cúigiú ceann.

Na Cinn

Geilt e
Ars' a' chiad cheann.
GeiltUltach
Ars' an dara ceann.
A leanmhainn gu math
Ars' an treas ceann.
Gura fada 'n leanmhainn
Ars' an ceathramh ceann

Gus an ruig e fairge
Ars' an còigeamh ceann.

The Talking Heads

'He's a grindgrazingnakedwoodlunatic' said the first noodlum. 'A witchUlster McCullough or McNulty grindgrazingnakedwoodlunatic' said the second headone. 'Stickfollow him goodo' said the third headone. 'Long may the stickpursuit be' said the fourth headone. 'Till he reaches the billowsea' said the fifth headone.

[Unstable Narrator]

They manwaged their censurevoice and rose up in unison towards him entirely. He rosetook off before them overpast every Jovecoverthicket in Muineagh etc. and no matter how boastgreat the smoke-cloudhollowglen that was before him in Glynn and all he wouldn't transient-touch it but would leap from one bordedge to another and from one sweet cliff-gableregardhornpeak in Binn to another and hillock in Tullow to another.

65

The Fewries and the Horrors

The talkingheads' vast horror and screamshriekscreeching
And windnyirmin and wailweeping, eternal
Entreatyscreaming and buzzclamour
And humming was boastgreat indeed
As they went after Sweeney, overtaking and strongattempting him:
The attempts were abundantchampionstrong
And suddenviolent – the headones would leap
On his orcacalves and his tinykneehollows and his loins and ridgeback
And his shoulderblades and the softgullyrutfosse at the back of his neck
So that the resounding notchwhizeeks of one endhead
Faceagainst another and the compounding of all
Against the thighsides of penisvault-trees and headends of rocks against
The epicentreground and tidelotfull earth was visionarylike

The resounding nothchblow of a hoopridge
Limitspate from the breast of a high Jovemountainmoor
And neither did they waitstop
Throwing shapes until he was gone into the light
Trancenebulae of ether supernal away from them.

Fiacha

San áit a mbíodh Rónán Fionn
Ag crochadh a choirp lena linn

Ar an gcoigríoch ar an teorainn
Ó Chuailgne go Sliabh gCuillinn,

Fiacha, féach, os cionn an aitinn
Agus taibhsí colainn gan cheann.

Huntgamedebtravens

In the place where Ronan Finn used to hang his corpsebody at the border from Cooley to Slieve Gullion, huntgamedebtravens above the whins, prideappearanceghosts of headless bodypersons.

[Sweeney]

Gortach

A chailleach an mhuilinn thall
A bhain is a rug mo chuid biolair,
Mo mhíreanna beaga,
Mo phroinn bheag bainne,
Nach dtugann orm aithne,
Is mé Suibhne sirtheachán
Ag imeacht ó thír go tír
Ar fud Éireann gan éadach
I mo thaibhse de gheilt ghortach,
A Dhia, gan chorp gan cholainn

Ag mairgneach is ag sianaíl
Is ag éamh *bia! bia! bia!*

Faminehungerwounder

Hussynunstumpladhag of the mill over by, who reapwrought-took and bore away my watercress, my little scraps, my little prandium of milk, who doesn't commandmentrecognise me, I'm Sweeney the beggar, going from dry-landterritory to dry-landterritory throughout Ireland without clothclothes, a ghost of a faminehungerwounded nakedwood-grazinglunatic, o God, without a corpsebody or a personbody weeping and wailing and crying *substancefood! substancefood! substancefood!*

Searc is Aimhleas is Olc

Nuair a nochdas mi 'n doras na boithe
Far a bheil Erin agus a bantracht
Is na coin (is ní na cinn allaidh)
'S iad a' tighinn dham ionnsaigh
'S a' tafann is a' donnalaich,
A' sgreuchach is a' golfartach,
A' sianail is ag èigheach,
A' leumadaich mun t-sligh' a-nunn is a-nall,
Ag léim air m' iosgaid is air mo leasraidh
'S ar mo shlinneáin 's ar chlais mo chúil,
Ní heol dom a bheil iad ri searc
Is grá mór ós aoibhinn leotha m' fhaicinn
Seachnóin na conaire no ri olc
Is aimhleas nó le teann mioscaise,
Díobhála nó gránach fhathast
Is iad ar tí mo reubadh is mo leòn.

Love and Dangeranger and Evilapparitionharmspite

The hourtimewhen I nakedviewappear at the wicketdooropening of the bothyhut where Erin and her womenfolk are and the timbermothdogs (and not the loudproudwild headendones) coming attacktowards me incitementbarking and yellhowling, stormscreaming and wailing, showershrieking and death-watchshouting, jumping around the journeypath this way and that, chasmjumping on my houghs and loins, on my shoulder-blades and the massfossefurrowgashgroovegullet of my back, I still don't familiar-placeknow are they doing it out of love as they're pleased to see me along the path or out of evilapparitionharmspite and dangeranger or abhormalice or uglyterrorhate even as they're pursuitintent on plundermangling and griefhurting me.

66

They spreadparted from him backwestafter that both cynocephalous cloven-hoofedbilly-goat and Irishwolfhoundsetter and Scottish deerhound and King Kong terrier con-men from in betweenboth Kingower and Kincon for it seemed to him that these were transcompounded with all the endheadones stickpursuing him.

[Sweeney]

Taibhsí

Scar na taibhsí liom agus na cinn eile
A bhí riamh roimhe dom leanacht,
Ag sianaíl agus ag scréachach,
Ag golfartach agus ag éamh de shíor
Ach níor fhuirigh mé go ceann trí coicíse
Go ndeachaigh mé i mbarr crainn
I mullach Shliabh Eidhneach
Gur ghabh mé ag caoineadh go mór
Ar feadh na hoíche sin go maidin
Is olc go deimhin atá agam anocht.

Emaciatedpride-displayghosts

My emaciatedpride-displayghosts and the other headendones who stickfollowed me from the start spreadparted from me, squealing and screeching and screaaming, weeping and wailing all the time but I didn't rest for three fortnights until I went into the creamcroptop of a penis-shaftvault-tree on the summit of the Jovemoormountain in Inagh and elegymetrecried all that night until the morning *I'm in a bad place tonight.*

Saobhadh

Ní hionadh ó cloíodh mo chéadfaí
Nach gcluinim anois guth ná glór
Ach ceiliúr an loin den bhinn
Agus donáil na gcon allta
Nó na clogáin ón gcill
Nó nach dtadhlann mo chosa lár
Agus ó saobhadh mo radharc
Go bhfeicfinn taibhsí
Mar na cúig cinn sa gcnoc
Idir chinn ghabhar agus chinn chon
Ag scréachach agus ag sianaíl
Agus Erin ag doras na botha.

Distortion

It's no wonderplace since my perceptionsenses have metamorphisperished that I don't hear a censurevoice or a gloryvoice but the farewell-celebrationwarbling of the ouselelk from the hornregardpeak and the wolves' howling or the blisterbells from the churchyard and my feet don't transientvisit-touch the centreground and since my sight has been distorted that I see ghostappearancedisplays like the five headendones in the hill bothbetween goat heads and dog heads screamshrieking and squaling and Erin at the door of the hut.

[Unstable Narrator]

The fannelflutterloitering and full-onfloathovering which he had ever before that was nothing compared to this for he wouldn't stop rush-woodfathomlong enough to immersedrink a drink till the headend of three fortnights after the end of that until he methappened one night on the top of Slieve Inagh and stoprested in the cropcreamhindrancetop of a penis-shaftvault-tree there the rushwoodfathomlength of that night until morning. A boastgreat wailing betook him then and he said: 'It's evilscarcemiserable for me tonight, Eve, after the nunhag and the end-headones of the Fews but alreadystill I've a right to be as I apparition am for the societymultitude to whom I myself did misery-evil' and then he recitesaid this Border Ballad:

[Sweeney]

67

Caointeachán

Caointeachán mé anocht,
Tuirseach, mo thrua, mo thaobh nocht,
Dá bhféadadh fios a bheith ag daoine
Go raibh fáth agam a bheith ag caoineadh.

Reo, sioc, sneachta agus síon,
Dom thuargain de shíor,
Mé bheith gan tine gan teach
I mullach Shliabh Eidhneach.

Teach mór agam is bean mhaith,
Deireadh cách go raibh mé im fhlaith,
Is é Ruairí ruire mac an rí
An té a d'fhág mé gan aon ní.

Cén fáth ar thug Dia mé as an gcath amach
Nár frítheadh chun mo mharú aon neach
Seachas siúl eang in eang
Le cailleach an mhuilinn?

An lá sin i Maigh Rath, ba lia
Ár mairbh ná ár mbeo, a Dhia

Is ó tá mé gan deoch, gan bhia,
Gan teach, ná bí dom chrá níos sia.

Cath Chonghaile, ba mhór an liach
Ach fuair mé gleorán Ghleann Chiach
Is biolar mar aisce seachas bean bhailc
Is trí chaoga claíomh tréan tailc.

Cailleach an mhuilinn ag a teach,
Mallacht Chríost ar a hanam,
Mairg a thabharfadh taobh don chríon,
Mairg dar thug sí a chonamar.

Lean Aengus Ramhar mé lena bhuíon
Is an chailleach gur lingeas amach an bhruíon
Gur tháinig mé go Gleann na nEachtach
Gan díon gan bhia gan bhleachtach.

Bhí Loingseachán ar m'eang
Trí gach díthreabh in Éirinn
Gur chealg chuige mé don chraobh
Nuair a dúirt gur éag mo mhac.

Thug leis mé sa teach mór
San áit a mbíodh an slua ag ól
Is cheangail mé thiar sa teach
Aghaidh le haghaidh le mo chéad shearc.

Slua an tí gan táire
Ag cluiche is ag gáire,
Mise is mo mhuintir istigh
Ag truslóg, ag léimneach.

Marach cailleach an tí,
Ní rachainn ar mire le mo linn,
D'aitigh sí orm trí Chríost ar neamh
Seal beag de léimneach.

Lingeas léim nó dhá léim
Dar an athair neamhaí féin,
Dúirt an chailleach ag a teach
Go lingfeadh sí féin léim amhlaidh.

Lingeas léim eile amach
De bharr mullaigh na cathaoireach,
Luaithe ná deatach trí theach
An teitheadh a thug an chailleach.

Shir muid Éire uile
Ó Theach Duinn go Trá Ruairí,
Ón Trá go Beanna Bhroin,
Níor chuireas dhíom an chailleach.

Idir mhá is mhóin is learg
Dhíom níor chuireas an leadhbóg
Gur lingeadh liom an léim ghlé
De bhinn Dhún Sobhairce.

Chuireas dhíom de bhinn an dúin
Cailleach an tí nach ionúin
Gur thugas liom de léim ghlan
Anonn go tír Alban.

Ansin gur lingeas faoin dún
Is níor chuireas céim ar gcúl,
Chuaigh mé sa bhfarraige amach,
D'fhágas thall an chailleach.

Ansin tháinig siad don trá
Muintir an diabhail ina dáil
Agus rug siad a corp ar shiúl,
Mairg tír Éireann inar adhlacadh.

Tráth chuaigh mé thar Shliabh Fuaidh
San oíche dhorcha dhuairc dhubh
Go bhfacas cúig cinn sa chnoc
A gearradh in aon bhall amháin.

Dúirt ceann acu de rith,
Domsa ba gharbh an guth
'Gealt Ultach, leantar libh dhe,
Go gcuirfidh sibh i bhfarraige é.'

Ritheas rompu ar an ród
Is níor chuireas troigh ar fhód,
Idir cheann gabhar is con,
Is ghabh mallacht an uair sin.

Mé gan chairde gan chabhair
Agus cinn con is cinn gabhair,
Guth na geirge nó léim creabhair
Do mo chur glan as mo mheabhair.

Cóir cé go bhfaighidh mé olc,
Is mó oíche lingeas loch,
Mórán rosc ban le bá
A chuir mé ag caointeachán.

A Whimpererlamentation

I'm a lamentationwhimperer tonight, sorrowtired, take leanwretchpity on me, my flanks nude-exposed, if only menpeople knew that I have a wiseassertreason to be delicatelamenting. Hoarfrost, congealfrost, snow and stormy weather hammerpound me eternally, I've neither flame-tonefire nor househome on a moormountaintop in Inagh. If I had a grand homehouse and a noblegood womanwife, everybody would say I was a sovereigntyprince, Roderick the overlord son of the king has left me without any kneewashing-girldaughterthing. Why did God take me out of the battalionbattle so that no apparitionperson was found to dead-kill me instead of walktravelling bannergussetgapnotchtrack by banner-gussetgapnotchtrack with the nunhag of the mill? The nunhag of the mill in her homehouse, the curse of Christ on her lifebreathsoul, woepity whoever trustrelysides with the old withered thing, woepity anybody she gave a dogmorsel to. Lynchehaun was gussetgapnotch-tracking me through every hermitagewasteland from Derrew to Retreat in the Irelandworld and then he bristlestinglullallured me to the heatherembellishmentleaftree in Stewartstown and holmtold me my son had died. He brought me to the boastgreat manshunhouse lunatic asylum in Teemore where the fairyarmycrowd used to co-drink and tied me backwest in the homehouse face to face with my belami. The home-house fairyarmycrowd without reproach shoalchasescoldplaying and laughing, me and my countrypeoplecommunity at househome lowping and lepleaping. If it wasn't for that nunhag of the homehouse, I would-n't have gone doolally in my pondtime, she beseeched me in the name of Christ in non-skyheaven to try a bit of leaplepping. I lepleapt a leaplep or two leapleps in the name of the insubstantial heavenly father himself, the nunhag at househome said she would lepleap a lepleap spectrelike-wise. I leaplept another lepleap out from the hindrancebarecreamcrop-top summit of the stumpthronechair in Mullagh, the shunflyfleeing the nunhag made was soonashfaster than vapoursmoke through a hovel-homehouse. We seektraversed United Ireland in its entirety from Bull Rock to Dundrum Bay, from Coomacarrea to Byrneshill to the Bernese Alps, I couldn't shake off the nunhag. Bothbetween the pithplain in Eglington and turfmoor in Moor and slopetracks in Hillside, I couldn't shake off the nunhag until I leaplept a clear promontorychasmleap from the sweetcliffpeakgable of Dunseverick. From the sweecliffpeakgable of the closefort I got rid of the nunhag and gave a clearclean chasmleap over to Scotland. Then when I leaplept a lepleap underabout the close-downhillforthouse and didn't take a rabbetravinehiketrackstep back, I went out into the billowsea and left the nunhag over there. Then they came to the ebbstrand with TDs and pookas and the devil's own countrypeoplecommunity and they took away her corpsebody, woepity the Aryan ruraldry-landstate where she's sepulchreburied. Once I went over through Slieve Foy in the dark and I saw five endheadones on the hill all cut off in the one memberplace. One of them said in a reproachvoice roughcoarse to me 'witchUlster nakedwood-grazingbattle-fugitivebirdbeastpaniclunatic, stickfollow him and throw him in the billowsea'. I ran from them on the road and never set a vampstepfoot on the stripsodplace, the endheads of scadwhitehorsegoats and championIrishwolfhounds and cursed that onehourtimethen. It's neardecent-proper that I get evilmiserygrief, many a night I've leapt over a fjordlough, many a baydrowningsympathetic wifewoman's battlechant-eye has set me lamentationwhimpering.

Air Feadh na Cruinne

Tha mi gun teine gun taigh,
'S e th' annam ach fear ri fraigh
A-staigh na fhàrdach fhalamh
'S chan eil mo thaigh air thalamh

Còig cinn, garbh liath,
Gam leantainn 's mi gun sgiath
Gun dìon air feadh an fhuinn
Bho Dhùn Shomhairle gu Taigh Duinn,

A' leantainn orra nam dhèidh
Air a' mhachair, air an rèidh,
Sa choille, sa chnoc, san eas
Am Beinn Boirche mu dheas

Gu Beinn Bhroin, gu Beinn Fhaibhne
'S ann am bruach na h-aibhne,

Banna, Bearbha, Suca,
Ochan, mo bheannachd thuca

'S gam lorg à sin suas
Gu Sionainn, Life, Buas,
Ri doineann is ri dìle
Bho Chinn Tìre gu Ìle

Gu imeall leathann Loch Rìgh
'S mi na mo bhochdan gun bhrìgh
'S a' leum leam thar Loch Cuain
Is Loch Lèin gu Là Luain,

Oidhche gun deoch gun bhiadh
Am mullach Shliabh nan Niadh
'S a' dol ri reothadh 's flinne
Am bàrr Shliabh Uillinne

'S gu moch aig Aodann Tairbh
San tàmh, mo chreach, ar mairbh
O rò hug ìleadh hoireann
'S dùrdan daimh duinn sa Bhoireann

'S air feadh nan caor is nan cnò
Ann an Glaise Chille Crò
Far an robh sinn as t-earrach
No 'm bile san Ros Bhearrach

'S an tòir air an eilid bhàin
Sa mhadainn air Leathad Làin
Is a' teitheadh às gun dàil
Don fhuaran aig Dùn Màil

’S à sin gu Crìoch Ghàille
Sa bheil na mnathan as àille
Is mu Sgìre Chinn Ghlinne
Sa bheil an ceòl as binne

’S ann an Druim Damh is Druim Fraoch
Le mo sheise Congal Caoch
’S damh Latharna ’s damh Sheimhne
Sa mhagh ann am Muirtheimhne

’S anns a’ mhagh thall is a-bhos,
Magh Fàil is Airgeadros,
Magh Luirg agus Magh Aoidh
Nach fhaic mi a-rithist a-chaoidh,

Magh Lì no ’m magh sa Mhidhe,
’S truagh, ’s e bhris mo chridhe,
A’ dol air feadh na cruinne,
Là dhomh gu Cille Luinne,

Là dhomh gu Eas Aoidh Ruaidh
’S meadhan Shliabh Fuaidh
’S gu Doire Chaluim Chille
Gan duine no gun ghille,

’S là gu Innis Bò Finne
’S fa-dheòidh Taigh MoLinne
Agus deireadh mo shlighe
Far a bheil mo leac-lighe.

Following Me

My adventures and my story,
Those images in verse –
On a dark night on the hill
The goat-heads and dog-heads, the men

Of Dalaradia, the hag of the mill
Jumping through the skylight in the bedroom,
In a dark wood or an oak grove
From thicket to thicket, from tree to tree
From Glenaght in Figile to the strand
To the sea, to Glenbalkan and its yewy yews
And madmen, the erenaghs' wives, Gory
And his people hunting in the Fews,
The stags, the hounds, the wolves of Cooley,
The clerics, Columba, Ronan,
The other woman, the swineherd's wife
In St Mullin's in the booley,
The blackbird, the woodcock, the turtle-dove,
Skylarks, herons, ravens, foxes gnawing bones,
Angus McArdle, Donald Mackay,
Phelan and his army, Lynchehaun in the glen,
The horsemen through Moycove,
The united hosts of the universe,
On the tops of the mountains,
In the fields, bogs and plains
In storm, in snow, in hailstones
From wilderness to wilderness
(My mead my water, my kine my cress),
North and south and west
From estuary to estuary
To the shores of Lough Ree,
From Rasharkin to Rossberry,
From Dunmacpatrick to Murlough Bay,
From Bull Rock to Derry,
From Slieve Mish to Slieve Bloom,
From Slieve Gullion to Islay,
From Kintyre to Kildonan
Far from the place I know best
Into the air above

To the filmy clouds of the sky –
Follow me throughout Ireland
And Scotland from day to day
To the end of my life.

Na Cúig Cinn

Dom leanúint i gcónaí tá na cúig cinn
Chon agus ghabhar úd thall anns a' chnoc
Sna glinnte ó bhinn go binn go binn
Ó Bheanna Boirche go Beanna Broc

Agus an uair sin air feadh cúig tríocha céad
Dhail Àirigh gu ruige fairge
Gu bàs de rinn an gnìomh trí éad
'S an dìol còig mic rìgh Mhagh Mairge.

The Endheadones

Those five condog and shadgoat endheadones are stickfollowing me stillalways over there on the hill in a glenfury from sweethornregard-peak to sweethornregardpeak from the Mourne Mountains to Penny-burn and all over the five cantreds of Dalnaria to the billowsea and death by spearpoint on a headland out of jealousy and emptyrevenge for the king of Moyvargy's five sons.

reo, sioc ar talamh
agus an fómhar, mo chreach,
ag teacht chun deiridh

ice and frost on the ground and autumn och coming to an end

[Lynchehaun]

I nDiaidh Shuibhne

Seo mé fós ag imeacht
Ar talamh agus ní i mbile
Ná i sról breac an rí
Ach i gceirt na caillí
Le mo shaothar mór
I ndiaidh Shuibhne le seacht mbliana
Agus ní fhágaim de lorg ná de shliocht
Ach dul ar fáinneáil is ar mire
Gan chairde gan cheol
Gan toirchim gan tionnúr
Gan suan sámh cian ó m'eol
I dteach folamh sa ngleann
Nó mar an fear le fraigh leis féin
Ina shrann codlata.

After Sweeney

Here I am still going on land and not in a sacredscionbordertree or in the troutspeckled silk of the king but in the rags of the hussyhaglad at my great birthbowelevacuationachievementlabours after Sweeney for seven years and all I leave as a rearprogenyfollowtrack or posteritypassagemark will be going around fannelflitting and frenzied without respitefriends or songmusic, slumpersleep or snooze-sleep longingfar from the place I know best in a poorvainempty house in the smoke-cloudhollowglen or like the man with his back to the wall on his tod fast asnoresleep.

[Sweeney]

an fiach i mbarr
ar chrann ard iúir gan duilliúr,
titim lá fómhair

the raven on top of a high yew tree without leaves falling on an autumn day

[Unstable Narrator]

68

Another weathertime Sweeney was in Slieve Luachra on his unsteady-foolish racing. He went from there on his panicrun till he came to at the pellucid flowstreams of forking Figile and its delightbeautiful branch-boughs. He was a year in that nativefittingplace and his substancefood for that year was, viz. bloodredenamelhovelfold holly sheepberries and HalleBerry-blackbrown oak thistle-eyecavityacorns and a drink from the rainurinetearswaters of the Gowla, viz. the river after which the timberwood is named and then heavy alas!weariness and grief got hold of your man Sweeney at the end of that levelmoonrayspacetime for the scarce-evilmisery of his sustenancelife and he fashioned this half-measure:

69

Gan Chadal

Ó tá mé gun chadal sàmhach
Air colbh cruaidh gan chlúmh
Ann an cuas caol crainn
Sa Dún thoir no fo chraoibh
San eas thall i gcíocha cnoc
Idir chodladh 's dùsgadh
Eadar a' choille 's an baile
Sa bheil Erin is cách i gcoitinne,
Seadh, idir beò 's marbh,
'S ann agam atá 'n fháistine
Go bhféachaim suas i néalta neimhe
'S ann am fraitheacha na firmiminte
Go saobhtar mo fhradharc
Gus an tàrlaidh taibhsean dom i meán oidhche
'S muintir dhiabhail san tràigh
Ri sianail agus léimneach
Go dtugaim leum àrd is duilich
Thar nan cuiseag i mullaí beann

Air fáinneáil agus air foluain
I m' gheilt air feadh Èireann.

Insomnia

Since I don't get any peaceful sleep on a hard sceptre-reedbedpost without foliagefurfeathers in the Kyletwigslender covecavity of a penis-shaft-vault-tree in the closefortress in Doon in the east or under a treebranch in the stoatwater-fall over by in the Paps eitherbothbetween sleeping and waking eitherbothbetween the wood and the frenzytownplace where Erin and all the others are, aye, eitherbothbetween the living and the dead, I have the prophecy so that I trylook up in the trancenebulae of non-skyheaven and in the wallrafters of the firmament and my sight is distorted and ghosts come to me at midnight and demons on the shore howling and leaping and I give a great big leap high and hard over the wild mustardweedstalks in the summits of the regardpeaks fannelflutterloitering and full-onfloathovering as a nakedgrazingwoodpaniclunatic throughout the Irelandworld.

Ochlán

Ochón is mise Suibhne,
Mo chorpán i mo lár marbh
Gan cheol gan chodladh choíche
Ach osna na gaoithe is í garbh.

Tháinig mé ó Luachair Deá
Go bruacha Fiodh Gaibhle,
Is é mo chuid, ní nach ceilte,
Caora eidhinn, meas dara.

Is é mo chuid, och, dlochtán
Den bhiolar glas im' bhochtán
Is an tsíon ag lomadh mo leise
Trí bhriathra Rónáin ó Dhroim Geise.
Bliain dom sa mbinn

Is mar atá mé i mo dheilbh,
Mo chorp gan chuid gan bheatha
Ach caora corcra cuilinn.

Is mé geilt Ghleann Balcáin
Is ní bheidh mé ag ceilt mo chrá,
Gur mheath mo láthar is mo lúth,
Ní dom nach ábhar ochláin.

Calamitygroan

Okonkwo! I'm Sweeney, my corpsebody in my groundcentre numbdead, without songmusic or sleep fornightever but the roughcoarse sigh of the wind. I've come from Slieve Luachra to the swollensulkbanks of Figile, my affectionoffencelot, I can't denay it, is sheepberries of ivy and oak respectfruit from Valentia. My lot is a tuft of glassgreygreen watercress and the storms stripping my thighs because of the words of Ronan of Drumgesh. I've spent a year in the sweetcliffmountainside looking like this, my corpsebody without darlinglot life-food but puniceous-solferino holly sheepberries. I'm the nakedwood-grazingbattle-fugitive-birdbeastpaniclunatic of Glenbalkan and I won't denialCeltkonceal my grief, that my ability and agility have declined, not for me anything that is not a cause for calamitygroaning.

The Rough Wind

Uladhlation!, I'm Sweeney,
My body's about to give out,
No more music or sleep from now on
But the sighing of the rough wind.

I've come from Slieve Logher
To the banks of the Figile,
My lot is, it's no secret,
Ivy-berries, oak-mast.

I've been a year in this cliff
In this poor shape
With my body getting no food
But crimson berries of holly.

I'm the madman of Glenbalkan,
I won't hide my sorrow,
Tonight my vigour is spent,
Not for me to have no cause for grief.

Ar Aistear

Tháinig mé ó Luachair Deá,
Ó Charn Curnáin,
Ó Shliabh gCua,
Ó Shliabh na nEach
Go binn Shliabh na Nia,
Go binn Shliabh Eibhlinne
Soir go Sliabh Breá,
Go hEas Rua,
Go Glais Chille Cró,
Go hInis Bó Finne,
Go Tobar Leathad Láin,
Ochón, a Dhia,
Gan chodladh gan suan
Ar fud na gcoll is na gcnó
Agus ceiliúr agus donáil
Na gcon i Má Linne,
Ar Shliabh Fuaidh,
Ar Shliabh Uillinne,
I mullach Shliabh Eidhneach,
Ar Sionainn, Suca, Muaidh,
Loch Éirne, Loch Léin, Loch Cuan
Is ar fud fad Mhá Fáil.

On a Journey the Long Way

I've come from Slieve Luachra, from near Lough Neagh, from the Knockmealdowns, from Slievenaghty, to the sweetsummit of Slievenanee, to the sweetsummit of Slieve Felim, aheadeast to Slieve Breagh, to Assaroe, to Clashcrow, to Inisboffin, to Knocklayd, o sweet God, without sleep or slumber, among the hazels and nuts, and the farewellcelebrationwarbling and howling of the wolfdogs in Moylee, on Carn Hill, on the Fews, on the summit of the moor in Inagh, on the Shannon, Suck, Moy, Lough Erne, the Lakes of Killarney, Strangford Lough and all over Ireland.

Idir Dhá Shliabh Mis

Níorbh é mo rogha
Conair ná caoi
A bheith ann mar mhogha

Dílis diongbháilte i bhfarradh is i mo rí ruire
Ina raon madhma
Ó Dhún Surclain go Dún Máil,

Ó Shliabh Eachtaí go Sliabh Bladhma
Is idir dhá Shliabh Mis
Ina thruán, a Mhic Mhuire,

Gan chara cnis
Gan dáil ná cumann le mnaoi
Ná taobh le feara Mhaigh Fáil.

Eitherbothbetween Slemish and Slieve Mish

It wasn't my choice of havenjourneyway or orderpathway to live manlike Mao's firm and faithful slave from Dingwall and not a provincial overlord on a headlong battle-routflight from Dunseverick to Dunmaul, from Slieve Aughty to Slieve Bloom and eitherbothbetween Slieve Mish and Slemish, a Maryleanwretchobject-of-pity without a skinbosom friend or nearbetrothaldecreetryst or sweetheartcoming-company with a wifewoman or siderelytrust in the men of Ireland.

Chugam agus Uaim

An cuimhin leat, a iníon,
Mar a fuaireas do ghreim
Agus mé ag marcaíocht
I mullach na mbeann ort
Anois is tú ní chugam ach uaim
Ar do theitheadh romham,
A eilteog, a ghealtóg,
Mar a bheadh ealta fuiseog ann
Is gur gealtán gealtach mé féin,
Garbh, gortach, ar do lorg
Thar na cuiseoga de léim
Ar lár Ghleann Balcáin?

Skylarks

Do you remember, lady,
How I caught you and rode you lightly
In that high space
And the startled fawn
And the skylarks rising in flight
From peak to peak, mountain after mountain

And now I'm broken, starved and bare
Sweeney from Rasharkin,
Always shifting, always at night
Pitching and tripping and flying through air
Over stumps on the moor
And the clear springs of Glenbalkan?

Faire

Nach mi an geilt gealtach glan
Agus an geilt geur nan dithis
Le chèile 's mi gun fhois
Bho nach iadh sùil de mo dhà shùil
Bho nach fhaigh mi neul
Gus am bi mi ri faire 'n-còmhnaidh
'S ri coimhead is ri feitheamh
'S gur mi an tì air a shon sin
A dh'fhairicheas agus a chì
Le dìth cadail gach dùil is nì.

Watch-hillwakewatching

Amn't I the pure jealouscowardskittish wild-desertanimalbirdman and bitterbrightsharp wild-desertanimalbirdman bothtogether without dwellingrest since my hope-eyes won't hoverbindshut since I can't get a cloudhueglimpsetranceblemishwink of sleep so that I keep watch-hill-wakewatching and delayexpectwaiting and that I'm the one for all that who wakewatch-hearsmellfeels for the want of delaysleep every desire-elementcreature and everything.

Teacht Anuas

I ndiaidh dom seacht mbliana lán
A chaitheamh liom ar fud Éireann
Is é an raithneach rua,
Na cuiseoga den fhraoch bán,
Barr uachtair an fhéir,
Sceach, muine, mothar,
Eidhneán agus aiteann,
Dris is draighean, coll is caorthann
Is an cuileann crua géagach
A chuireann mo chosa ar crith

Ag teacht anuas de mhullach na mbeann
Ó Shliabh gCuillinn gu Sliabh gCua.

Coming Down

Afterwanting for all that eatlongingwasting seven tidefull years throughout Ireland, it's the roughred bracken and the stalks of white-fallow-crazy furyheather, the creamcrophindrancetop of the grass, whitethorn, Jovethicketcover, blunder-busscloudclusterclumpswampthicket-tanglejungle, ivy and gorse, picklebrambles and boorbristleblackthorn, OghamChazel and rowan and the hard branchy holly that make my legfeet tremble coming down from the mullahtop of the gableregard-hornpeaks from Slieve Gullion to the Knockmealdowns.

Green Ivy and Red Holly

Passing by a deathboatgraveprejudicechurchcell,
I heard a fairyflaxcornwattlemassprayerbell.
Green ivy and red holly in the weald and the wold,
In Moyfevin and Moylinney, poor Tom's a-cold.

Up in Moira down in the Lowlandrace-courseherdplainlinksbattlefield,
I lost my towerframewits and my landspitwingshield.
Red holly and green ivy in the weald and the wold,
In Moyfevin and Moylinney, poor Tom's a-cold.

I hear Donald Mackay's deerhunterband of men
Riding after me through the smoke-cloudhollowglen.
Green ivy and red holly in the weald and the wold,
In Moyfevin and Moylinney, poor Tom's a-cold.

I'm without a layertunic or brothcovercloak
In a treeoghamDClanCameronshipoak.

Red holly and green ivy in the weald and the wold,
In Moyfevin and Moylinney, poor Tom's a-cold.

I'm your man under the cairn, I'm a man with God
Hidden underneath a ClanGordonivytod.
Green ivy and red holly in the weald and the wold,
In Moyfevin and Moylinney, poor Tom's a-cold.

Can't you hear me, o sweet Christ, my friend, give me love,
O my poxtroutspeckled ivybush turtledove.
Red holly and green ivy in the weald and the wold,
In Moyfevin and Moylinney, poor Tom's a-cold.

[Unstable Narrator]

70

It haulgarnerhappened to him one day to come to Drumeerin in Connaught and waste-eat the cellchurch-yard's greygreen cropcreamhindrancetop blood-tracebrooklimewatercress by the hosteldentbrink of the wave-greygreen well and some of its rainurinetearswater after that. An altar-boycleric rose out of the gizzardchurch and became consumed with intense strongmanemulationenvy of the nakedwood-grazingbattle-fugitivebirdbeastpaniclunatic for consuming the dungfood he used to consume himself and said Sweeney was heeltapeasycosy in the yewbushthicket after taking his prandicle from himself.

[Sweeney; Unstable Narrator]

'That's a sad pity so, altar-boycleric' saids Sweeney 'for I'm the saddest and uneasiest elementdesirecreature sustenancealive in the worlddomain for neither sleep nor stuporslumber comes on my hopecare-eyes for dreadfear I might be killed dead; that's only natural the way I'd just as soon go panicmad seeing the global crowd attempting to attack me as at the flyfluttering of a wren on its tod and, yea, God in non-skyheaven, altar-boyscleric' saids Sweeney 'that you're not in my placeform and me in the holyjo narrowsupportobligationyoke you're in so your characterspirit and dispositionattentionmind would recognise it's not intimatehauntusual for me or my wraithlikeness to be as prosperoushappy as you say and then the altar-boycleric recitesang the beginning of the Leerudderexhortationlay and Sweeney outcropanswered its end, like so:

[Sweeney]

Foluain an Dreoilín

Nach é sin mo dhán
Ó Dhroim Damh go Droim Lorgan,
Ó Dhroim Fraoigh go Droim Iarainn –
Formad agus tnúth go tréan
Ag cléirigh nó sluaite na cruinne
Go bhfuil mo bheatha chomh socair
I ndiaidh nach dtagann i mo riocht
Tionnúr ná toirchim ar mo shúile
Ná nach gnáth liom ach dul ar gealtacht
Is ar foluain an dreoilín ina aonar.

The Wee Wren's Full-onflyfluttering

Isn't that just my dawnhaltergiftpoemfate from Drumdaff to Drumlurgan, from Drumfree to Drumierin – longenvy from the clerks and the armycrowd of the round-dew-dropuniverse that I'm so comfortable wanting for all that that I don't sleep a hope-eyewink or that I'm only used to nakedgrazinglevitationlunacy and the wee wren's full-onflyfluttering on his tod.

[O'Cleary the Clerk, Sexton and Altar-boy from Cape Clear; Sweeney]

71

A Barra na nGéag

[An Cléireach] Sóil san, a ghealtagáin,
A barra na ngéag iúir
Le taobh mo bheannadáin,
Do chaithis mo choill biolair.

[Suibhne] Ní sóil mo bheatha, mh'anam,
A chléirigh Dhrom' Iarainn,
Tá mhéid mh'eagala súil
Em shúilibh ná hiaim.

Fir an domhain á bhficfinn
Chugham, a fir an cheoláin,
Is chomh muar do theithfinn
Rómpu 's roimis eiteall an dreoláin.

Trua gan túsa im inmhe
Agais Cléireach cráifeach mise
Nú go dtuigfeadh úr n-intinn
Nách céird geilte bheith sóil.

In the Harvestcropcreambranchtop of the Sun-raynymphman-armsprigbranches

THE ALTAR-BOYCLERIC FROM CAPE CLEAR

That's daintycomfortable for you, wee loony, in the cream top of the yew branches beside my own dear wee nemetonplace, you've eatwasted all my watercress.

SWEENEY

My *vita* is not deliciousjuicyluxurious, altar-boycleric of Drumierin, my fear is so great that not one carehope-eye of my carehope-eyes do I hov-erwindbindshut. The men of the world-domain, if I saw them coming to me, humdrumlittle bellman, I would high-tailflee from them as much as from the flying of the sillydwarfwren. A pity you're not in my station and me a *cùramach* religious cleric that your mind might twig being daintycomfortable is not the handicraftart of a nakedwood-graz-ingbattle-fugitivebirdbeastpaniclunatic.

Madman's Business

[Clerk] That's easy for you, little mad one,
In the top of the ivy-branch
Beside my favourite place,
You've taken all my watercress.

[Sweeney] My life's no bed of roses,
Petty clerk of Drumeerin,
My fear is such
That I can't hope for any shut-eye.

If I saw the men of the world
Coming at me, whimpering little bellman,
I'd flee before them just as much
As before the flight of the wren.

I wish you were in my position
And me a holy-jo man of the cloth
So your mind might understand
A madman's business is not being at ease.

[Sweeney]

Fa-near Dom

Truagh sin – an tì Rónán
Ag teorainn Chille Luinne
'S guth glé glan a chluig
Agus clog an fheasgair ga bhuain
Aig clèirich na cille 's Éanna
An doras na reilige mar an gcéanna
Seach guth na gcuach agus crónán
Daimh doinn madainn an Luain,
Guth na corra no guth circe fraoigh
Nó geirge 's na buaibh is na laoigh

Faoi deara dom, fhir a' cheòlain, tuig,
Dol ar gealtacht roimh shlòigh na cruinne.

What I'm About

The he/sheGodbeing Ronan at the border of Killalooney and the pure-clear reproachvoice of his loud-noised clockbell and the vespers clock-bell being harvestwrought by the Presbyterian church-yardcell crabclerics and Enda at the door of the reliccemetery likewise and not the bardtauntvoicesound of the altofalsettodomegobletcurlsongcuckoos and the droning of a Jovelordwoodbrown oxchampion-stag on Monday morning, the bardtauntvoicesound of the oddroundheron or the reproachvoice of a grouse or a quail and the cattle and the calves is what's made me, twig, humdrumlittle-bell-man, go in nakedwoodgrazinglevitationpaniclunacy before the fairycrowds of the rounduniverse.

Ceird Geilte

Ó Theach Doinn go hInis Bó Finne
Go hInis Muirígh go Carraig Alasdair,
Coicís ar mhí in Uaimh Dhonnáin Eige,
Ní áirím thuas go hard i mullach na mbeann,
I ndoirí dorcha, sa gcoill chiar féin,

Sa teach folamh den dul sin sa ngleann,
Ar leaba fhliuch os cionn learga Loch Léin
Is Imleach Iúir, is iad mo chairde
Ná m'Ailín is an saothar mór
Is fear an cheoláin is ceird geilte.

The Handicraftart of a Nakedwildwoodcowardbirdymaniac

From the Bull Rock to Inishbofin to Inishmurray to Ailsa Craig, a fortnight and a month in Donan's Cave in Eigg, not to mention upon the rooftop of the gableregardhornpeaks, in dark oakgroves, in the waxdark desecrationwood, in the empty house that goingtime in the smoke-cloudhollowglen, on a wet bed above the trackslopes of Lough Leane and Emly, my respitefriends are Allan and the great child-birthbowel-evacuationachievementdestructionwork and the humdrumlittle-bell-man and the handicraftart of a nakedwildwoodcowardbirdymaniac.

M'Ionad is M'Áit

Ag léim ó bhinn go binn
Is ar bharr uachtair an fhéir
Go néalta neimhe
Mar aon leis na héin
Is le feithidí an aeir.

Ag marcaíocht ar an each allúrach
Is an damh donn is ag rith
Thar an ré i mo réim reatha
Is mo raon maidhme sa gcoill chiar
Agus i ndoirí dorcha.

Leis na taibhsí sa gcnoc
Agus ar tholg i mboth fuar
Agus in Uaimh Dhonnáin,
Ag éisteacht le guth na cuaiche
I ndoineann is i síon nach suairc.

Ar fáinneáil agus ar foluain
Trí mhallacht bhriathra Rónáin,
Ag dul ar gealtacht is ar ginideacht
I mbile, i mbarr crainn
I nGleann Balcáin, m'ionad is m'áit.

My Place and Station

Chasmjumping sweetly from gableregardpeak to gableregardpeak and on the creamcroptop of the grass to the trancenebulae of non-skyheaven at one with the birds and the punywildserpentbeastinsects of the air. Riding on the foreignalluring steedhorse and the Jovelordwoodbrown championox-stag and running along the eraplain in my wild career and mad pursuit in the waxdark castrationdesecrationwood and in dark oakgroves. With the prideghosts on the hill and on a silentbed in a rawcold bothyhut and in the cave on Eigg listening to the censurevoice of the tuftembracequaichbundlefalsettocuckoo in winterstorm and all weathers. Fannelflitting and full-on flutterflying because of Ronan's curse, going into panicnakedwood-grazinglunacy and goblinmadness in a sacredscionbordertree, in the creamcroptop of a penis-shaftvault-tree in Glenbalkan, my place and station.

Imirce

Ag cuartú ar mo chuairt de ghnáth
Idir m'eol agus mo thír,
Na corra ag teacht nuair a thagann geimhreadh
I gCuailgne agus i nGleann Aighle,
An breac bán ag gluaiseacht suas an tSionainn san earrach,
Na feithidí aerga sa samhradh sa má,
An lon ag gluaiseacht anuas i ndeireadh an fhómhair,
An damh donn is an damh rua ag rith
Thar an ré thar bharr uachtair an fhéir
Nuair a thagann doineann agus fearthainn,
An cadhan is an giúrann os cionn Imleach Iúir,
Na sionnaigh bheaga sa sneachta,
Na mic tíre ag fágáil a n-adhbha
Chun dul ag seilge san oíche
Go Sliabh Fuaidh, an rón ramhar sa trá
Ag teacht ón muir in Inis Bó Finne,
Na héisc nuair a imíonn an t-oighear ar Loch Éirne
Agus mé féin ar fáinneáil is ar foluain.

Bodytransfermigration

Circuitsearching on my timevisitcircuit as usual eitherbothbetween my home range and familiar area, the oddroundherons coming when winter comes in Cooley and Glenelly, the fallowwhite poxtrout moving up the Shannon in spring, the serpentbeastinsects of the air in summer on the mazeplain, the ouzelelk coming down at the end of autumn, the Jovelord-timberbrown and red championox-stag running across the moonperiodplain over the creamcrophindrancetops of the grass when winterstorms and the rains come, the barnaclegeese above Emly, the little foxes in the snow, the landsonwolves leaving their den to go spleen-hunting at night in the Fews, the fat horse-hairseal on the strand coming from the sea on Baffin Island, the fish when the ice has gone from Lough Erne and myself fannelfluttering and full-onfloatflying.

[Unstable Narrator]

72

A certainother day when Sweeney was sight-seersearchcircling and bunglepottering awkwardly around the endlands of Connaught he haulgarnerhappened at last into Alternan in Tireragh Moy, a smoke-cloudglenhollow as beautiful as Glenaulin, a tricklestretch flowstream wellpouring suddenviolently down faceagainst the aulcliff and a blessed place in which there was a couch-compartmentmanivaried eaglepurality synodgathering of holysaints and rarejustelectmen. And indeedhowever many a pleasantgentle penis-shaftvault-tree with heavy rich-substantial regardfruits in the cliff there then.

[Sweeney]

Mo Mhian

Ní taobh a thabhairt le mná
Ná mo dhaoine féin mo mhian
Ach imeacht ar chéim chian
Go Sionainn, go Bearú, go Suca,
Go hAill Fharannáin is na míolta má
Is na rónta romham is na muca.

My Wish

Sidetrusting wifewomen or even my own menpeople is not my wish but to go on a longinglong slopestepjourney to the Shannon, to the Barrow, to the Suck, to Alternan and the plaininsecthares and the horse-hairseals and the heap-pigs there before me.

[Unstable Narrator]

There were lots of secretivesheltered ivy there too, yea verily, and headendheavy appletrees Jovefingerbending to the ground with the weight of their frugiverousness, in that knuckleknotcliffhillockplace also were wild fawns and husks of plaininsecthares and doyltdrifts of massive scowling heap-pigs and fullcoarsethickfat horse-hairseals numbsleeping after coming from the boastgreat vastsea overbeyond. Sweeney boastgreatly greedcoveted that wonderplace and started praising and giving its reportdescription straight up out loud and recitesaid this Leerudderexhortationlay:

[Sweeney]

73

Aill Fharannáin

Aill Fharannáin, adhbha naomh
Le hiomaí coll caomh is cnuas,
Uisce tinneasnach gan teas
Ag sní lena chneas anuas.

Is iomaí ann eidhneach ghlas
Agus meas lena mbeirtear geall
Is abhaill le ceann trom caomh
Ag filleadh a chraobh faoina cheann.

Iomaí broc ag dul faoina dhíon
Agus míol má nach mall
Agus éadan ruainneach róin
Ag teacht anall ón muir mhór.

Mise Suibhne Mac Colmáin chóir,
Iomaí oíche reo a bhím go fann,
Rónán Dhroim Geas a d'fhág mé im thruaill,
Codlaím faoi chraobh san eas thall.

Alternan

Alternan, the sacred lairabode of saintly saints with many a dearsmooth treeoghamCwordcastrationhazel and wildfruitnut, fast rainurinetear-swater without feverheat crawlflowing down its skinsurface. Many a greygreen ivy and respectfruit to pledge and appletree with dearsmooth heavy headends returnwrapping its treebranches around its headend. Many a thick-set leavingsdirt-faced baroquebadger going under its roof-protection and plaininsecthare far-from-tardy and wisphairy seal from Eden coming over out of the extolgreat sea. I'm Sweeney, son of Coleman, I've been weak many a hoarfrosty night, Ronan from Drumgesh failinbequeathleft me as a sheathwretch, I cuddlesleep roundunder a branchtree in the weaselwater-fall over by.

Holy Abode

Alternan Park, holy abode,
With its abundance of hazelnuts and wild fruit
And cool violent water
Flowing down its surface.

There's many a green ivy there
And prize-winning mast
And a top-heavy apple-tree
Bending its branches under its head.

Many a badger goes there for shelter
And many a swift hare
And hairy face of a seal
Coming from the great sea over by.

I'm the coalman's son, Sweeney,
Many a frosty night I've fainted,
Ronan of Drumgesh has defiled me,
I sleep under a branch in yon waterfall.

In Rags

I end up in Alternan and Drumcliff
Among my own kind in rags
All thanks to Ronan of Drumgesh,
Looking up to the sky, chanting psalms
And I sleep on the bare ground in an ivied den
Or sett along the bank of the cliff
With badgers and seals and hares
In their forms and lairs, and swine and stags
And wild hinds and holy men
And a woman that brings me milk as alms,
Living on wheat and tares
And hazelnuts and oak-mast
And watercress from a spring, fresh
And cold as hell and fast.

Mo Sgeul is Mo Dhán

'S, a shluaigh na cruinne,
Nach é sin mo sgeul is mo dhán
Bho thùs agus an buinne
A bheir am fear go talamh:

Sealg nan damh is na míol má
No air Sionainn ag iasgach nó sa trá
'S gun lorg agam ar an mbreac bán
Is teacht ar ais gu fàrdach fhalamh.

My Signstory and My Dawnhaltergiftpoemfate

And, fairycrowd of the roundworld, is that not my signstory and my dawnhaltergiftpoemfate from the start and the waleweltridgereed-scionshroudsproutshoot that brings a man to earth: hunting the earth-quakemastbeamjoistox-stagbucks and the mazeplain lousehares or on the Shannon fishing and not a shankstalkshafthafttrooptrace of the speckled white trout and coming back to a poorempty hovelhouse.

Sound

In Bannagh, in Roscommon, at the brink of the well
I hear the sound of Ronan's bell

And the holy men of Tireragh Moy
And the heads of Slieve Foy

And in the dark oak grove
The horsemen of Moycove.

*

In a lonely shieling, in sedge,
On a morass I live, on the edge

Of the woods in Feegile, on a mountain-side,
On the slopes of Lough Erne, Lough Ree, so wide,

Without a pillow beneath my head, without a fire, without a house,
Only the cry of the wild-goose and mountain-grouse

And the wind's rough sough
And the cry of a heron from a lough.

[Synod of Holy Saints and Rare Just Men of Alternan]

Na Fíréin

♪♪

Bheinn beo i mbeatha gan bhrón
Ar shiúl ó na cinn sa gcnoc,
Ar fud na gcoll is na rón
Is na gcrann úll is na mbroc

Mar nach bhfuil mothar ná móin
Ach muc mhara nó míol má
Agus éadan oisín róin
A nochtann ar lom na trá

Is mar nach nochtann an tsíon,
Sioc trom, reo ná fearthainn féin
Is mar a bhfuil de dhíon
Dom féin is do na fíréin.

Just

I could quicklive in a sustenancelife without sorrow, walking away from the headendones on the hill and the hazels and frothseals and apple trees and badgers and where there's neither a blunder-busscloudcluster-clumpswampthicket-tanglejungle nor a moor but seapigwhales and plainlousehares and the Ossianic face of a frothsealpup nakedappearing on the bare strand and where the violent weather dosn't nakedappear, frost or ice or rain and there's roofprotection for myself and the rarejust.

Ionad Naomh

♪♪

Gleann álainn is ionad naomh
Mar a mbíonn sinne fíréin
Gan iníon is gan bhean chaomh
Gan taobh lenár ndaoine féin.

Eidhneán glas ann agus meas
Is mórán d'úlla sa ngleann
Gan teach gan tine gan teas
Gan seastán gan séis na gceann.

Iomaí crann agus craobh chrom,
Iomaí sruth milis nach mall,
Iomaí rón ramhar is muc throm
Ina gcodladh san eas thall.

Holysaint Place

A lovely glen and a holysaint place where we are just men without a daughtergirl or a wifewoman or sidetrusting our own menpeople. Lots of glassgreygreen ivy and lovefruit and apples in this smoke-cloudhollow-glen without a homehouse or a fire or heat or the hum of the headendones. Lots of penis-shaaftvault-trees and Jovebent treebranches, lots of sweet streams, lots of fat frothseals and pigs sleeping in the waterfall over by.

[Unstable Narrator]

In Aill Fharannáin

In Aill Fharannáin in Iarthar Chonnacht
Oíche reo, nach álainn:
Iomaí broc agus muc mhór,
Iomaí míol má is oisín róin ramhar,
Iomaí naomh agus fíréan
Agus iad go léir ina dtost.

In Alternan

In Alternan in West Connaught on a frosty night, beautiful: many a dirt-badger and great swine, many a plainlousehare and Ossianic froth-sealpup, many a holysaint and rarejust men and all of them silent.

Aistriú

Athraím leam bho bhàrr croinn
Gu ceann eile, aistrím bho thìr
Go tír bho inbhir go hinbhear
Bho ghleann gu gleann
Ó Ghleann Balcáin gu hÌle,
Bho bhinn go binn ó gach dinn
Go dinn bho Chinn Tìre go Boirche
Faoi mar a aistríonn mo ghné
Nam oisín allta no mo mhíol má
No mo mhuc throm no ròn reamhar
Mar a bha mi 'n Aill Fharranáin
Air neo le guth glan geirge
No giùrain os cionn Imleach Iúir
Faoi mar a bhíos arú inné
Nam fhear allaidh làn feirge
Gun taobh ri mná
No nam thoirchim i mo thocht
A-staigh taobh liom fhéin anocht.

Transpositionshiftingtranslationjourney

I change from the hindrancecreamcroptop of one penis-shaftvault-tree to another headendone, I translationjourneyshift from ruraldry-land-state to ruraldry-land state from estuary to estuary from smoke-cloud-hollowglen to smoke-cloudhollowglen from Glenbalkan to Islay from sweetgableobservationhornpeak to sweetgableobservationhornpeak from height to height from Kintyre to Mourne justabout as my species-form translationjourneyshifts as wild Ossianic fawn or plaininsecthare as I was in Alternan or thickheavy scowlheap-pig or thick horse-hairseal or with the cleanclear censurebardvoice of a quail or teredo-barnacle-goose above Emly justabout as I was the day before yesterday, an angry man not given to trustsiding up to wifewomen in a slumberstupor in mattressquiet in at househome beside myself tonight.

An Lá Sin

Chuaigh mé lá go Fiodh Gaibhle,
Lá eile go Binn Fhoibhne.
Chuaigh mé lá go Dún Sobhairce.
Chuaigh mé lá go Sliabh Eachtaí,
As sin go Sliabh Bladhma,
Go hInis Muirígh lá eile,
Go Sionainn, go Suca,
Go Beanna Boirche, go Loch Rí.
Chuaigh mé lá go hInis Bó Finne,
Go hEas Rua lá eile.
Is fíor: níor fhág mé má ná mothar,
Machaire ná muine ná móin,
Cnoc ná cabhán ná coill chluthar
In Éirinn an lá sin gan taisteal.

That Day

I went one day to Figile, another day to Benevenagh. I went a day to Dunseverick. I went a day to Slieve Aughty, from there to Slieve Bloom, to Inishmurray another day, to the Shannon, to the Suck, to the Mournes, to Lough Ree. I went one day to Inishboffin, to Assaroe another day. It's true: I didn't didn't fail-leave a pithplain from the Moy to the Maze or linksbattle-field in Maghera or turfbog in Moor or Jove-coverthicket in Muineagh or blunder-busscloudclusterclumpswamp-thicket-tanglejungle in Moher, a hill in Knock or a yellow-waterlily-maimcavity in Cavan or a secretivewarmwarp-solid castration- wood in the Irelandworld unhackletravelled that day.

[Unstable Narrator]

74

Sweeney came at endlast to the frenzyvisionhometownplace where Moling was, viz. Moling's House in St. Mullin's.

ag Tigh Moling, iúr,
bíodh nach ann don tobar,
ag fás as an úr

at Moling's house in St Mullins a yew though the well has gone growing anew

[Sweeney]

Claochló

Agus na cinn úd ar mo shliocht,
Chuaigh mé leis na héin
Gur chlaochlaigh mé cló agus cruth,
Deilbh agus dath, mo riocht,
Mo ghné agus mo ghuth
Gur athraigh mo cheol
Gurb é seo mo thír féin
Feasta gach aon lá
I bhfearann glas cian ó m'eol
Idir an choill chiar agus an mhá.

Ecotone

With those headendones on my progenytrack, I went away with the birds and my typeapearrance and embryoform morphed, my statue-shape and colour, my capabilitystate, my speciesaspect and my censurevoice and my songmusic changed so that from now on this is my dry-land territory every day in a glassgreygreen land bothbetween the waxdark castrationwood and the mazeplain.

[Unstable Narrator]

Moling had St Kevin's tramplepsalter in his witnesspresence before him then and was reading and incantationteaching it to the science-episode-lessonones.

Moling's Oratory

Moling of Graiguenamanagh and Argidross
With his eyes to the non-skyheavens above
His altar and his upturned palms

Could be Cranach the Elder's Christ on the Cross
Or Kevin praying and resting on a portal dolmen
Above Glendalough, or your man from Dromiskin

Waiting for a blackbird or collared dove,
Or a robin or aberdivinesiskin
To alight in his witnesspresence and land

And lay and nest in a stretched-out hand
As he reads and sings with his congregation of men
From his linenlined illuminated book of psalms.

[Sweeney]

Turas

Ag teorainn chille i nDál Araidhe,
Arna mhárach go Cill Deirbhile,
Go héadrom aerga go Cill Riáin
Go ráinig mé Cluain Cille ar an gcoigríoch,
Go himeall an tobair i nDoire Cholm Cille.

Tharla dom i gCill Uí Shuanaigh,
I mo chaora gan lias i mbile Chill Lughaidh
Ina ndéanaim suan sámhach,
Coicís ar mhí in Uaimh Dhonnáin,
Ag scarúint is ag triall go hEas Dhubhthaigh,
Lá eile go hAill Fharannáin,
Go dtí Teach Moling faoi dheoidh.

Pilgrimagejourney

Roodmarking at the boundary of a cell-churchyard in Dalnaria, the next day to Kildervla, light and airy to Kilrean till I reached Clonkilly on the alienborder, to the edge of Columba's well in Derry; I've happened in Killaloony where I soundly sleep a sound sleep, a fortnight and a month in Donan's Cave; parting and trygoing to the Falls of Duthac; another day to Alternan, to Moling's house in St. Mullen's at last.

Ag Teach Moling

Ó nach bhfuil i mo dhán
Bheith i gCluain Creamha
Ná i Ros Earcáin
Mar a raibh maithe Dhál nAraidhe lena linn

Is i dTeach Mhic Ninnidh feasta
Ná sa mbaile mar a raibh Erin,
Ós mioscais liom gach ionad ina mbínn,
M'fhearann, mo thír agus mo chríocha,

Agus ós minic mé ar an bhfaiche seo sa maidin
Ag feitheamh leat de chéin,
Ní mé nach mbeinn chomh sáil socair céanna
San ionad seo thar gach ionad in Éirinn?

At Moling's House in St Mullin's

Since I'm not dawnhaltergiftpoemfated to be in Clooncraff or Rasharkin where the great and good of Dalnaria were in their pond-day and in Taghmacninny anymore or in the hometownplace where Erin was, since I hate everywhere I've been, my territory and endland and as I've often been on this fortfield waitwatching you from a far for a longinglong time, mightn't I be just as soulhappy in this place as in any place in Ireland?

Ar Loingeas

Nach mó lingeadh doiligh sin a lingeas le mo linn
Ar loingeas i néalta neimhe dom in Éirinn

I mo dhuine le Dia ó Shliabh Mis ó thuaidh,
Thar Dhún Ruairí, thar Shliabh Fuaidh,

Thar choill agus chabhán agus chnoc,
Thar mhóin is mhuine, thar iomaí loch

Ó Loch Rí leathan anuas go Loch Léin
Ar m'ais go dtí an baile seo féin

Faoi dheoidh le longadh go moch
Gan tásc ar mhac tíre ná damh ná broc,

Lon, cú ná rón ach cléireach ag teagasc an cheachta,
Agus lucht an léinn ina fhianaise mar chuideachta,

As duille leabhair álainn mín
De chuid mo chomhalta Caoimhín.

In Sea-roverfleetexpeditionexile

I've startattackjumped so many distressdifficult startattackjumps in my pondgenerationtime in sea-roverfleetexpeditionexile in the tranceneb-ulae of non-skyheaven in Ireland as a man with God from Slemish from in the north, morethanoverby Dundrum Bay, morethanoverby the Fews, morethanoverby Kalendscastrationdesecrationwood in Kill and yellow-waterlilymaimcavity in Cavan and hill in Knock, morethanover-by turfbog in Moor and Jovecoverthicket in Muineagh, morethanover-by many a fiordlough from Lough Ree down to Lough Leane backagain to this very frenzyvisionhometownplace at last to cavityvesseleat early with no deathreport of a landsonwolf or an ox-stag or a messbadger, an ousel-lullelk, a herohound or a horse-hairseal but an altar-boycleric giving a lesson, and learningstudentsons in his witnesspresence for company, out of an eye-lidleaf of one of my jointfellowfoster-brother Kevin's longflowing books.

[Unstable Narrator]

Sweeney came westafter that onto the spreading-groundstratumbrink of Tubridy's well in the witnesspresence of the altar-boycleric and went-took to gormandising on blood-tracebrooklimewatercress. 'That's early swalloweating, wee grindgrazingnakedwoodlunatic' said the altar-boycleric; and then Moling recitesaid and Sweeney outcropanswered him:

[Moling; Sweeney]

Ceiliúradh Cóir

75

Och, is mise Suibhne Geilt, a fhir oirní,
Le gealtacht ar fud Éireann thall agus abhus
Trí mhórán de shíonta, trí mhórán toirní
Ar fud na gcrann is na ngéag, na luibh is na lus.

[*Moling*] Moch sin go tráth, a ghealtagáin,
Le ceiliúradh cóir.
[Suibhne] Cé moch leat, a chléireacháin,
Tháinig teirt sa Róimh.

[M] Cá bhfios duit, a ghealtagáin,
Cathain a thig teirt sa Róimh?
[S] Fios thig dom óm Thiarna
Gach maidin is gach nóin.

Is eol dom féin príomh is teirt,
Gach mothar is móin.
Taithím i dtráth orthu beirt
Gach maidin is nóin.

[M] Inis trí rún ráitsí
Scéal Tiarna na tíre.
[S] Agat atá an fháistineacht
Más Moling thú dáiríre.

[M] Cad a thug duit m'aithne,
A gheilt ghníomhach ghéir?
[S] Minic mé ar an bhfaiche
Ó chuaigh mé as mo chéill.

[M] Tuige nach ndéanann tú cónaí
Go buan, a mhic Cholmáin Chuair?
[S] Is fearr liom a bheith faoi shos
I mball amháin sa mbeatha bhuan.

[M] Mo thrua, an sroichfidh t'anam
Poll Tí Liabáin?
[S] Ní thugann Dia orm
Pian ach a bheith gan támh.

[M] Gluais anall agus beir
Ar chuid a bheas milis leat.
[S] Dá mb'fhios duit, a chléireacháin,
Is doiligh a bheith gan bhrat.

[M] Béarfaidh tú mo chochall
Nó béarfaidh mo leann.
[S] Inniu cé go bhfuilim im chróch bán
Bhí mé uair a bhí ní b'fhearr.

[S] Ochán, is minic m'ochlán
Gan bhia gan leann
Gan leann agam ná cochlán
I mullaí na mbeann.

[M] An tú an Suibhne scáfar
A tháinig as an gcath gan rath?
[S] Más mé, ní rathaítear
A ṅ-ithim go moch ná a dhath.

[M] Conas a tharla m'aithne
Duit, a ghealtáin ghéir?
[S] Minic mé anseo ar an bhfaiche
Ag feitheamh leat ó chéin.

[M] Álainn duille an leabhair
Seo saltair Chaoimhín mo ghrá.
[S] Áille duille m'iúir féin
I nGleann Balcáin bán.

[M] Nach suairc leat an roilig sa má
Lena scoil sciamhach dath?
[S] Ní suairce ná m'oireacht
Ar maidin ar Mhaigh Rath.

[M] Rachaidh mé go ceiliúradh
Go Glais Chille Cró.
[S] Lingfead crann eidhinn glan,
Léim ard, is í ba mhó.

[M] Saothrach dom san eaglais
Thar ceann tréan is trua.
[S] Saothraithe mo leaba
I mBinn Fhoibhne fhuar.

[M] Rachad don chill le hÉanna
Thar ceann trua is tréan.
[S] Rachadsa mar an gcéanna,
Mo chreach, i reilig fíréan.

[M] Cá háit ina dtig do bheatha
Go crích, i gcill nó i loch?
[S] Aoire de do mhuintir féin
A mharós mé go moch.

Brahmin and Shaman

MOLING

That's an earlyearly prayermealhourtime, little grindgrazingnaked-woodlunatic, for neardecentright vanishfarewellwarblegreetcelebration.

SWEENEY

It might be early bird time for you, little altar-boycleric, milking-grazingtime sunrisetierce has come at the hallowed burialdwelling-place in Rome.

MOLING

How do you know, little grindgrazingnakedwoodlunatic, when milking-grazingtime sunrisetierce comes at a hallowed burialdwelling-place in Rome?

SWEENEY

I get word from Milord every matinsmorning and nonesnoon. I know prime and terce, every thicket and moor, I visit them at matins and nones.

MOLING

Tell us in dearprattlesecret the storynews of the Masterlord of the ruraldry-landstate.

SWEENEY

You're the one who's got the gift of prophecy, Brother Moling, Massa, if that's really who you are.

MOLING

How do you commandrecognise me, busy feat-performing soursevere-keensharp woodloony?

SWEENEY

I've often been in the greenfield in Faha since I lost my wits.

MOLING

Why don't you make your alwaysdwelling permanent, son of Coleman Corr?

SWEENEY

I'd rather be at reliefrest in one memberplace in the soiledeverlasting sustenancelife.

MOLING

God pity you, will your animist soul reach Hades?

SWEENEY

God gives me no griefpain except I never get any idleplaguesilencerest.

MOLING

Shift over here and partake of flatterhoneysweet foodbits.

SWEENEY

If you only knew little altar-boycleric, it's distressfulhard for me to be without a brothcovercloak.

MOLING

Take my mufflebushy hacklescrotumnetpodhood or take my alemantle.

SWEENEY

Though I'm emptygrasslandpalewhite and saffron today, things were better one hourtime.

MOLING

Are you that timidfrightful Sweeney who came scot-free from that pointless catbattalionbattle in Moira?

SWEENEY

If I am, Massa, what I eat earlyearly is not guaranteed.

MOLING

How did you commandrecognise me, sourseverekeensharp little wood-loony?

SWEENEY

I've often been in the greenfield in Faha waitwatching you with O'Kane from afar a longinglong time.

MOLING

The eyelidgloryleaf of this book are delightbeautiful, the tramplepsalter of Kevin that I love.

SWEENEY

The eye-lidgloryleaf of my own yew in the palewhite-emptygrassland of Glenbalkan are more delightbeautiful.

MOLING

Isn't the relicgraveyard on the pithplain agreeable to you with its beautiful coloured school?

SWEENEY

No more agreeable than my territoryassembly that morning in Moira.

MOLING

I'll go vanishfarewellwarblegreetcelebrating in the cellchurch of Clashacrow.

SWEENEY

I'll leap a high chasmleap straight up into a shrillweedclear ivy penis-shaftvault-tree, that's greater.

MOLING

It's labouredlaborious for me in the gizzardchurch in Aglish on behalf of the strong and the weak.

SWEENEY

My bed in rawcold Binevenagh is even more labouredlaborious.

MOLING

I will go to the cellchurch-yard with Enda on behalf of the weak and the strong.

SWEENEY

I will go likewise to the relicgrave-yard of the just.

MOLING

Where will your sustenancelife territoryend, a cellchurch-yard in Kill or a fjordlake in Lough?

SWEENEY

A whipherdpastor of your countryfolk-community will deadkill me earlyearly.

[Sweeney]

Teirt agus Fios

Is éard a fuair mé, mo mhairg, mar aisce
Beatha nam aonar aig teine gun fhadadh
Ó chaill mé, mo mhairg, m'Erin mo thaisce
'S gu bheil mi gun bhròg 's gun aodach gun chadadh.

Ní bheidh mé mar rí Dhál Araidhe feasta
Bho dh'fhàs air mo chorp is mo thaobh mo chlòimh
Ach ag feitheamh gach maidin go síoraí seasta
Gus an tig teirt agus fios thall san Ròimh.

Milking-grazingtime Tierce-sunrise and Soothwordartscienceknowledge

What I got as a gift is a life on my lone tod by an unkindled furzefireplace since I lost my Erin and I'm without a brogueshoe or clothclothes or tartan. I won't be the king of Dalaray anymore since downhair has wastegrown on my corpsebody but watchwait every morning forever till milking-grazingtime sunrise-tierce and soothwordartscienceknowledge have come over in Rome.

aon duille amháin,
bile iúir i nGleann Balcáin
agus leabhar Chaoimhín

one leaf a yew tree in Glenbalkan and Kevin's book

Ar Mo Dhia

Trí ghabháil na rann
Is na laoithe sin is na salm
Le Rónán is a mhuintir i gCill Lainne,
Le Moling agus na mic léinn
I dTeach Moling sa bhfeascar,
Trí ghrá mór is trí chuimhne,
Trí ghealtacht is trí mhire,
Seo mé agus aithne agam
Faoi dheoidh tar éis an aistir
Ar Dhia is ar dhaoine.

My God

By reciting verses and those lays and psalms with Ronan and his followers in Killaloony, with Moling and his students in St. Mullin's at vespers, through love and meditation, through ecstasy and madness, here I am knowing at last, after all that journey, God and people.

As Mo Shaltair Féin

Caithim biolar agus uisce,
Déanaim ranna, deirim
Laoi bheag nó gabhaim sailm
I m'thost as leabhar Chaoimhín
Arís agus arís eile
Nó as mo shaltair féin
I mboth fhuar i Sliabh Bladhma
Nó in Uaimh Dhonnáin Eige

Nó lá eile in Eas Rua,
Gan chodladh, ag seachaint daoine,
Go dtagann sionnaigh bheaga
Amach ón gcoill chluthar dhlúth
Agus gach damh alla
Nó go gcluinfidís mo ghuth.

Out Of My Very Own Tramppsalter

I waste-eat watercress and rainurinetearswater, I make partitionverses, I say a wee rudderlay or I go psalms without a word out of Kevin's book again and again and again or out of my very own tramppsalter in a raw-cold booth-hut in Donnan's Cave on Eigg or another day in Assaroe, without sleep, fleeshunning menpeople, and little foxes come out of the secretivesheltered Kalendscastrationdesecrationwood close by and every shoutwild championox-stag to hear my censurevoice.

feascar, Tigh Moling –
abhus gráice gráice cloig
is i gcéin gu-gúg

at vespers at Moling's house in St Mullins nearby a bell tintinnabulating and over there a cuckoo

Ar an bhFaiche

Nuair a tháinig mé faoi dheoidh go dtí an baile
Mar a raibh an cléireach
Ar an bhfaiche i m'fhianaise
Ag teorainn a chille ina chríoch is ina fhearann
Agus mé ag feitheamh de chéin
Gur tháinig mé ar shraith an tobair
Gur ghabh mé ag ithe biolair,
B'fhios dom nach raibh dhá dhéanamh aige
Ó tharla aithne dom ó chuaigh mé mar aon leis na héin
Ach mar a dhéanaim féin i mbile

Gach maidin go moch agus gach nóin
De rann is de cheiliúradh.

Ar Bhruach na Bearú

Is fearr liom ná duille leabhair
Nó saltair Chaoimhín ag lucht an cheachta
Nó lucht an léinn léim creabhair
Nó dhá léim idir mhá, mhóin is learg
I m'Fhear Coille le ginideacht is ar mearú
Le síon is le sioc is le sneachta

Nó guth feadóige nó glao coirre sa loch
Nó guth giúrainn is guth glé na ngearg
I mbarr uachtair an fhéir is i gcuasa caola cloch
Is guth na gcuach ar bhruach na Bearú
Ná guth cloigín – olc an séan! –
Agus meigeallach cléireach is fíréan.

Censurevoice-sounds

I prefer to the eye-lidgloryleaf of the scholars' pliant exercise-book or St Kevin's tramplesalter a chasmleap by a gad-flywood-cock or two chasmleaps eitherbothbetween the plain in Eglington, the turfmoor and the hillside in my mad wandering as a Wild Man of the Woods in storm and frost and snow or the censurevoice-sound of a whistleplover or the call of a hollowpointeelheron on the lake or the censurevoice-sound of a teredobarnacle-goose or the clear curkling of a cormorantquail or shelduck-corncrake in Lemonfield and on the creamcroptop of the grass in Barroughter and in kyletwignarrow cupcovecavities of castleshorestones in Coose and Keale and Clogh and the censurevoice-sound of the tuftembracequaichbundlefalsettocuckoos on the swollenbanks of the Barrow to the censurevoice-sound of a blisterbell – evil denyomen! – and the bleating of altarboy-clerics and righteous men.

On the Fieldgreen

When I came at last to the frenzyhometownplace where the sextonaltarboycleric was at the boundary of his endlands and quarterlands as I waitwatched longing from afar and I came to the spreadingbrink of the well and ate watercress, I knew he was only, as commandmentknowledge happencame to me since since I went off with the birds, doing what I do in a scionbordertree early every morning and nones as partitionversifying and farewellcelebrationwarbling.

[Moling]

76

Feascar

A Shuibhne, tá i ndán duit
Bheith anseo is do shaol
Teacht ann agus do scéal
Is t'imeachtaí a fhágáil ann
Is t'adhlacadh i reilig fíréin.

Cibé áit ina mbeidh: Beanna Boirche,
Inis Bó Finne thiar i gConnacht,
Sliabh Mis thuaidh nó theas nó Eas Rua,
Nascaim ort bheith i dTigh Moling san oíche
Go scríobhtar liom do scéala.

Mo Scéala

Gach lá go moch i bhfianaise
Moling agus cléirigh na cille
Mar aon leis, bíonn lucht an léinn
Ina dtost le ceiliúradh cóir
Agus duillí an leabhair
Agus ní hé saltair Chaoimhín
Le ciumhais d'ór álainn
Á n-iompú go mall

Fuireachair le lámha glana
Agus é i dtoice dom is i ndán
M'imeachtaí a fhágáil
Ina seoid is ina maoin anseo
Go scríobhtar mo scéala,
Mo ghníomh is mo bheatha leo.

My *Testimonio*

Early every day in the witnesspresence of Moling and the altar-boyclerks of the cellchurch-yard with him, the scholars are vanishfarewellwarble-greetcelebrating silently and the pages of the book and not the trample-salter of St Kevin with its lovely gold binding being turned slowly by clearclean hands lateslowly and vigilantdeliberately as it's my dawnpo-emfate and fortune to leave my comings and goings as tittlejewels and wealthtreasuregifts here and my story, my factacts and my sustenancevi-ta with them is written by them.

In the Journey-book: *Vita*

'*Dé do bheatha*, Sweeney, you're more
Than happywelcome here,' said Moling,
'As it's dawnhalterfated in a poem for you to be
Here and to bring an end to your secular worldlife,
To leave your storynews and your spotcomingsandgoing
And to be sepulchreburied
In the relicgraveyard of the rarejustelect,

And I nexusbind you,' says Moling, 'however greatelate
Your neverendingtour every layday in the Irelandworld,
You come every vesperevening to me
So I can write yourself and your stories with me out
And dePict you in the journey-book here.'

[Sweeney]

Sounds

Without a home or house,
Without a fire, stopped still
In a dusky wood,
All frosty and starry
At night in the dark
And gloomy oak grove
As dark as Acheron,
Without clothes, without food
But berries and hazelnuts
And holly, I hear sounds:

The cooing of the turtle-dove
High up in a yew tree,
The cry of a heron,
The cry of the mountain-grouse,
The plover and skylark,
The stag of Cunghill,
The stag of Island Magee,
The wolves and packs of hounds,
The madmen in their huts
Back west in Rossbarry.

Nasg

Ged a tha mi saor
A dhol air fainneal agus air foluain
'S mi ri cuartachadh is ag imrich
Gach àirde de dh'àirdean Èireann,
Chan eil mi saor bhon a tha 'n dàn dhomh
Gun cuir sibh orm nasg
Ged a bhiodh e gun chuibhreach
Gun ghlas agus gun gheimheal

A bhith 'n seo gach là 's gach feasgar
Agus tighinn thugaibh, a Mholing,
Ach an cuir sibh sìos mo shaoghal,
Mo sgeul 's m' imeachdan ann an sgrìobhadh.

Airsealringchained-dogtie-bandpledge

Though I'm free as a joiner to go fannelignorancebewildermentastray and giddyrunskipping as I visitwhirlabout and emigrateflit through every airtpoint of the airtpoints of Ireland, I'm not free at all as it's poemfated for me that you put an airsealringchained-dogpledgetie-band on me even though it has no slaveryharness or watergreengreyfetterlock or prisonchain to be here evey day and night and come to you, Moling, so that you can put down my worldlife, my story and my placeboundaryjourney in writing.

Ceiliúradh na dTráth

Fuar dom i mbarr crainn ar feadh na hoíche gach tráth go maidin,
An tráth sin ag moladh rí neimhe is talún agus crainn Éireann,
Ag baint clog na prímhe i ndoras na reilige an tráth sin,
An tráth sin biolar an ghleanna mar mo shásamh faoi theirt,
An tráth sin ag déanamh an oird nóna ag Snámh Dhá Éan,
An tráth sin gach lá go Tigh Moling is clog an fheascair á bhaint.

Farewellwarblecelebration of the Canonicalmealprayertimehours

It's rawcold for me in the creamcrophindrancetop of a penis-shaftvault-tree all night every canonicalmealprayerhourtime until matins, that canonicalmealprayer-timethen mollypraising the king of non-skyheaven and earth and the penis-shaftvault-trees of Ireland, reapringing the blisterbell for prime in the door of the relicgrave-yard that canonicalmealprayer-timethen, that canonicalmealprayer-timethen watercress from the smoke-cloudhollowglen as my satisfactionfood at tierce, that canonicalmealprayer-timethen nones at Swim-Two-Birds, that canonicalmealprayer-timethen every day to St. Mullin's and the warpvespers blisterclock being wroughtrung.

I Leaba na Naomh

Ní haon ionadh mo shaol a theacht i gcrích
Agus éag is imeacht i néalta neimhe naomh –
Nár chaith mé mo shaol ar chomhairle
Cholm Cille mhaith, fáidh feasa na fírinne,
Nó le leabhar Chaoimhín álainn i m'fhianaise,
Le guth clogáin is fearta Rónáin Fhinn,
Le mo chumann an gheilt naomh Ailín
In Eas Dhubhthaigh de dheas do dhún rí Bhreatain,
Coicís ar mhí in Uaimh Dhonnáin Eige,
I mbeannad is ionad naomh Aill Fharannáin
Agus ag friotháil feascair gach oíche
Theas ag Tigh Moling – is aige atá an fháistine féin! –
Agus nach minic mé ar an bhfaiche
Le ceiliúradh cóir ag feitheamh leis de chéin?

In the Place of the Holy Saints' Bed

There's nothing wonderstrange about my secular life coming to a regionend and dying and going off and on to the holy saints' trancenebulae of non-skyheaven – haven't I spent my worldlife according to Columba the true seersayer's counsel or with Kevin's lovely book in witnessfront of me, with the censurevoice of Ronan's blisterbell and his miracles, with my dear associate the saintholy nakedgrazingwoodlunatic Allan at Essduich southnear the king's closed fort in Dumbarton and sixweeks in Donnan's Cave in Eigg, in the holy place in Alternan and attending vespers every night in Saint Mullin's with Moling who sees the future and all and see how often I've been out on this green farewellwarblecelebrating like I should and watchwaiting for it and him from longingafar?

Críocha

Ó bhrú tobair i nDroim Iarainn
Go sraith tobair i Ros Comáin,
Ar an gcoigríoch

Idir Tír Chonaill is Tír Báinigh,
Ó bhruach na glaise
In imeall Fhiodh Gaibhle
Nó imeall leathan Loch Rí,
Thar an mhuir fhairsing ó Éirinn
Go Críoch Bhreatan idir tuile is trá,
In Inis Bó Finne dom lá
Is as sin go hInis Muirígh,
In Eas Rua lá eile dom,
I Sliabh Mis lá eile
Go Tigh Moling san oíche,
Ag doras na heaglaise
Nó doras na reilige,
Bím ag lingeadh liom is ag léim
Anonn is anall ar mo shlí
Chun mo chríocha féin
Idir neamh agus talamh.

Territoryboundaryends

From the womb-bruisebrink of a well in Drumeerin to the stretch-spreadstratum of a well in Roscommon, in a strange place in neighbouring territory amongbetweenboth Donegal and Banagh, from the bankbrink of the brook in Glasha and on the edge of Feegile or the broadopen edge of Lough Ree, across the wideabundant sea from Ireland to Britain amongbothbetween strandebb and floodflow, a day in Inishbofin and from there to Inishmurray, in Assaroe another day, on Slemish or Slieve Mish another day to Timolin and St. Mullin's at night, at the door of the church in Aglish or the door of the relicgraveyard, I chasmjump and springattack and start back hitherways and thitherways back and forth on my way to my own territoryboundaryends amongbetweenboth non-skyheaven and a spot on dry land on surface-soilcountry earth and all creation.

[Enda McBracken]

Sailm, Rainn agus Laoithe

Tar isteach, iaigh linn, a dhuine,
Atha i ndoras na reilige,
Ionad dín agus dídine
I gcoinne doininne is fearthainne
Agus mar leaba oíche

Mar a ngabhann muid cléirigh na cille
I bhfolach ar shluaite na cruinne
Sailm, rainn agus laoithe
Mar a bhfuil de luibheanna sa muine
Agus de thorthaí ar fud na conaire,

Biolar is fochlacht i mbruach na glaise,
Úlla, caora, creamh is airne,
Sméara, sú craobh, dearcáin sléibhe,
Lus bian, maothnatán, mionán, meille
Is mónadán mar mhéid ár bproinne,

Crainn choill, darach agus bheithe,
Eas ag sní de bhéim buinne,
Glao coirre de loch glas uaine,
Fearán eidhinn le taobh na linne,
Fuarán ina lár agus tobar uisce,

Ealaí binne ar bhuaic toinne
Is ealta d'éin go hard i mbile
Ag ceiliúradh is ag moladh rí neimhe
Agus talún agus mac Muire
Choíche agus go brách na broinne.

Come in, damenclosejoin with us, manperson, for a while in the doorway of the relicgrave-yard, a place of roofprotection against winterstorms and rain and a bed at night, where we the altar-boyclerics of the cellchurch-yard go coverhidden from the armycrowds of the universe and sing our psalms, partitionverses and laypoems, where there are so many herbplants in the Jovethicket and fruits all along the trajectorypath, watercress and brooklime in the swellingbank of the glassgreengreystream, apples, sheepberries, garlic and kidneysloes, smearbrambles, raspberry, Jovemountain acorns, herb viands, mallow, meadow saxifrage, atriplex and cranberries for our prandium, woodhazel, oak and livingbeech penis-shaftvault-trees, a stoatwaterfall winding its way down in torrentblows, an oddroundheron's cry off the lake, a turtledove beside the generationpond, a coldfountain in the groundcentre and a rainwater well, peaksweet swans on the crest of a skinwave and a flock of birds uphigh in a sacredscionbordertree vanishfarewellwarblecelebrating and mollypraising the king of non-skyheaven and earth and the son of Mary now and forever.

[Unstable Narrator]

77

As regards the nakedwood-grazingbattle-fugitivebirdbeastpaniclunatic backwestafter that, he was during that year accustomfrequenting Moling. He dh'fhalbhanted one day to Inishbofin in the remoteposterior of the westland of Connaught, another day to weepsmooth Assaroe, another day to the delightbeautiful smoothgrasslands of Slemish or Slieve Mish, another day to the permastingcold Mournes; whichever of those he would go to every day, he would prepareattend at espartovespers every night at Moling's house in St. Mullin's.

[Sweeney]

Horae Canonicae

Cluinim i Luachair Deá
Agus in imeall an fheá
Gráice gráige agus cling
Thall ag an mbeannán Moling

Mo chuid *Horae Canonicae*:
Go hInis Bó Finne gach maidin is gach nóin,
Go Sliabh Mis faoi theirt,
Ag imeacht gan bhróg is gan cheirt,
Gan éadach lín, gan éadach róin
Ar fud Éireann ó Ros Earcáin go Tigh Doinn
Agus biolar agus uisce mar mo phroinn
Go dtagaim ag deireadh gach lae
Go Tigh Moling is é socair sáil seascair
Agus Éanna Mac Breacáin ag baint clog an fheascair.

Horae Canonicae

My own *Horae Canonicae*: to Inishbofin every matins and nones, to Slieve Mish or Slemish at terce, going without a brogueshoe or an apple-treerag, without sackcloth or haircloth throughout Ireland from Rasharkin to the Bull Rock with blood-tracewatercress and rain-urinetearswater as my prandium, till I come at the end of each day to St. Mullin's, cosy and sheltered, and Enda McBracken reaping the vespers bell.

Gàir na Gairbhe

Alltan àlainn aoibhinn
A' lìonadh le bainne làn,
Am mac-talla 's mìorbhail
Is gàir binn na Gairbhe.

Ros Bhroc is Tonn Ruairidh,
Druim Leathad agus Dairbhre
'S èisteachd ris an aifreann
Far am buailear clag gun bhailbhe.

Dùrdan daimh duinn Dàmhair
Oidhche fhuar gheamhradail
Is Inbhir Dhùghlais oidhche fhuar
Is dearcan donn air darach ann.

An sìon air bhàrr Beinn Boirche
'S gàir muir na fairge
'S ceilear aig eòin-chalaidh,
'S oirfeid dham anam e.

'S binn leam loin a' ceileireadh,
Osnadh gaoithe 's ceòl nan salm ann
Mar fhuaim doininn fon darach
Air leacannan Ghleann Bhalgain.

Eas Ruaidh gu Eas Dhubhthaich
Gus an tug mi ceann mo bhàire,
Guthan aoibhinn eunlaith,
Cò 'n eas as glaine gàire?

The Resoundroar of Fiercerough Garf Water

A beautiful hotcockle-streamlet linen-netfilling with a tidefull milk-dropcurrent, the cliffsonecho is a miraclemarvel and the hoppermelodytruesweet resoundroar of fiercerough Garf Water. Dungarvan and Dundrum Bay, Drumleid and Darvery and listening to the chapel-housemass where not-so-dumb-bells are rung. The teasingmotesing-songmurmur of the surlybrown oxbeamstag rutting in October on a rawcold wintry night and Inveruglas on a rawcold night with pregnant-brown eyeberries on a treeoghamDoaktree. The stormweather on the harvestcropcreamtop of the bison-elk Mournes and the resoundroar of the stormsea and the sonnetwarbling of the ferrybayharbourshore birds are music to my soul. I love the blackbirds warbling, the soughing of the wind and the music of the psalms there like the sound of the storm under the oaks on the slopes of Glenbalkan. Assaroe to the Falls of Duich till I came to the headend of my ruttingbattlegamepath, the sweeteven bardvoice of the birds, what water-fallstream is a purewhiter resoundroar?

[Unstable Narrator]

Moling hammerarrangeordered a wee surfeitprandium for him that levelmoonrayspacetime and so he said to his female dairyfarmsteward to give him a no-thing of the alas!beaucow's groinmilking. Her name was Muriel, womanwife of the cowherd Mangan. The amount of the refection the care-takerwifewoman would give him was, viz. she would stakethrust and kneadwedge her voluptuous soilheel up to the ankle-joint in the cowpat from the edge of the dung-yardmilking-place conearest to her and spillpour and leave its tidelotfill of beestings in it for Sweeney. He would come timidly and cautiouswatchfully to the inter-wild-desert of the dung-yardmilking-place to drink the new milk.

[Sweeney]

Triall

Agus má fhiafraíonn mo dhaoine
Mar sin *Cá bhfuil do thriall?*
Nó *Cár imigh tú uainn, a Shuibhne,*
A dhuine? Ní hansa:
Ní dhéanaim ach cur i gcéill:
Siar go hInis Bó Finne
In Iarthar Chonnacht, go hEas Rua,
Go Sliabh Mis, go Beanna Boirche.

Journeysettingout

And if my menpeople ask like that: *So, where are you journeytrying for?* or *Where have you losscrossed over and gone away wantingfrom us to, Sweeney, manperson?* that's dearesteasy: all I do is pretend-tell: *Backwest to Inishbofin, to the Falls of Assaroe, to Slemish, to the Mountains of Mourne.*

Ar M'Imirce Arís

Tá mé sáil socair i mbile
Thar chách i gcoitinne
Nó ar m'imirce
In Uaimh Dhonnáin Eige
Nó ar an each donn ar Mhá Linne
Nó siar go sléibhte Boirche
Nó in Inis Muirígh nó Inis Bó Finne
Gan neach i m'fharradh gan chairde
Gan teach gan tine
Mar a bhí an gheilt eile
Mo dhuine Fear Coille
Nuair a ráinig sé Fiodh Gaibhle.

Emigrationflitting Again

I'm happy in a sacredscionbordertree unlike the others or in flitemigration in the cave in Eigg or on the Jovelordwoodbrown steedhorse in Moylinney or back west to the Jovemoormountains of Mourne or Inismurray or Inishboffin without an apparitionperson with me or respitefriends, with neither house nor home nor hearth, as the other nakedgrazingwoodlunatic was, my man Woodman when he came to Figile.

biolar is uisce,
glan is glas is coisricthe
mar chuid na hoíche

watercress and water clear and green and holy for my lot at night

Nasc

Bhínn ag teacht is ag imeacht i ngach maighean
I mo rí cúige tráth dá raibh
Ó thuaidh idir Sliabh Mis álainn mín
Is Dún Sobhairce thíos in Ultaibh
Is Inis Bó Finne in Iarthar Chonnachta
Agus féach anois mar a d'éirigh:
Mé ar mo choimeád cian ó m'eol
I dTigh Moling faoi Learg Laighean
Mar a raibh Congall rí Uladh is Colmán,
Scannlán is Uibhne, liom féin i gcillín
Gan chodladh sámh gan cheol
Go scríofar mo scéala leis na cléirigh
I bhfianaise lucht an cheachta
Gach oíche mar nasc mar dhán.

Bind

I used to come and go to every place as a provincial king once fromin the North between Slieve Mish and Slemish and Dunseverick down in Ulster and Inishbofin backwest in Connaught and look what arose: kept far away from the place I know best in St. Mullin's (or Timolin) underabout Mount Leinster on my tod in a churchcell without sleep or music to have my story written down by the crabclerks in the witnesspresence of students every night as a bindinghalterpoem.

New Milk

Lying down, I sing an old aria
For Erin, I who was once a king
In garments with a girdle of chequered silk
And satin as I take my new milk
In the presence of Muriel and Moling
In an empty space far from Dalnaria.

[Unstable Narrator]

Last Supper

So then, Sweeney, that's it:
Your last supper and for your prandium
Beestings the colour of cum
And for your mead cowshit
In a grazing-field in an empty space
For your eternal resting-place.

[Sweeney]

Mo Dhalta

Ó ghoin tú mo dhalta
Gur mharaigh tú d'aon urchar é,
Tú féin is na cléirigh chráifeacha
Le formad agus tnúth
Mar mhilleadh coimirce
I bhfianaise bhur mac léinn
Agus lucht an cheachta
Ag teacht d'ionsaí na heaglaise,
Ó d'imrís an bás air, a mhic Dé,
An tráth a theilg a leabhar álainn
I ndomhain sa linn lán,
Mo mhallacht ort, a Dhia,
Is go bhfaighe tú ní bás de rinn
I gcoill nó i gcill nó i loch
Is adhlacadh dá réir i reilig fíréin
Ach tú a dhul ar aon leis na héin
Ar gealtacht is ar ginideacht
Ar fud Éireann, ar foluain
Is ar fáinneáil, a Dhia neimhe,
Gan furtacht ná fóirithint
Gan chabhair gan chairde
Gan chodladh sámh go bráth bán.

My Petfosterstudentdisciple

Since you scrapstingstabbed my petfosterstudentdisciple and deadkilled him with one shot, you and the devout sextonaltar-boyclerks in envy and jealouslongingvying violating a protectionguarantee in the witnesspresence of your sons of learning coming attacktowards the church, since you playinflicted death on him, o God, the canonicalhourtime you soundcondemncast his lovely book in to the depths of the tidefull generationpond, curse you, o God, and may you die not by spearpoint in a castrationdesecrationwood or churchyardcell or a lake and being buried accordingly in the relicgrave of the just but by going off with the birds in paniclunacy and goblinmadness all over Ireland, full-onfloating and fannelfluttering, o God in non-skyheaven, without any comfort or help or respitefriends or sleep till the crack of doom.

Sireadh

Samhalta liom ag críoch mo bheatha
Mo chliamhain Aonghas Mac Fheargail i raon madhma
Thar na srutha milse, ag sireadh na mbeann,
In Uaimh Dhonnáin, i ndoirí dorcha,
Sa gcoill chiar gur tháinig sé go Gleann Earcáin
Don teach mór agus doras an tí
Nó go ndeachaigh sé suas i mbile.

Nó – an cuimhin leat, a iníon? –
Mar a chuaigh Guaire don seilg an lá sin
Agus mar an dobhrán i ndomhain an locha
Faoin linn lán úd nó ag iomramh loinge
Gan laoi thar an mhuir mar a bhfuil na taibhsí,
Ar a thuairisc trí bhith síor ó d'éag m'athair
Le dhul ina dháil arís ina theach thiar.

Travelseeking

The end of my life is virtualvisionarylike my son-in-law Aeneas MacFergal in his mad career over the sweet streams, seektraversing the gableregardhornmountains, in Donan's Cave, in dark oakgroves, in the waxdark castrationdesecrationwood until he came to Glen Arkin to the big house and the door of the pursuithouse where he went up in a sacredscionbordertree. Or else – do you remember, girl? – how Gory went spleenquesthunting that day and like the dim-wittedotter in the depths of the lake under that tidefull generationpond or voyage-tale rowing a housebedship without a laydayoar across the sea where all the appearancedisplayghosts are, looking for him forever since my father died to go and asemblymeet him again in his house back in the west.

[Unstable narrator; Muriel]

78

One day westafter that, a mutual reviling and rooley-booley garnerhaul-happened at night between Muriel, wifewoman of Buckley the cowherd, and another woman in the boolydungyard and the other woman said: 'It's worse for you that you're fonder of another man and that you don't prefer your own man coming to you than your man the nakedgrazingetc. who's been in the habit of visiting and consorting with you for this last year past'.

[Unstable Narrator; Moira]

The sister of the herdboy, Moira, heard this but she holmtold nothing of it till the morrowmorning when going giftbringing the milk for Sweeney to the cow-dung conext to the fieldbarrierhedge where he was. Fromsincewhen the herdboy's Suirsister saw that, she came in and said to her brother: 'Your blone is at the haggardfieldbarrierhedgevallum beyond the pale east over there with another man, you milksop' she said.

[Unstable Narrator]

Jealousy seized the herdboy on hearing that and he came out and he rose up suddenimpulsively and evilangrily and his hand drew a half-spear that was on the rack in the house and went to aimattack the nakedwood-grazingbattle-fugitivebirdbeastpaniclunatic. The nakedwood-grazing-battle-fugitivebirdbeastpaniclunatic had his side towards him lying waste-eating his collation out of the cow-dung. Then the herdboy gave a stakethrust of the Christ-side piercing spear out of his hand and jinkscrapstingwounded your man Sweeney's left Dun-cownipple and the divisionpoint went through him and burstbroke his beamridgeback in burntwo. Some said it was the gablepoint of a wildJovestag's horn the boyherd set under him, where he would drink his swallowdrink out of the cow-dung so that he fell on it and that's how he died.

[Sweeney]

Dawnhalterfategiftpoem

After the Battle of Μοῖρα when I came to strifehate,
For all I was only implicated in the slaughter,
Everywhere I'd been my love for Erin didn't falter
(Or my mother, father, brother, sister, son and daughter).
It was my dawnhaltergiftpoemfate and wench-chance as well
That I should die in Saint Mullin's by the point of a sword
As I lived according to Ronan's miraclecurseword
Not as I killed a man in his chuch but dared desecrate
And woundpierce the altar-boycleric's precious vesper-bell
On his breast and Saint Kevin's lovelylined tramplepsalter.

Flight

A man who bore the yoke of piety and fulfilled God's command
And endured persecutions was marking out a church in my territory
and land;
I heard the sound of Ronan's bell and seized Ronan's hand.

With the words of Ronan, I set off in my headlong flight,
Wandering and flying throughout the world in the sough of the winter
night;
My talons are feeble, there is no strength in me for fight.

I would not shake the dew from the top of the grass
In the glen, in a lonely shieling, on sedgy land, on a morass,
Throughout the wood and the climb to the deer-pass.

Little foxes yelping, the skylarks, my sister's son and my hound,
The cry of the heron, wolves at their rending, I flee at their sound
Through the ivy-trees through the thicket to the ground.

The curse of Christ on your mouth, I had rather, hag,
Hear the voices of the cuckoos and the belling of the stag
In a storm in Slieve League under the shelter of a rag.

Throughout every wilderness in Ireland, Lynchehaun was on my track.
In the cow-dung at Moling's house, the herd seized a spear on a rack,
The shaft sprang off it up in the air, the point went through me, breaking my back.

[The Other Woman]

Sa bhFál Sin Thoir

Ní call duit féin bheith socair sáil
Agus do bhean dhil sa bhfál
Sin thoir nó thall sa mbuaile,
A mheatacháin, ag fear eile
Le beagán bainne a fháil
Ar maidin le bliain anall

Ach dul ar foluain is ar fáinneáil
Ar fud Éireann i d'fhear buile
Ó Dhún Sobhairce go Dún Máil,
Ó Ghleann Balcáin go Gleann Aighle,
Gach ball ó Mhaigh Lí go dtí Magh Fáil
Is go bhfaighir bás agus ifreann thall.

In That Haggardfieldbarrierhedge Over East

You've no call to be heeleasy with your little woman in that haggardfieldbarrierhedge over east or over in the dungyardmilkingfold, you puny coward you, with another man to get a bit of milk in the morning this past year but rather go off full-onfluttering and fannelflying all over Ireland like a madman from Dunseverick to Dunmail, from Glenbalkan to Glenelly, every ballmembermarkplace from Moylee to Moyfail and may you die and go to hell.

[Unstable Narrator]

Leis

Agus fuair sé bás go hobann trí shá ga
De ghoin in odhar a chíche clé
I bhfogas dá chroí
Sa mbualtrach sa mbuaile ina luí
Agus a thaobh leis is ansin ar fhleasc a dhroma
Gur briseadh ina dhá leath é.

With a Haunchthigh of His Exposed Also

And he died like that by a raydart stakestab mortally bitbitewanewounding him in his left nipple near to his heart in the booleydung in the booleydungyard lying down with a haunchthigh of his exposed also and therethen on the wreathwandstriplingsplinterfilletflat of his ridgeback so that it and him broke in two.

Dúnadh

I ndiaidh dom gan dul
Ar aíocht go teach duine
Ar droim dhomhain,

Tháinig mé romham faoi dheoidh
Go Tigh Moling, ní hionann
Agus na tithe óil

Mar a bhfuil slua an tí
Is a gcaitear saill is feoil
Agus iomaí cuach is cupán

Agus beann buabhaill
Ag coirm leanna,
Seo mé i mo luí

Ag caitheamh mo phroinne -
Ní beag bainne, lán leamhnachta -
Sa mbualtrach sa mbuaile

Is ó nach bhfuil mo theach ar talamh,
Gabhaim romham go doras na heaglaise
Go gcuirim mo ghualainn leis an ursain.

Jambprop

After wanting for all that and going without hospitality in any manperson's homehouse on the ridge of the world I came at last to Moling's house, not like the drinking houses where the fairyarmycrowds are with their fleecefat and fatflesh and cuckooquaichs and cups and buffalohorns, here's me lying down eating my collation of milk or tidefull beestings in cowdung in the dungyard and since my househome is not on this earth I go over to the door of the church and put my shoulder to the propjamb.

Glorious Kingdom

I was a prince, I was a good, great king
On a kingly circuit throughout Ireland, Moling.

Then Ronan came to my country, marking out his church
Glorifying the king of heaven and earth.

I heard the sound of Ronan's vesper-bell
By the brink of the clean-banked, green-flecked well.

Now I'm without a house, without a title,
Without power, and I give thanks to the king above,

Seeking him in the glen, from peak to peak, over meadow and sward,
In a tree's narrow hollow, in the cowdung in the milking yard.

[Unstable Narrator]

79

Gheibh mi bàs, chan ann le bàthadh
An Eas Dhubhthaich ach le sàthadh
Den ghath le làmh an aoghaire
Mu dheas an Laighin Laoghaire

It was there and then that an altar-boycleric of Moling's countrypeo-plecommunity, Enda McBracken, was reapringing the prime blister-clockbell in the door of the relicgrave-yard there then when he saw the greatly distressing slaughterfeat that had been done there.

Time

When you behold Enda McBracken
As he appears at the door of the yardcell
To bear witness for Moling and to ring prime
And tierce and sext
And then none and then all the skies blacken
And you hear the tolling of the compline bell,
Then you know that it's that time
And you know what's coming next.

Then he recitesaid the Leerudderexhortationlay:

[Enda McBracken]

80

Teachd Fa-dheòidh

Truagh sin, a Mhungain nam muc,
Rinn thu gnìomh truagh is olc,
Mairg a mharbh a los a neirt
An rìgh, an geilt naomh 's an naomh geilt.

Thig gu dìleann olc dhut às
Teachd fa-dheòidh gun aithreachas,
Bidh t' anam an seilbh aig na deamhain
Gun tighinn air do chorp sleamhain.

'S ionann ionad air nèimh
Dhomhsa 's dha fhèin, fhir nach sèimh,
Gabhar sailm Dihaoine
Airson t' anma le daoine.

Bu rìgh gun lochd e, bu gheilt glan,
Fear glè uasal 's fìor a bh' ann,
Sin thall na lì a leac-lighe,
A thruaighe 's e bhris mo chridhe.

Coming and Going at Last

That's balepitiful, McSwiney, Moling's swineman from the Isle of Muck, you have done a balepitiful sickaching peat-stackdeed, oftwoe betide who deathkilled on account of his power, the king, the Holy Gael and the Fool for Christ's sake. Evilapparitionloss will come of it Flood-forever for you to come and go at last without repentance, your soul will be possessed by demons, not to mention your slippery corpsebody which won't be found. It'll be the same place in heaven for me and him, man, Psalms of Ascent will be sung by folk for your soul on fastFriday. He was every bitinch a king, without harmfault, he was a greatclear wildwood-dwellingbird, he was the most clear, finepreciousproudno-blepatrician and duniwassal and true manone, over there is his happy-huejewelled graveslab, o mercy the pathos has burstbroken my heart.

Bás Gan Sagart

That is just sick, Moling's swineherd,
You've done a selfish violent deed,
Pity anyone that by his strength would kill
The king, the saint, the fool for Christ's sake.

You'll get your comeuppance
And in the end a *bás gan sagart*,
Demons will possess your soul
And beasts and serpents and insects take your corpse.

The self-same place in heaven
Will be there for him and for me, man,
At Friday fasting, psalms will be sung
For the soul of the true guest.

He was every inch of him a king,
He was a madman, pure and complete,
There's his resting-place lit bright,
The pity of it has broken my heart.

[Unstable Narrator]

81

Enda changeturned late to the other side and holmtold Moling that Sweeney had been killed to death by Mangan, Moling's swineherd. Moling rose up immediately the firsthourtime with the altar-boyclerics with him to the armsplace where Sweeney was and Sweeney admitconfessed his corriecauldronpitfault-transgressions and confession to Moling.

[Moling]

Éacht

I ndoras na reilige chualas an t-éacht:
Tháinig chugam Suibhne saor
Nuair a bhí sé ag baint na gcaor
Dé Domhnaigh gur tugadh a dhá lán
De ghoin do mo ghealtagán.

Agus ní mhaireann ach do chuil,
Do shionnach, a bhean, is do chat
Agus do dhreoilín ó shlat go slat

Abhus agus t'fhear thall in ifreann
Gan trócaire ag faí is ag gol
Gan beannacht ar a cheann.

Ach fuil na geilte níor théacht.
Ar an treas lá éireoidh a chneas
Ón bhfód is a chorp gan chol
Gan locht agus feicfidh cách,
Thiar is thoir, thuaidh is theas,
Im' chill i dTigh Moling a fhuil
Ar an leac go fóill is go brách.

Slayingfeat

At the entrance to the relicgrave-yard I heard the slayingfeat: Sweeney came to me when he was picking berries on Sunday and was mortally wounded. All that's living is your fly, your fox, wifewoman, and your cat and your wren in this life and your man in merciless hell in the next, crying and lamenting without a blessing on his head. But the madman's blood didn't congeal. On the third day his perfect body will rise up from the earth and everyChristbody will see, east and west, north and south, in my cellchurch-yard St. Mullin's his blood on the gravestone still and forever.

[Unstable Narrator]

I nDiaidh Shuibhne

Cuimhním ar mo dhuine, Moling is Rónán ina dtriúr
Agus a gcoirp ar crochadh san iúr

I Ros Béarach agus in ifreann thall
Is i nGleann Balcáin úd na sruth milis nach mall

Is ar m'ainm bunaidh, mo bhunús is mo shloinne
Sa mbualtrach dom ag caitheamh mo phroinne.

Après Sweeney

I mind-think of your manperson, Moling and Ronan all three and their corpsebodies hanging in the yew in Rossbarry and over in hell and in Glenbalkin with its fastsweet streams and of my basic name, my origins, my patronymic and family name in the cow-dung as I waste-eat my prandium.

[Sweeney]

Admháil

Coisric mé, a chléirigh,
Mar go ndearna mé cionta is coireanna.
Thug mé ainm Dé gan fáth.
Bhris mé coimirce i Maigh Rath gur mharaigh mé fear
Gach lá agus fear eile gach tráth nóna.
Mharaigh mé rí Uí bhFaoláin
Is cúig mic rí Mhaigh Mairge.
Mharaigh mé dalta de mhuintir Rónáin.
Bhí fios agam de bhean fir eile.
D'ól mé deoch d'uisce glan i ngoid as an tobar.
Shantaigh mé gleann álainn
Is ionad naomh Aill Fharannáin.

Conformityadmission

Bless me, Father, for I have sinned. I took the name of God in vain. I violated the guarantee at Moira and killed a man every day and another man every evening. I killed Whelan and McRee's five sons. I killed one of Ronan's followers. I knew another man's wife. I drank a drink of pure water I stole from the well. I coveted the holy place and beautiful glen of Alternan.

Aithrí

An bás a gheobhad is cuma
Cén ceann sa deireadh thiar thall –
In aice Lann Rónáin Fhinn,
Titim leis an aill in Aill Fharranáin,
I mbuinne díleann Eas Dhubhthaigh,
De bhinn Dhún Sobhairce díreach
Go ndéantar bruar is conmar díom
Nó le ga trí mo chneas, trí mo chíoch,
Trí mo chroí – nach olc an gníomh! -
Nó go ngointear is go mbristear mo dhroim
I ndó nó le beann chongna fia.

Agus seo mé ag iompú i ndiaidh mo thaithí
Agus gach coir á cur i bhfaoistin bhéil
Is á hamhdachtáil agam, ag caitheamh uisce
Is Corp Chríost in áit an bhiolair, ag aithrí,
Mo chúis, ag glacadh le hungadh
Is ag fáiltiú le Dia mar a bheadh sé riamh
Mar dhán dom le cléirigh na cille.

Repentance

The kind of death I'll receive doesn't matter in the heel of the hunt – death on the battlefield at Moira, falling down the cliff or the waterfall in Alternan, Duffy's Falls in hoopshootspoutspate or in Dunseverick or death by javelintroopray or by a rayspear through the skinsurface, the breast, the heart or a deer's antler that wool-wastewanewounds my ridgewavecarapaceback and breaks it in seartwo. And here I am turning after all I've experienced, confessing all my crimes, partaking of water and *Corpus Christi* instead of blood-tracebrooklimewatercress and wel-comerejoycing to God like the church-yardcell altar-boysextonclerics had it as my halterfatepoem all along.

Salmairí

Amhail is a chraith na cléirigh
D'uisce coisricthe orm is a chan
Chun a rí féin a mholadh
Sailm ón saltair líneach álainn
Gur theilg mé sa duibheagán í,

Seo mé féin ag iompú chun aithrí,
Ag gabháil na salm
Céanna Dé hAoine
Is an lá ag gabháil ó sholas orm
I bhfianaise Dé is daoine.

Rantbeggarpsalmists

As the altar-boysextonclerics wavesprinkled churchconsecrated rain-urinetearswater on me and sangsaid to praise their own king psalms from the lovely linenlined greatgospelpsalter until I soundcondemnthrew it into the darkdepths, here I am turning and repenting, chanting the very same psalms on Friday in the fading light in the witnesspresence of the daygod and menpeople.

Confessional

I'm your man behind the curtain and man at the wall
In the Falls and in Derry and Berlin.

When I have to go and tell it all,
I'm a Sexton, Berryman or Snodgrass.

I'm *Song of Myself* and *Leaves of Grass*.
I'm *Life Studies*. I'm the work of Sylvia Plath.

I'm Lailoken. I'm *Georgic et Merlin*.
I'm a walking sociopath.

[Unstable Narrator; Sweeney; Mangan; Moling]

82

The herdboy came piercelooking for him. 'That's a black peat-stackdeed you've done, Buckley, *a bhuachaill*' saids Sweeney 'viz. killing me numb-dead without affectionguiltoffence for I can't shunfleefly through the haggardfieldbarrierhedge anymore because of the jinkscrapstingwound you kickflingfrolicgave me'. 'Holy Moly, If I'd known it was you,' said the herdboy, I wouldn't have jinkscrapstingwounded you at all even if you meant to harm me.' 'By Christ's holy spear, manperson,' said the dying Gael, 'I never harmed you at all at all in life whatever you might imaginethink or done harm to any manperson on the beamridgeback of the domainworld since God burysent me into paniclunacy and little harmloss to you me being in a haggardfieldbarrierhedge here and getting a little milk for God's sake from that wifewoman and I wouldn't sidetrust your wifewoman or all the wifewomen on earth for the all the fruits in Fruitlands.' 'The male-diction of Christ on you, cowherd boy,' said Moling, 'that's an evil peat-stackdeed you've done, short worldlife to you in this world and hell in the next life for doing the peat-stackdeed you've done.' 'There's no baydrowningsympathy for me in that,' saids Sweeney, 'for your stingtreacheries have surrounded me and I'm a dead man from the jinkscrapstingwounds you that have been kickflingfrolic-given to me.' 'There'll be retribution for you there,' said Moling, 'viz. the same span as me in non-skyheaven for you'.

[Sweeney]

For All That

I do not wish you, cowherd and pious cleric,
A short life here in this world for all that nor hell
In the next but that there is not a holy bell
Of yours to be heard here now nor your church standing
And I'm still here for all that I'm a petty king
Is my retribution and weregild and eric.

Gan cheol

Binne liom ná comhrá
Ciúin na muintire ná stocaireacht
A dhéanann fir is mná
A chluinim go moch,
Guth mná áille, guth cléireach
Ag méileach is ag meigeallach
Ná bhur mac léinn in bhur gcill
Ó chuaigh mé le gealtacht gan cheol
Gan chairde gan chodladh
Choíche bheith i mo thost.

No Songmusic

I prefer to the quiet conversation of folk or the scroungetrumpeting that men and wifewomen make I hear early, the censurevoice of a beautiful wifewoman, the censurevoice of altar-boyclerics chatterbleating and whimperwhining or of your sons of learning in your cell-churchyard since I went off in nakedgrazingwoodbirdlunacy without songmusic without respitefriends without sleep forever to be restsilent.

[Unstable Narrator]

An Lorg

Chaidh mi 'n lorg air Suibhne seang
Aig an robh 'n sgiath bhreac air a mhuin
Agus lèine den t-sìoda 's den òr
'S mi seachd bliadhna ri saothair mhòr,
Tuath, deas is siar air eang
Thairis air feur is air fonn,
Ga shiubhal bho Shamhain gu Bealltainn,
Samhradh is geamhradh, a' sealltainn
Is a' sireadh bho ghleann gu gleann,
San t-sliabh 's am mullach nam beann
Bho Shliabh Mis gu Sliabh Fuaidh,

Bho Bheinn Iùghaine gu Beinn Bhroin,
Air feadh Èireann bho bhathais gu bonn
Is air feadh an domhain gu lèir gu cruinn
'S cha d'fhuair mi ann ach sgal an luin
Is an donnalaich a nì na coin,
Gàir agus ceilear an daimh dhuinn
'S air an rèidh dùrd an daimh ruaidh.

Blindwomanthighfoot-print-troopsearching

I went blindwomanthighfoot-print-troopsearching for leanmeańn Sweeney who had the wingshield on his mountainbrambleback and a shirt of silk and gold and I was seven years at the great tidal-island-labours, farmcountrypeoplenorth, neatnearsouth and backwest on his nookmeshlegtrack over the grass and the melodydesireland, deathtravelseeking him from one end of the year to the next, summer and winter, showlooking and seekroaming from glen to glen, in the mountainmoor and in the rooftop of the binheadhills from Slieve Mish to the Fews, Benone to Benbourne, throughout Ireland from tip to toe and throughout the whole wide world and all I got was the calfsquallyell of the ouzelelk and the dogs howling, the crying and concealerhumming of the surlybrown earth-quakemastbeamstag and on the easyoverplain the sullenmutterbuzzing of the brownred one.

[Unstable narrator]

And then in trinity, viz. Sweeney, Mangan and Moling, recitesaid this rudderexhortationLeelay:

[Sweeney; Mangan; Moling]

83a

Cumann Triúir

[Suibhne] Rinne tú gníomh, ní suairc sin,
A bhuachaill Mholing ón Luachair,
Ní fhéadaim dul faoin bhfál
Ag an ngoin a ghoin do dhá lámh.

[Mongán muicí Moling] Abair liom má chluinir, a fhir,
Cé thú, a dhuine, go deimhin?
[S] Is mé Suibhne Geilt gan oil,
A bhuachaill Mholing ón Luachair.

[M] Dá mb'fhios dom sin, a Shuibhne sheing,
A dhuine, dá n-aithneoinn,
Ní thabharfainn ga faoi do chneas
Cé go bhfeicinn thú dom aimhleas.

[S] Ní dhearnas thiar ná thoir
Aimhleas duine ar droim dhomhain
Ó chuir Críost i dteinne mé ó m'thír
Ar gealtacht ar fud Éireann.

[M] D'inis dom, ní nár bhréag,
Iníon m'athar is mo mháthar,
Tú a fháil sa bhfál sin thoir
Ag mo mhnaoi féin ar maidin.

[S] Níor chóir dhuit a chreidiúint sin
Go bhfionnta féin a dheimhin,
Mairg gur tháinig dom ghoin i leith
Nó go bhfeicfeadh do shúile.

Cé go mbeinn ó fhál go fál,
Ba bheag duit a dhíobháil,
Cé go mbéarfadh bean dom deoch
De bhainne beag i mo dhíol déirce.

[M] Dá mb'fheasach dhom a bhfuil de,
Do ghoin trí do chíoch, trí do chroí,
Ní ghoinfeadh mo lámh thú go brách,
A Shuibhne Ghleann Balcáin.

[S] Cé gur ghoin tú mé sa bhfál,
Ní dhearnas ort aon dochar,
Ní thabharfainn taobh le do mhnaoi dhil
Ar talamh gona thorthaí.

Mairg a tháinig atha ón teach
Chugat, a Mholing Luachra,
Ní ligfidh dhom dul faoin gcoill
An ghoin a ghoin do bhuachaill.

Mallacht Chríost a chum gach clann
Ort, arsa Moling lena bhuachaill,
Trí éad i gcroí do chnis,
Is trua an gníomh a rinnis.

Ó rinnis é, fuafar an gníomh,
A dúirt Moling lena bhuachaill.
Rachaidh duitse thar a cheann
Gairide shaoil is ifreann.

[S] Cé go ndéanfá díol as,
A Mholing, ní beo mise,
Níl mo chabhair ann,
Tháinig bhur gcealg i m'thimpeall.

Rachaidh éiric ann duit féin,
Arsa Moling, *seo mo lámh,*
In aon fhaid liom ar neamh
Duit, a Shuibhne, ón Tiarna.

Beidh maith duitse, a Shuibhne chaoil,
Tusa ar neamh, arsa an buachaill,
Ní hionann agus mé féin abhus
Gan neamh agam, gan saol.

SWEENEY

You've done a peat-stackdeed that's no pleasant thing, Moling's cowherd from Slieve Luachra. I couldn't go underabout the fieldwall-hedge for the blackhanded wound you wounded me with.

MANGAN

Tell me if you hear, man, who are you, manperson, indeed?

SWEENEY

I'm Mad Sweeneywithout reproach, Moling's cowherd from Slieve Luachra.

MANGAN

If I'd known that, leanmean Sweeney, man, if I'd recognised you, I wouldn't have set a spear on your skinbody though I used to see you doing me harm.

SWEENEY

West or east, I never did harm to any manperson on the ridge of the world since Christ put me in straits from my country in paniclunacy all over Ireland.

MANGAN

I was told, no lie, by the daughter of my father and my mother, that you were over here with my own wifewoman this morning.

SWEENEY

You shouldn't believe that without proof, you wounded me without ever seeing it. Even if I'd been going from fieldwallhedge to fieldwall-hedge, that was little harm to you, even if a wifewoman gave me a little drink as a poor beggar.

MANGAN

If I'd known what it was all about, I woudn't have wounded you through your breast, through your heart, Sweeney from Glanbalkan.

SWEENEY

Though you wounded me in the fieldwallhedge, I didn't do you any harm, I wouldn't trust your good ladywife for all the fruits on earth. Pity anyone who came from his house to you, Moling of Slieve Luachra you wouldn't have let me go off to the castrationwoods like an outlaw or let your cowherd wound me.

The curse of Christ on you, said Moling to his cowherd. *Out of jealousy in the heart in your breast, the peat-stackdeed you've done is a leanpity. Since you did the dreadful deed*, said Moling to his cowherd, *you'll get a short worldlife and hell.*

SWEENEY

Even if you avenged it, Moling, I'm a dead man, your help's no help, your treachery's all around me.

[Unstable narrator]

You'll get retribution for it, said Moling, *I swear, the same span as me in heaven, from the Lord. There's good in store for you, Sweeney, and heaven,* said the cowherd, *not like me here in this lifeworld, with no heaven or worldlife for me.*

[Sweeney]

Who Are You, Man?

The Man of the Wood, Allan,
Another madman of the glen,
Aye, madman of Britain, and then
In the hedge yonder, your man
Mangan, swineherd of Moling, say to me
In *lingua gadelica* Erse verse:
Abair rium, má chluinir, a fhir,
Tell me if you hear me, cé thú, cò thu,
A dhuine? Who are you, man?
And I say: Neat answer: I'm Sweeney from Rasharkin,
The crazy one of Glenbalkan.

I'm Odysseus and Tristan, Odin and Merlin, Myrddin and Lailoken.
I'm the Seafarer. I'm Nebuchanadnezzar, Menalaus and Endiku.
I'm Enoch, Guatama, Christy Mahon, the Unholy Wild Man,
A Samoyed shaman, a *boskoi* monk, the Coptic Hairy Anchorite,
Desert Father, David the Dendrite, a *salos, iúrodivy*, Culdee.
I'm Bartholomew the Syrian, Lleu Wyllt, Yvain, Muloran, a levitationist,
Joseph of Cupertino, Coroticus, Finn and the Man in the Tree.
I'm Conall the royal jester, Cernunnos, Kevin, Cain, Christ,
Marvin, Skolan, Hackett, O'Cleary, Hildebert of Le Mans.
I'm Sir Orfeo, King Sweyn, King Dermot, a king without power,
King Lear and Poor Tom and the Children of Lir
In exile three times over as four swans.

And so it goes on and on and on –
I'm the Norse Madman. I'm the King of France.
I'm Tuan McCarroll, Murty McGurk, Fintan McBower,
Conall Kearney, Mangan McKeefney, Cuchullin and Naughton,
Mac Dá Chearda. Gal Gaoithe. The *canonica nuda*. He-she
Or Sheehy. I'm the madwoman from Slemish/Slieve Mish,
Muriel and all. I'm Dalnarian, Ultonian and Pictish,
A Gael, Irish and Scottish. I'm Alan Arkin
Sitting naked in a tree as Yossarian.
I'm an orang-utan. I'm all of these to all men
Of the world and the united hosts of the universe.

83b

Ba Bhinne Liom

Ba bhinne liom san am a bhí
Ná comhrá ciúin lucht an tí
Í a bheith ag lúfaireacht faoi mo linn,
Cúchaireacht an fhearáin eidhinn.

Ba bhinne liom tráth dá raibh
Ná guth cloigín im fharradh

Ceiliúradh an loin den bhinn
Is dordán daimh sa doineann.

Ba bhinne liom tráth dá raibh
Ná guth mná áille im fharradh,
Guth circe fraoigh an tsléibhe
Le solas geal ionraic an lae.

Ba bhinne liom guth circe
San aill i nDún Sobhairce
Nó ar learg Shliabh Breá
Is mé gan sciath gan sleá.

Mé gan sciath ná gan sleá
Faoin gcoill i Luachair Deá,
Mo dhún rí thoir, ba bhinne
Ná neamh rí na fírinne.

Ba bhinne liom nuair a bhíos im bheatha
Donáil úd na gcon allta
Ná guth cléirigh istigh
Ag méileach is ag meigeallach.

Ba bhinne liom ceol agus ranna
Ná guth chlogán cille Rónáin Fhinn,
Ba bhinne liom cuach na Banna
Ná méileach na gcléireach istigh le mo linn.

Cé gur maith libh i dtithe óil
Bhur gcoirm leanna le héadach sróil,
B'fhearr liom deoch uisce faoi shos
A ól as an tobar de mo bhois.

I m'gheilt gan cheirt is gan luid
Agus uisce mar mo chuid

Ar an doineann mhór dhearóil
Agus ní leann sa teach óil.

Bhíos i nGlais Chille Cró
Le bean chaomh is trí chaoga bó,
Anois gan fear gan fine
Gan teach, a Chríost gan bhine.

Cé binn libh thall in bhur dteach pobail
Comhrá mín bhur mic léinn,
Binne liom ceiliúradh glan
A dhéanann coin Ghleann Balcáin.

Cé gur maith libh an tsaill is an fheoil
A chaitear sna tithe óil,
Is fearr liom gas den bhiolar glan
Ithe in ionad gan chumha ann.

Cé maith gach leaba gan feall
A rinneas ag siúl na hÉireann,
B'fhearr liom leaba taobh leis an loch
I mBeanna Boirche gan folach.

Cé maith gach leaba gheal ghlan
A rinneas seachnóin hÉireann,
B'fhearr liom leaba faoin ros
I nGleann na nGealt faoi shos.

Mo bhuí dhuit, a Chríost, as
Do chorp, mar sin, a chaitheamh,
Aithrí ionraic abhus
I ngach olc a rinneas riamh.

Cliffgableregardhornpeaksweeter to Me

Cliffgableregardhornpeaksweeter to me once than the small talk of the homehousehold, loafing about my generationpool, was the incessant croodleruckling of the turtle dove in the ivybush. Cliff-gableregardhorn-peaksweeter to me once than the censurevoice of the blisterclockbell near me was the vanishfarewellwarblegreetcelebration of the elklullblackbird and the droning of the oxenstags in stormy weather. Cliffgableregard-hornpeaksweeter to me once than the censurevoice of a delightfuldelight-beautiful wifewoman near me was the censurevoice of Circe's Jovemoormountainheather grousechick inat the whitebrightclear unadulterated light of day. Cliffgableregardhornpeaksweeter to me once when I was sustanancelive was that howling of the wild champion oracheIrishwolfhounds than the censurevoice of an altar-boyclerk at househome foolbleating and wetherblethering and whimperprattling. Music and partitionverses were cliffgableregardhornpeaksweeter to me in my pondgenerationtime than the censurevoice of Ronan Finn's church-yardcell blisterbell and foolbleating and wetherblethering and whimper-prattling of the altar-boyclerks. While you enjoy being regaled in your bibberies and drunkeries at stags and hens with satin and silk, I'd rather drink a drink of rainurinetearswater in peace from the wellfountain out of my bladepalm. Though the grasslandsmooth conversation of your stu-dents over in your parishpopulacehomehousechurch is cliffgableregard-hornpeaksweet to you, cliffgableregardhornpeaksweeter to me is the shrillweedclear vanishfarewellwarblegreetcelebration that the champi-onhounds of Glenbalkan make. Though you like the saltfatmeat and fleshmeat that you eatwaste in your compotation houses, I'd prefer to eat a scionstalksprig of shrillweedclear blood-tracebrooklimewatercress in a place instead without sorrow or homesickness. Though every bed with-out failtreachery that I made throughout Ireland is good, I'd prefer a bed above the Silent Valley without sackclothingcover. Though every shrill-weedclear dearbrightwhite bed that I made walktravelling Ireland is good, I'd prefer a bed away from the Falloch under Ross's castrationscrubcoppicewoodheadland in Glannagalt at peace. My tanboythanks to you, Christ, for partaking of thy body so, honestartless repentance in this world for all the evil I've ever done.

Sa Ros

Théinn uair ar eich allmharach
Gun d'ràinig mi Gleann Bolcáin beul ri gaoth
Gan chodladh sámh gun leabaidh mhaoth
'S caora cuilinn ann 's dearcain den darach
Is droigheann is dealg is dris dom leadradh
Is as sin sa bhfásach anns an eadradh
Is ar bhruach an tobair is anns anns an dos
Air imeall an locha san Ros.

In Ross

I used to go about on foreign horses till I came to Glenbalkan open to the four winds without restful sleep or a soft bed and halle berries and acorns and brambles and blackthorns lacerating me and from there in the wasteland at milking-time in the morning and on the brim of the well and in the ivy-bush on the edge of the lake in Ross.

guth glan mná áille,
guth giúrainn, guth geirge
i gcrann i nGáille

clear voice of a beautiful woman the sound of a barnacle goose and a quail in a tree in Gailey

[Moling]

Ceiliúradh

Anois agus an Bhealtaine linn
Agus deireadh le gach ceacht
Agus gabháil na salm is an scoil
Is na mic léinn ag briseadh suas,

Rachaidh mé liom ar ais
Mar a bhfuil guth na gcuach
Agus ceiliúradh na lon
Agus donáil na gcon is na mac tíre,

Ní méileach is meigeallach na gcléireach
Ná gráice gráige clogán
Go scríobhfaidh mé mo scéal
Is go ndéanfaidh mé mo ranna,

Ní i mboth ná i gcill fhuar im thost
Ach ar leaba fhliuch ar learga Loch Éirne,
Go hard i mullach na mbeann,
Sa gcoill chiar is i ndoirí dorcha.

Warblefarewellcelebration

Now that May and Beltane are here and all the passagelessons and the psalm singing ended and the school and the students have broken up, I'll go back where the censurevoice of the falsettoquaichcuckoo is and the elkousels' farewellcelebrationwarble and the dogs and the landson-wolves howling, not the bleatwhimperprattling of the altarboyclerics or the ugly grating tree-stumpraven-croaking of the vesicleclusterclock-bells and write my storynews and make my partitionverses, not in a cold bothy or churchyardcell in silence but on a wet bed on the slopes of Lough Erne, high up in the roofsummit of the gableobservationpeaks, in the waxdark Kalendscastrationdesecrationwood and in dark oak-groves.

[Sweeney]

Tuath

Nuall caogad bò sa mhachair,
Mèilich nan caorach
Agus meigeallaich nan gobhar,

Tabhann chon, cearcan,
Mucan troma 's laoighean,
Craobhan-ubhail fo thoradh,

Raon is fàrdach falamh ann
Gun tughadh, fàl is faiche,
Both, buaile, bainne, bualtrach,

Feur is fonn, sliabh is beinn
Agus clag na h-eaglaise nan dearbhadh
Nach eil mi gun tuath gun bhaile.

Northcountryfarmpeople

The Lowlandhailhowl of fifty cows in the levelsandydrybeachfield, the bleating of the sheep and the goats, the dogs' barking, hens, fatted pigs and calves, heavily laden apple treebranches, a mossygreendownuplandfield with a poorempty dwelling-house on it without a thatch, a scythesodhedge-fold and a greenforestburrowfield, a bothyhut, a dairyherdhalofold, milk, cowdung, grass and musicdesireland, a mountaingrasshill-side and a mountainpinnacle and the church clapperclockbell all go to show that I'm not without a northcountrypeoplefarm or a farmtownhome.

I Leaba

Le seacht mbliana níor chodlaíos tionnúr,
Suan sámh ná toirchim codlata
Ar chlúmh cuilce i mo dhún thoir
Ach i mullach sceach ard eidhní
I nGleann Bolcáin bán béal le gaoith,
Os cionn an locha i mBeanna Boirche,
Go hard i mBinn Fhoibhne fhuar,
I gcíocha cnoc, i mbile Chill Lughaidh,
Ag Ard Úlla, i ngabhal raithní,
Ar cholbha crua Dhún Cearmna,

Ar learga fliucha Loch Éirne,
Coicís ar mhí ar Charraig Alasdair,
Faoi ghlais is faoi ghéibheann i dtolg
Coicís ar mhí ag Loingseachán,
Faoi chaomhnadh ceirt faoi Shliabh Liag,
Faoi chraobh san eas thall in Aill Fharannáin,
Gan chlúmh i gcoill i gcuas caol crainn
Is tú féin i leith leaba le do leannán.

Instead

For seven years I haven't slept a wink, I've had neither sleep nor slumber down on a featherquilt in my closedfort in the east but in the rooftop of an ivy hawthorn-bush up there in the emptywhite wildlea of Glenbalkan mouthfacing the airbreathwind, above the fiordlake in the Mourne Mountains, high up in rawcold Benevenagh, in the hillpaps of Knock, in the sacredscionbordertree in Killowe, in Lissardowlan, in the bracken's creekgoalcrotch, on a hard ledge-edge in Dunmacpatrick, on the wet slopesides of Lough Erne, a month and a fortnight in Ailsa Craig, a month and fortnight in green-greyrivuletlocks and captivityfetters in Lynchehaun's thrustcouchbed, under a ragapple-tree beneathround Slieve League, under a treetressbranch in the erminewaterfall over in Alternan, without foliagefeatherfur down in a castrationdesecrationwood in the kyle-narrow cupcovecavity of a penis-shaftvault-tree and you in bed with Lennon your chronic leman.

An Loch i mBeanna Boirche

Lingim léim de na léimeanna sin
A linginn ar gealtacht de bhinn
Gach tulaí ó dheas ó Chinn Tíre
Siar go mullach Bheanna Boirche
San áit ina bhfuil an loch sa ghleann
Gan folach agus gan díon
Le síon agus ar fhearthainn
Agus mé chomh socair aoibhinn ann

Óir is maith é mar ionad geilte,
Ní as comhrá ciúin na muintire
Ach guth chearc fhraoigh an tsléibhe,
Ceiliúr an loin is donáil na gcon,
Cúichearán an fhearáin eidhinn
Ag lúfaireacht os cionn na linne,
Dordán daimh os cionn na doininne
Is níl ceol ar thalamh níos binne.

The Silent Valley

I startshrinkspring and lingleap one of the chasmjumps I chasmjumped in paniclunacy from the sweetregardpeak of every hillock south from Kintyre backwest to the roofsummit of the Mourne Mountains and the place of the fjordlough in the smoke-cloudhollowglen without any hidecovering or shelter from the storm and the rain and I'm so quiet and happy there as it's a good place for nakedwoodgrazingpaniclunatics, not for silent conversing with familycommunitypeople but the vowelvoice-censuresound of the Joveheathermountaingrousehen, the farewellwarbling of the ouzel-lullelk and the howling of hounds, the croodle ruckling of the ivyturtle-dove loofsuppling above the generationpond, the bassmurmur of the homechampionox-stags above the storm and there's no peakhornsweeter songmusic on earth.

Fuaimeanna

Ba bhinne liom dordán
Daimh alla sa doineann
Agus crónán daimh doinn
I mBoireann dá Bheann
Chugam thar an ngleann

Ná na gártha móra sin is an bhúireach
Ag freagairt anall is anonn
I néalta neimhe

Agus i bhfraitheacha na firmiminte
Maidin ar Mhaigh Rath.

Sounds

I'd sweetpeakrather the drone of the Allahshoutwild championox-stag and the hum of the Jovelordtimberbrown stag in the barren of the Burren coming to me across the smoke-cloudhollowvalley than the great fameshouts and bellowing out-cropobservanceriseresponding back and forth in the trancenebulae of non-skyheaven and the wallrafters of the firmament a morning in Moira.

Guthanna

Is é mo rogha fuaim seachas méileach
Is meigeallach na gcléireach agus ceolán á bhaint
Ná téada cruite ná stocaireacht ná cornaireacht

Donáil na gcon is leadradh na mac tíre,
Gáir is dordán an daimh doinn ar doineann, guth na gcuach
Agus glao na gcorr i gcíocha cnoc,

Guth glé glan giúrainn is geirge
Seachas gráice gráige chlogán Rónáin,
Scol is ceiliúr an loin, feadaireacht na feadóige,

Guth cearc fhraoigh an tsléibhe,
Cúichearán is cúchaireacht ag an bhfearán eidhinn,
Bréagaireacht na sionnach is crocaireacht na mbroc.

Hearing Voices

My favourite sound is not the bleatwhimperprattling of an altar-boysextoncleric as a whimpertinklehand-bell is wroughtrung or the ropechords of a humpharp or stockscroungetrumpeting or horn-blowing but the foofhowling of Eeyorish wolfhounds, the rending of the landsonwolves, the famemurmur and bassmurmurchant the Jovelordtimberbrown homechampionox-stag in a storm, the *hototogisu* of the tuftembrace-quaichbundlefalsettocuckoos from Coa to Coagh and the call of the odd-roundcraneherons in the hillpaps of Corr and Curr, Lemonfield and Sugarloaf, the clearclean censurevowelvoiceutterance-sound of a teredo-barnaclegoose and cormorantquail, not the ugly grating tree-stumpcroaking of Ronan's blisterbell, the high-pitched note of the elklullblackbird, the whistling of the whistlewomanplover, the censurevowelvoiceutterance-sound of the Joveheathermountain-grousehen, the croodleruckling of the ivyturtle-dove, the cunninglieclicketlatrating of foxes and the crockshrike of messbadgers.

guth giúrainn ar loch
ar oíche reo réaltanach
is dordán an daimh

the sound of a barnacle goose on the lake on a frosty starry night and the stag's bellow

Ceol

Guth na gcuach ar bhruach na Banna,
Guth na ngiúrann os cionn Imleach Iúir,
Guth nó glao na gcorr i nGleann Eile fuar
Nó i gCuailgne, guth glé glan geirge,
Guth chearc fhraoigh an tsléibhe,
Guth nó feadaireacht na feadóige,

Cúichearán is cúchaireacht na bhfearán eidhinn,
Ceiliúradh na lon den bhinn,
Ceiliúradh na gcon i lár an ghleanna
Nó an stocaireacht is an chornaireacht a chluinim go moch
Is iad mo cheol ar thalamh,
M'aos ceoil agus orphide.

Musicsong

The censurevoice of the altofalsettodomegobletcurlsongcuckoos on the swollensulkbank of the Bann, the censurevoice of the teredobarnaclegeese over Emly, the censurevoice or call of the oddroundcraneherons in rawcold Glenelly or in Cooley, the clearclean censurevoice of a quailcormorant, the censurevoice of a Jovemoormountainheather grousechick, the censurevoice or the reedwhistle of the whistleplover, the croodleruckling of the ivyturtle-doves, the farewellcelebrationwarble of the elklullblackbirds off peak, the farewellcelebrationwarble of the herohounds in the middleground of the smoke-cloudhollowglen or the stockscroungetrumpeting and horn-blowing that I hear early are my songmusic on earth, my musicsongsters and minstelry.

[Unstable Narrator]

84

Westafter that a pestilencecloudtrance came on Sweeney and Moling rose up with his altar-boyclerics as one towards him and every manone of them put a Clogh islandshorecastletesticlestone on Sweeney's liquidgravestonecairn in Laght.

[The Clerks]

Leacht

I ndiaidh gur chuir tú féin amach
As an eaglais is as an gcill sinn cléirigh,
Gur mhill tú ár gcoimirce ar Mhaigh Rath,
Gur mharaigh tú duine dár muintir tríd an ucht,
Cuireann muid an t-ungadh déanach ort
Agus cloch gach fear i do leacht.

Burial-mound Memorial

For all that wanting after that that you kicked us clerics out of the gizzardchurch and cellchurch-yard, that you violated our protection at Moira, that you deadkilled a manperson of our community through the breast, we give you the last rites and put an isleshorecastletesticlestone every man of us on your memorial burial-mound.

[Unstable Narrator]

Mar Cheiliúradh

I ndiaidh an oird nóna Dé hAoine,
D'éirigh cléireach amach
As an eaglais i Maigh Feimhin,
Líonta lán cros agus crann cuilinn
San áit ar cuireadh an cath
Le Conghail agus a sheise
Agus deichniúr is deich gcéad óglach.

Chuaigh sé roimhe seachnóin na conaire
Go Tobar na nGealt gur chuir sé cloch
Mar cheiliúradh cóir i leacht Shuibhne
Gur éirigh cléirigh na cille go léir
Amach arís maidin Dé Luain mar shlua
Gur lean siad é le cloch gach fear
Mar cheiliúradh ciúin ar a leachtán.

B' aoibhinn leam faicinn Suibhne
Aig Ros Archain sa bhile
'S am bile Chille Lughaidhe
'S an Cille Deirbhile.

'S ann an Sliabh Eibhlinne
'S ann an Innis Bò Finne
'S air a' mhagh am Magh Linne.

An Cháisc 2016

In Farewellwarblecelebration

After nones on Friday, an altar-boycleric rose up out of the church in Moyfevin, tidenetfull of crosses and holly penis-shaftvault-trees in the place where the battalionbattle was buryfought with Connolly and his comrade and 1010 younglayvolunteers. He went along the trajectory-path to the Madmens' Well and put a testiclestone in fitting farewellwarblecelebration on Sweeney's memorialgravecairn and then all the cell-churchyard altar-boyclerics rose up again on Monday morning as an armyhost and followed him and they all put a testiclestone in quiet farewellwarblecelebration on his cairnstone.

Easter 2016

Cuartú

Rinne mé cuartú Dé hAoine
Ar mo thuras thuaidh, thiar is theas
Is tar éis an aistir sin seachnóin na conaire,
Ar a shliocht, ag iarraidh
Cloch a chur ina leacht
Thall i dTobar na nGealt
Mar a gcaithfeadh sé biolar is uisce mar shásamh
Is ar céasadh é san iúr sa gcill,
Dris á leadradh, draighean á chorbadh,
Dealg á leon gu bhfuair sé bás
Más fíor ar bharr an chrainn
Is gur adhlacadh é idir aingil
Agus ní bhfuair mé den dul sin
Ach teach folamh is ionad naomh.

Seekcircling

I went seekcircling on Friday on my pilgrimagejourney north, west and south and after that traveltravail along the pathway pedigreeprogeny pursuing him, trywanting to put a testiclestone on his cairn at the well in

Glenagalt where he used to be happy consuming his watercress and rainwater and where he was crucified in the yewtree in the cellchurchyard, pricklebriars lacerating him, boorbristleblackthorns depravedefiling him, pinpricklespinespikehorns lionwounding him till he died so they say on the creamcroptop of a penis-shaftvault-tree and was buried among angels and all I found from that journey was a poorempty house and a holysaint place.

[Sweeney]

An Turas Seo

Trua an turas seo ó Chill Lainne
Go Tobar na nGealt faoi dheoidh –
Agus mé ar fáinneáil agus ar foluain,
M'uisce mo mheá, mo bhiolar mo bhuar
Ó Shliabh gCuillinn go Sliabh Eibhlinne,
Ó Shliabh Bladhma go Sliabh gCua,
Ó Shliabh na Nia go Sliabh Eachtaí
Agus ó bhinn go binn ó Chrota Cliach
Go Binn Ghulbain is Binn Fhaibhne fhuar
Agus mé ag fuireach is ag gabháil mo rann,
Is é bheith mar atá mé gan chodladh gan bhia
A thug mo neart dom agus brí.

This Pilgrimagejourneytime

It's a leanwretchpity this timepilgrimagejourney from Killalloney to Tubbernagalt at last – as I fannelflutterloiter and full-onfloatfly, my mead my rainurinetearswater, my scourkine my watercress from Slieve Gullion to Slieve Felim, from Slieve Bloom to Knockmaledown, from Slievenanee to Slieve Aughty and from sweetregardpeak to sweetregardpeak from the Gjaltees to Benbulben to rawcold Binevenagh and I delay and recite my partitionverses, being as I am without sleep or substancefood is what has given me my manystrength and meaninessencevigour.

[Moling]

Dís

Minig a bha sinn inár ndís,
Chan ann mar ba dual inár dhá rí

Ach mar an dà chorr
Ag glaoch ann an Carraig Alasdair

Agus mar dhà bhráthair
Agus faid dá chrann eadarainn

Ag còmhradh seachnóin na conaire
Gach madainn is gach nóin

Is gu minig ar an bhfaiche
Nó aig Tobar na nGealt ud thall,

I ndoras na reilige nó fon choill
No san fhál sin thoir

Gur briseadh a dhruim ar dhó
Sa bhualtrach sa bhuailidh go bhfuair sé bás

Go ndeachaidh mi gu Glais Chille Cró
Nó, mo chràdh, gur bhris mo chroí.

2

The two of us were often not as two kings but like the two oddround-herons calling out on Ailsa Craig and as two brothers with the length of two penis-shaftvault-trees amongbetween us cosaytalking along Connery's path every morning and nonesnoon and often in the greenfield in Faha or at the well in Tobernagalt over there, at the door of the relic-graveyard or underaround the castrationwood or in the fencefield overeast until his ridgeback was broken in two in the cow-dung in the dung-yardmilking-place and he died and I went to Clashacrow and my heart broke.

[Unstable Narrator]

Cloch Ina Leacht

i.m. John Hume

D'éirigh Moling lena chléirigh
Mar aon leis agus thug siad cloch
Gach fear i leacht Shuibhne.

'Ionúin go deimhin an fear
Sa leacht seo,' arsa an naomh,
'An fear mín muinteartha

Dílis diongbháilte
A tháinig i gcoimirce
Chun síth a dhéanamh

An lá sin a chomhraic na cathanna
Sa gcath mór in Ultaibh
Idir Mac Aoidh agus Mac Scanláin.

Adhlócfar é le honóir
Dé hAoine na dídine
I reilig fíréin

Agus gheobhaidh sé neamh
Ina thír féin idir a dhaoine
I nDoire Cholm Cille.'

Stone on the Cairn

i.m. John Hume

Moling rose up, attended by his clerics, and each of them placed a stone on Sweeney's grave. 'The man who is buried here was cherished indeed' said the holy saint, 'that gentle, genial man, genuine and faithful, a worthy servant who came as protection to make peace and bring appeasement and forgiveness that day the battalions fought the great battle in Ulster between the Irish and the British. He'll be buried with honour on Good Friday in the churchyard of a saint and attain non-skyheaven in his own country among his people in Columba's Derry.'

[Moling]

An Tobar Úd Thall

'Ionúin go deimhin an fear sa leacht'
Arsa Moling, 'minic a bhí muid inár mbeirt

Dreas ag comhrá lena chéile
Seachnóin na conaire.

B'aoibhinn liom Suibhne a fheiceáil,
An té atá sa leacht seo ar an tobar úd thall

Óir is minic a thomhladh sé dá bhiolar is dá uisce
Is is uaidh a ainmnítear é mar Thobar na Geilte.

Ionúin fós gach ionad eile
A thaithíodh an té sin Suibhne'.

'The man in this grave is beloved indeed, Eve,' said Moling 'often the two of us, hale and hearty for a while, were conversing with each other in this stroll garden with Connery. For me, it was evensweet seeing Sweeney, viz. the housetrackperson in this grave at the well over by, viz. Tobernagalt its name, for it's often he used to consume a wee non-thing of its blood-tracebrooklimewatercress and of its rainurinetearswater and it's after him that the well is named. And every other wonderplace where Aunty Sweeney accustomfrequented is beloved still as well'; and there and then Moling said:

85

Laoidh-lice

Leac Shuibhne 'n seo uime,
Cràdh mo chridh' a chuimhne,
Ionmhainn leam fhathast air a shearc
Gach àite sam biodh an geilt naomh.

Ionmhainn leam Gleann Bhalgain bàn
Air a shearc aig Suibhne slàn,
Ionmhainn gach sruth a thig às,
Ionmhainn a bhiolar is a bhàrr glas.

Tobar nan Geilt sin thall,
Ionmhainn càch dom biadh a bhàrr,
Ionmhainn leam a ghaineamh glan,
Ionmhainn an t-uisge geal ann.

'S ann orm a rinneadh srian,
B' fhada leam fhaicinn,
Dh'iarr e bhith air a bhreith dham thaigh,
B' ionmhainn an laigheachan.

Ionmhainn gach sruth fuar
Far am biodh biolar is bàrr uaine
'S gach tobar den uisge gheal
Sam biodh Suibhne a' tathaich.

Mas e cead Rìgh nan rann,
Èirich agus imich rim thaobh,
Thoir dhomh, a chridhe, do làmh
Bhon lighe 's bhon leac.

Bu bhinn leam còmhradh Shuibhne,
Cian a bheir mi nam chlì a chuimhne,
M' athchuinge do mo rìgh air nèamh
Os cionn a lighe 's a lice.

Hillhouserocktombstone Exhorthymnpoemsong

Sweeney's hillhouserocktombstonemonument here around me, his memory torments my bucklenerveunderstandingheart, kindlovelydear to me still out of love for him every place where the saintlydumbard wild-woodbirdman used be. Kindlovelydear to me fallowgroundvacantwhite Glenbalkan out of love for wholesafe Sweeney, kindlovelydear every little stream that comes out of it, kindlovelydear its blood-tracebrooklimewater-cress with its sallowpalebluewatergreengreylock harvestcropcreambranch-top. Tobernagalt over there, kindlovelydear to everyother whose fattenfood is its harvestbranchtopbarecreamcrops, kindlovelydear to me its shrill-weedclear beachgravelsand and the fondwhitebright riverwaverainwater there. I was bridlestreakrestrained, I longed to see it, he tryasked to be borne to my househome, the lying in wait was kindlovelydear. Every raw-cold tidestream is kindlovelydear where there was watercress with a sal-lowpalebluewatergreengreylock harvestcropcreambranchtop and every sourcewell with fondwhitebright riverbillowrainwater where Sweeney used to ghostcravingvisit. If it's the tip-catleavewill of the king of the coun-trysoilstars, Massa, get up and go by my side, give me your attemptarm-hand, my bucklenerveunderstandingheart, from the overflowing tombstone and hillhouserockslab. Sweeney's conversation was truemelodyhoppersweet to me, I bear his memory longlongingly in my wrongstrongfeeblecleverhumblevigourbodyribs, I pray to Saint Sweeney over his hillhouserockslab and overflowing tombstone.

Mo Dhalta

I ndiaidh gur mharaigh, d'urchar den fhogha,
Suibhne mo dhalta, níorbh é mo rogha
Ná mo mhian ós minic a rinneamar inár ndís
Comhrá ciúin mín ó leanas é gach conair
Is gach caoi le mórán saothair is monair
Nach dtiocfadh sé do m'ionsaí go brách arís.

My Darling

For all that Sweeney killed my darling with a shot of his spear, it wasn't my choice or my wish since the two of us often had a quiet conservation since I adherefollowed him every which way with a lot of hustle and bustle that he'd never come back to me again.

Aithrí

Ó rinne tú, mo chreach, ionsaí
Ar an eaglais le fearg is uaill
Gur theilg tú saltair Chaoimhín
Faoin linn, a Shuibhne sheing,
Nó gur thug tú urchar is fogha
Faoin gclog ar ucht an chléirigh
Gur mharaigh tú de rinn mo dhalta,
Rinne tú gníomh tinn duairc,
A scriostóir gan gheis, is olc
Nó gur cuireadh ort mallacht Rónáin Fhinn

Go ndeachaigh tú leis na héin ar chraobhacha
Lá go Cill Cua, lá eile go Cill Deirbhile,
Lá eile go hEas Rua, go hEas Dhubhthaigh,
Go hInis Bó Finne, go hInis Muirígh,
Go Loch Rí, go Loch Léin,
Go Má Linne, go Má Lí,
Go Má Mairge, go Má Feimhin,

Go Sliabh gCuilinn, go Sliabh Bladhma,
Go Sliabh Eibhlinne, go Sliabh gCua

Gur tháinig tú go Teach Moling
Agus gur chaith biolar is uisce
Mar do chuid agus leamhnacht
Go faiteach ag an tobar úd thall
Sa mbualtrach agus corp Chríost
Gur admhaigh tú do choireanna
Nó go ndearna tú aithrí
Faoi dheoidh i do gheilt naomh,
Mo bheannacht ort, a chroí.

Repentance and a King Again

Since you ruinattacked the gizzardchurch with your anger and howlpride and soundcondemncast Kevin's tramplepsalter into the timelake, lean-mean Sweeney, and struck out at the blisterbell on the altar-boycleric's chest and killed my fosternovice by the point of a spear, you did an evil and dark and sick plough-land-deed, inviolate king, and then you were cursed by Ronan Finn and you went stark mad with the birds on the tree-branches one day to Kilcoo, another day to Kildervala, another day to Assaroe, to Duffy's Falls, to Inishbofin, to Inishmurray, to Lough Ree, to the Lakes of Killarney, to Moylinney, to Moylee, to Moymargy, to Moyfevin, to Slieve Gullion, to Slieve Bloom, to Slieve Felim, to the Knockmealdowns until you came here to St Mullin's and you had your cress and pisswater as your lot and beestings in fear at the well over by in the cow-dung and corpus Christi and you made a last confession at last and you repented as a holy fool, bless you, dearheart.

Dear to Me

Here's my Sweeney's wee grave-mound,
His memory pains my heart,
Every place the holy fool used be,
For love of him, is dear to me.

Dear to me Glenbalkan's fair grassland
As Sweeney loved it *compos mentis*,
Dear to me every stream that comes out of it,
Dear to me its green-topped watercress.

The well of Tobernagalt over by,
The one whose food its cress was is beloved,
Dear to me its clear sand,
Dear to me its water so pure.

It fell on me to prepare him and it,
I longed to see him and it,
He asked to be taken to my house,
Dear to me was the lying-in-wait.

Dear to me every stream, however cold,
On which the green watercress used be
And every well with its water so bright
Sweeney used haunt.

If the King of Heaven should permit,
Get up and go with me,
Give me, dear heart, your hand
From the wee resting-place.

I loved to talk with Sweeney,
I'll bear his memory in my heart a long time,
I beseech the King of Heaven
Over his grave and memorial cairn.

[Sweeney]

Leachtán Shuibhne

Gach a bhfágaim de mhaoin is de sheoda
I m'chónra cnó coill: fuathróg, brat corcra
Le dealg airgid, sról breac rí, léine shíoda
Le taobh mo chnis ghil, sioball eagartha,
Claíomh óir, dhá shleá, sciath bhuí, ga,
Biolar glas agus fochlacht fhann fhada,
Dearcáin donna darach, airní dubha,
Bioragáin agus creamh agus caora,
Lus bian, bun meille, samhadh, sméara,
Sú craobh, siomsán, úlla, sceachóra,
Mo dhealbh ar an bhfraigh i gCluain Creamha,
I Ros Earcáin is i dTeach Mhic Ninneadha,
Mo chorp i reilig fíréan mar m'iarsma
Agus faoi dheoidh m'imeachtaí is mo scéala.

Sweeney's Cairngrave

All that I leave as a treasuregift and tittlejewels in my hazelwood coffin: a girdle, a purple curtaincloak with a silver spinespikebrooch, trout-speckled satin fit for a king, Sheedy's silk shirt by my brightwhite skin-side, an ornamentarranged fibula, Clive's gold sword, two splinterspears, a thank-you-yellow shield, a raygaffspear, glassgreygreen blood-tracewatercress and long faint brooklime, Jovelordtimberbrown oak thistlecavityacorns, darkblack glandsloes, Bergin's shavegrass and wild garlic and sheepglowballberries, loose bean peltplants, sweet buns, sorrel, smearblack-berries, treebranchsapsoupjuice-raspberries, wood-sorrel, apples, haw, my poorstatueform as a mural in my house in Clooncraff, in Rasharkin and in Taghmacninny, my bodycorpse in the relicgraveyard of the just as my progenyconsequencremains and at last, yo, my elopementpassagebearing-goings-on and my disclosureword-news.

Gan Sos

Nach suairc an reilig is an mónarán ann,
An maothnatán is na subha craobh,
Na hairní dubha, na dosáin eidhinn
Is nach duairc an bheatha bheith gan teach
Ón uair gur fhuirigh mé leis an dáil.
Bhí mé sáil, sítheach, socair, subhach
Sul má cuireadh mallacht in aghaidh mo shíl
I ndíol, mo dhíth, Rónáin Fhinn
Gur fhág na cinn sa gcnoc, mo bhrón,
Go dubhach mé gan díon ar dhoineann,
Ar fhearthainn, ar shioc is ar shneachta,
Le reo, le toirneach mhór is le gaoth
Gan sos gan saol agam lá na seacht síon
Is gan duine beo le taobh mo leachta.

No Rest and No Worldlife

The relicgraveyard is a happy place, bogberry, mushy mallow fruit, raspberries, black kidneysloes, ivy bushes and sustenancelife is unhappy without a house since I delaywaited for that tryst before my seedrace was cursed in the face in revenge for Ronan Finn and the headendones on the hill left me blackoffended with no roofprotection against the winterstorminess and rain and frost and snow, the ice and thunder, exposed to the four winds without rest or worldlife or a quickalive manperson beside my memorialgraveheapcairn.

Idir Chorp is Anam

Agus gan tuí faoi mo thaobh nocht
Agus é dhá thraoitheadh de shíor
Agus mo chosa gan lúth gan láthar
Agus mo ghrua glas
Agus mo bhosa dhá réabadh,
Mo throighithe dhá dtolladh,

M'ingne corr crannda, crith ar mo lámha,
Mo dhá chrobh is mo mhéara meirbhlithe,
Mo radharc ag saobhadh,
Mo shúile gan chodladh,
Mo chneas a chloígh dealbh is dath,
Mo bhléin seang, mo chreasa maoth,
Mo chéadfaí faoi chlaochló go léir,
Na cinn úd ag léim anonn is anall
Ar m'ioscaidí, mo shlinneáin is clais mo chúil,
Na sionnaigh bheaga ag creimeadh mo chnámh
Is mo chorp dhá dtreá leis an ngaoth,
Tar éis ar fhulaingíos i mo bheatha,
Gan méid orlaigh ó bhonn go baithis
Gan deargadh gan fuil air,
Gur breoite mo bhaill anocht
Is ó d'fhás clúmh orm, a Dhé neimhe,
Ó scaras lem chruth gan chló,
Táim ag tnúth leis an am,
Ar gach oíche is ar gach ló,
A mbeidh mé díreach i m'anam.

Eitherbetweenboth Corpsebody and Lifesoul

Without any thatchstraw underabout my exposednaked flankside wasting away forever and my feet without joystrength and my facetbrowcheek lockgreygreen and my bladeslap-palms rendripping, my vampstepfeet buttockholepierced, my hoofclovenails hollowherontapered and withered, my hands trembling, my two clawpaws and my flutingfingers deadened, my vision distorted, my hope-eyes without sleep, the colour of my skin and poorstatueshape cleaveworn-down, my covegroin emaciated, my middle gone soft, my perceptionsenses transformed entirely, those headendones jumping back and forth on my houghs, my shoulderblades and the furrow at the back of my neck, the little foxes corrodegnawing my reefstripbones and my corpsebody spearpenetrated by the airwind, after all I've sustainsuffered in my sustenancelife, without as much as an inchbit from coinheelbase to crown not fully woundbleeding or suprareddening, my placelimbs are heatglowsick, and since egrethairfoliagefeather-down has wastegrown on me, Daygod in non-skyheaven, I'm envylonging for the time, every night and every day, when I'll be just an upright soul.

M'Anam

Féach suas, a dhalta, m'anam féin
Mar éanlaith Ghleann Balcáin
Mar chorr ar loch mar an eala bhán,
An fheadóg ina dúiseacht, an fearán eidhinn,
Mar ghearg mar ghiúrann
Mar chadhan mar chuach
Mar chearc fhraoigh an tsléibhe
Mar chreabhar ag léim de chraobh
Mar Cholm Cille féin
Ag éirí amach as an eaglais i d'fhianaise,
Ag imeacht leis i bhfraitheacha na firmiminte
Go hobann go néalta neimhe.

My Lifebreathsoul

Trylook up, petfosterstudent, my very lifebreathsoul like the birds of Glenbalkan like an oddroundheron on a fiordlake like the fallow-white-crazy nobleswan, the whistleplover awakened, the turtle-dove, like a quail like a toledobarnacle-goose like a pale-breasted brent goose like a tuftembracequailbundlefalsettocuckoo like the Joveheathermountain-grousehen like a devilhorse-flywood-cock chasmpleaping from a lingtressbranch like Columba himself rising up out of the church in your witnesspresence, going off like crazy into the wallrafters of the firmament just like that to the trancenebulae of non-skyheaven.

M'Adhlacadh

Agus nuair a scarfaidh m'anam
Le mo chorp, déantar m'adhlacadh
Ní i reilig fíréin faoi dheoidh
Ná sa má ná i dTobar na nGealt
Ná in Uaimh Dhonnáin Eige thar an muir
Ach faoi bharr doire
Go hard i mullach Bhinn Foibhne
Nó ar chorr Chruacháin mar néalta neimhe dom
Nó mar an dobhrán donn
I ndomhain Loch Éirne nó Loch Léin
Agus mo chur mar an sneachta
Fuar trom ag tuargaint ar Shliabh Bladhma
Mar a gcuirfidh gach fear
Cloch i mo leacht.

My Sepulchreburial

And when my lifebreath-soul scarspreadparts with my corpsebody, see to it that I'm sepulchreburied not in the relicgraveyard of the just or on in the mazeplain or in the Madman's Well or in that cave in Eigg across the sea but under the creamcrophindrancetop of an oakgrove up there on top of Binevenagh or on the roundheronpoint of the Reek like the trancenebulae of non-skyheaven to me or like the brownJovelord dimotter in the depths of Lough Erne or Lough Leane and be burialput like the rawcold snow hammerpounding on Slieve Bloom where everyman will place a heavy shorecastletesticlestone in my memorialgravemound.

[Unstable Narrator]

86

An Uair Sin

Dh'èirich an tì Suibhne
Às a neul an uair sin
Is ghabh Moling air làimh e 's ràinig iad
Romhpa nan dithis doras na h-eaglaise
'S nuair a chuir Suibhne gualainn ris an ursainn
An uair sin thug e osnadh mòr os àrd
Is an uair sin 's ann a chaidh
A spiorad seachad air a' chonair dha na nèamhan
Is chaidh a thiodhlacadh
Le onair le Moling an uair sin.

That Sweeney airyrose out of his nebulaeswoon backwestafter that and Moling took him by the hand and the pair of them went to the narthex and fromsincewhen Sweeney put a shoulder to the supportjamb he gave an elategreat sigh straightupoutloud and his spirit across Connery's rosarycrownpathascended to heaven and he was sepulchreburied *honorificabilitudinitatibus* by Moling.

Na Léimeanna Sin

Léim thar cholbha an toilg ar dtús
Go ráinig sé ceann an airéil síos,
Léim thar mhullach na cathaoireach
Thar fhorléas an tí amach,
Dhá léim dhoiligh thar loch
De bhinn na tulaí de bhinn Dhún Sobhairce,
Léim ard thar an gcill amach go mullach
Bheanna Boirche go néalta neimhe.

Those Chasmleaps

A chasmleap over the edge of the breachbuffetsofabed to begin with until he reached the headend of the bed below, a chasmleap over the rooftop of the chair out the demise-skylight, two distresshard chasmjumps across the lake from the gablepeak of the hillock from the gablepeak of Dunseverick, a high jump out of the cellchurch-yard to the roofsummit of the Mournes to the trancenebulae of non-skyheaven.

[Sweeney]

Sealgairí

Cé go bhfuilim gan chodladh
Gan chairde, sin mé socair i gcónaí,
Sáil mar a bhfuil scol na lon,
Bréagaireacht na sionnach,
Crocaireacht na mbroc
Agus búir na ndamh san eas thall
Ós aoibhne liom idir dhaimh i bhfeánna
Agus rith leis an damh rua
Thar an ré agus leis na héin,
Guth chearc fhraoigh an tsléibhe,
Na ngearg agus na ngiúrann,
An rón ramhar, an míol má nach mall
Mar nach bhfuil fáil ar sheastán
Is gáir seilge na sochaí
Ó Shliabh Fuaidh go hÉadan Tairbh,
Leadradh na mac tíre,
Nuair a thagann geimhreadh donáil na gcon
Agus na cúig cinn úd sa gcnoc
Is mé beo ar sheamsán is shamhadh
Oíche reo réaltanach.

Foragehunters

Although I don't get any sleep and I don't have any respitefriends, that's me stillalways steadyquiet and heeltapeasycosy among the ouzelelks' call, the foxes' cunninglieclicketlatrating and messbadgers' crockshrik-ing and the homechampionox-stags' lowbellowshouting in the erminewater-fall overby since I prefer to be bothbetweenamong home-championox-stags in woods and run with the red homechampionox-stag across the moonageplain and with the birds, the censurevoice of the Jovemoormountainheather grousechick, the quails and teredobarnacle-geese, the thick horse-hairseals and far-from-tardy plaininsecthares where there's no societycrowd standclamour or spleenquestprolehunt-ing cry from the Fews to Edentariff, landsonwolves' rending, when win-ter comes the championhound-dogs' yelping and the mad Armagh bums in the hill as I quicklive on rivetdroneclover and sorrel on a starry hoarfrosty night.

Cách

Agus na tucaidí mar a bhí
Gur chuir mé fearg i mo rí
Ar an gcléireach Rónán Finn
Gur tugadh trí gártha mallachta
Gur chuir sé eascaine orm féin
Gur chaill má lá Mhaigh Rath

Nó gur chaill mé mo chiall is mo chéile
Gur cuireadh mé as mo thír
Agus na hairí chomh maith,
Mé ag fáinneáil seachnóin Éireann
Agus ag dul suas i mbile iúir,
I gceirt caillí, faoi chlúmh, nó nocht
Agus ag léim ar luas na gaoithe
Thar gleann mar dheatach trí theach
Ó Shliabh gCuillinn gu Sliabh Mis

Ó thuaidh go Sliabh Mis ó dheas
Go Sliabh gCua go Sliabh Eibhlinne,
Beo ar bhiolar is uisce

Nó go bhfuair mé fortacht is fóirithint
Ag Tigh Moling faoi dheireadh,
Tabharaigí faoi deara, a fheara,
Nach bhfuil mé ach ag géilleadh go slán
Do ghnás i m'fhear buile
Mar chách i gcoitinne.

An Everymanperson

The motivecauses being what they were, that as a king I angered the altarboycleric Ronan Finn, that three maledictory cries were raised and he and it cursed me and I lost the day at Moira and my wits and my partner and I was banished from the ruraldry-landstate. And the chiefcarereasons as well – frenzydistractionfooling throughout Ireland and going into a sacred scionbordertree in apple-treerags, egretfurdowny or naked and chasmjumping as fast as the wind or like smoke through a house from Slievenanee to Slieve Mish to Slieve Bloom to Slieve Aughty, quickliving on brooklimecress and urinetearsrainwater till I found comfort and relief in St. Mullin's at last, just be aware that all I'm doing is yieldcomforming safe-fully to convention as a madman like every other common everymanperson.

[Unstable Narrator]

Sa Trá

Chuaigh mé siar ar a lorg
Agus linn lán ann ar maidin
Gur airigh mé scréach na bhfaoileán
Agus feadaíl na feadóige,
Tafann ag eilteog sa raineach rua,
Cuach go déanach i ndoire dorcha,

Daighear den ghaoth gharg
Is an ghrian fhann úd nach bhfanann
Ach gan sliocht bharr a throighe
Sa trá sa ngaineamh glan.

In the Strand

I went backwest on the track looking when there was a tidefull fulltide in the morning and all I hearfelt and feelheard was the gulls screeching and the whistleploverwhistling, a flighty young hind incitebarking in the brownred bracken, a lastlate cuckoocuckoo in a dark oakgrove, a dart of sharp airwind and that faint solumsun that doesn't stay and not an ancestorsign of the creamcroptop of his foot on the strand in the pure sand.

An Mhire Mhór

Ní haon ionadh
Mar go gcaithim de luibheanna –
Lus bian, sú craobh, sméar,
An raineach, an luachair, an tseisc –
Agus go bhfuil mé gan chodladh
Nach minic a bhaineann mo chosa
Leis an drúcht ar bharr uachtair an fhéir
Is mé ar fáinneáil is ar foluain
Ar fud sléibhte domhain donn,
Go gclaochlaíonn mo chéadfaí mar sin,
Mo cholainn agus m'intinn,
Go bhfeicim néalta neimhe
Nó na cúig cinn sa gcnoc,
Go n-airím guth chuach na Banna,
Guth giúrainn, guth glé glan geirge,
Guth coirre, fead nó guth feadóige
Nó guth chearc fhraoigh an tsléibhe
Nó go ndéanaim ranna.

Frenzy

It's no wonder as I wasteconsume plants – loose bean peltplants, raspberry, bracken, rushes, sedge – and I can't get any sleep that's it's unoften that my legfeet touch the dew on the creamtop of the grass as I fannelflutter and full-onfly throughoutamong the world-domain, that my senses change like that, my personbody and my mind, that I see the trancenebulae of non-skyheaven or the headendones in the hill, that I hearfeel the censurevoice of the cuckoocuckoo on the Bann, the censurevoice of the barnacle goose, the clear voice of the quail, the voice of the oddroundheron, the whistle or voice of the whistleplover or the voice of the moorhen or so I make partitionverses.

[Psalmists]

Fogha

♪♪

Ó tharla gur chuir tú do mhéar
I suaithne na sleá
Agus le fogha faobhrach géar
Gur mharaigh tú sinn le sá

Den gha in odhar na cíche clé,
Go dté tú féin sa spéir
Mar éan go néalta neamh Dé
Chun báis de rinn dá réir.

Dartdart

Since it haulhappened you buryput your finger in the splinterspear cord and, with a sharpshort dart, you dead killed us with a stakesawstab of the rayspear in the Dun-cownipple, may you go up in the skysphere like a bird to the dayGod's non-skyheaven nebulae and die at spearpoint in Ring.

[Michael O'Cleary]

Marginalia

God knows how I feel your pain
And cry, Sweeney Gelt,
Going like a madman at full pelt
As I work away, not on the Shannon in spring,
Fishing, but in Salamanca, Paris, Rome,
Prague and Lisbon, far from my home,
And Antwerp, Lille and Louvain
In the Low Countries at my long lines –
Recensions, interpolations, redactions, codicils,
Contractions, collations, accretions, apostils – for hours
On end on Ronan and Moling,
Communing with myself, weak and weary,
With O'Mulconry, *père et fils*,
Farfassa, Ward and the two Peregrines.

Yours
The poor brother Michael O'Cleary

[Sweeney]

Lámh ón Leachtán

Is duairc, a bhuachaill, an gníomh a rinnis
Gur ghoin tú mé trí mo chroí sa bhfál
Thoir ar maidin go bhfuair mé bás
Agus cé gur gairid mo shaol abhus
Is go bhfuilim i leacht ag an tobar úd thall,
Is mé go deimhin Suibhne Geilt
Agus tugaim duit mo lámh ón leachtán
Go n-éirím agus go ndéanaim imeacht
Chun éisteacht le guth na gcuach is an ghiúrainn
Is mo laoi bheag féin a rá. *Finis*.

Hand from the Tomb

That's a bleakblack peat-stackdeed you've done, herdboyo, stingwounding me through the heart in that fieldwallhedge facing the rising sun beyond so that I died and although my worldlife over here is closebrief and I'm in a clearmemorialgrave-mound at that well over by, I am indeed Mad Sweeney and I swear I give you my hand from the tomb and rise up and make to go to listen to the censurevoice of the falsettodomegobletcurlsongcuckoos and barnaclegoose and even singsay my own wee rudderpoem. *Finis*.

I gCill nó i Loch?

Och, a chléireacháin, ó ráinigh mé
Doras na heaglaise
Mar ar mithid dúinn scaradh

Mar is dual is mar a bhí i m'dhán
Faoi dheoidh, ní mo mhian triall
Anois go hEas Dhubhthaigh

Nó titim d'aill Dhún Sobhairce
D'oidhe d'éag ná bás de rinn
Trí bhriathra Rónáin Fhinn

Agus ní mo rogha go dtiocfaidh mo shaol
I gCill Cua nó i gCill Riáin
Ach i ndomhain sa loch fuar

Mar a bhfuil an dobhrán is an breac bán
Agus m'adhlacadh, ní le honóir,
A Dhia mhóir, i reilig fíréin

I dTigh Moling i ndeireadh mo ré
Ach go moch faoin linn lán
I Loch Rí nó Loch Léin.

In a Cellchurch-yard in Kill or a Fjordlake in Lough?

Och, little altar-boycleric, since I've hinnyreached the door of the gizzardchurch in Eglish where it's duetime for us to spreadpart as is my tresslot and dawnhalterpoemfate at long last, it's not my desire to attemptgo to Duffy's Falls or fall off the cliff at Dunseverick in a tragicviolent death or die at the last-wordplanetpoint of a spear in Ringsend through the words of Ronan Finn and it's not my choice that my worldlife ends in Kilcoo or Kilrean but in the world-depths of a rawcold lough where the dim-witotter and sea trout fallowblank speckledtroutcopybook are and to be sepulchreburied, not *honorificabilitudinitatibus*, extolgreat dayGod, in the relicgrave-yard of a justman at Moling's house in St. Mullin's at the end of my moonspacetime but early underabout the tidefull generationtimepond in Lough Ree or the Lakes of Killarney.

Is Mise Suibhne Geilt

Is fíor, is mise Suibhne Geilt
Ar fáinneáil agus ar foluain
Ar teitheadh dom as an gcath
Amach an lá sin i Maigh Rath
Trí mhallacht Rónáin Fhinn

Trí gach díthreabh in Éirinn,
Ag tuisleadh de bharr craobh,
Gan mhnaoi, gan éadach, mo thaobh nocht
Agus clúmh ar mo chorp, i gceirt,
Ag léim anonn is anall sa slí,

Níos luaithe ná deatach trí theach
Ar m'imirce gan sos ar fud Éireann
Agus taibhsí romham i meán oíche,
Mo bhiolar is m'uisce mo shásamh,
Gan chodladh, gan a bheith ar cuairt rí

Ach ag déanamh rann, ar an imeall
Is ar gcúl, ag seachaint daoine
Agus ag teacht faoi dheoidh
Go Tigh Moling agus ar mo chéill.
Is dearbh gur mise Suibhne Geilt.

The Irish Wild Man

It's true, I'm Sweeney the archetypal Irish Wild Man whose madness is occasioned by a battlefield experience and the curse of a *sacerdos*, taking to the wilderness, perching on trees and running along them, naked, hairy, covered with feathers and clothed in rags, levitating and performing great leaps, swifter than smoke through a house, restless, travelling great distances throughout Ireland, experiencing hallucinations at midnight, observing a diet of cress and water, losing status as king, avoiding public view, making verses, and coming at last to the house of Moling in St. Mullin's, his memory restored. For certain I'm Sweeney the Irish Wild Man.

[Daniel O'Duigenan]

O'Duigenan's Colophon

(Après Royal Irish Academy MS B IV I)

My life here as a poor Medieval Gaelic scholar, bard and copyist is tough
Shifting all the time from place to place – Shancough, Kingsborough,
Drumlaheen, Kilkere – cold, exhausted and aching to the marrow.

The cailleach of the mill – God break her legs! – can go to Clashacrow.
That Erin that I loved once upon a time's an old cow
And a foreign sow that eats her own farrow.

There's my Sweeney lying streteched out upon a pyre,
Run through by a swineherd at his byre
With a spear through the heart, like a dead wren or sparrow

Fallen out of his tree, beside a pre-Christian rath
And restored salvific millrace and bridle-path
From Graiguenamanagh to Saint Mullin's on the Barrow.

This is my lifetime's effort. As not even a writer, just a scribe,
My concern was never to putrify the dialect of the tribe
On my journey to the Big Houses from Belgarrow to Ballinacarrow.

There was a time I knew before my hand and feet went lame
When Brother O'Cleary and Morrissey were here (and my verse went the same),
Every gneeve, sessiagh, ballybetagh, davoch and collop here, every ballyboe, bog and carrow.

Packs of wolves and the red stag are the company that I keep,
Shunning mankind. Without womenfolk and without restful sleep,
The life God has vouchsafed me here is very bare, very narrow.

No matter anymore. It'll all be in the past soon
And I'll be buried at last in Geevagh, Heapstown Cairn or Ballindoon,
Poor bacach, or scattered out over Lough Arrow.

87

Finis

Gabhadh ar láimh mé gur éirigh mé as mo néal
Go bhfuair mé neamh go hard agus fad saoil.
Sin m'imeachtaí ó thús go deireadh, sin mo scéal,
Sin a bhfuil uaim anois, a chairde gaoil.

Agus ní féidir le duine, dá ndéarfainn é,
An scéal a chur i bhfolach nó faoi cheilt
Arís go deo. Is mé féin féin díreach an té,
Nach mé féin, a rinne scéal Shuibhne Geilt

Ar lorg na gcon sa ngleann i mbun donála
Is guth na gcuach is guth mná áille
Ó Chrota Cliach siar go dtí Críoch Gháille
Go Tobar na nGealt i ndeireadh dála. Dála.

Finis

I was taken in hand and I got up out of my nebulatrance and reached non-skyheaven and my length of worldlife. Those are my comings and goings from stem to stern, that's my story, that's it all from me, that's all I want now. And no manperson, if I say it myself, can conceal the story ever again. I'm the one, am I not, who made the story of Mad Sweeney on the progenymarktrack of the hounds in the smoke-cloudhollowglen howling away and the censurevoice of the tuftembracequaichbundle-falsettocuckoos and the censurevoice of a beautiful woman from the Galtees backwest to Galey to the Madmens' Well in the heel of the hunt.

88

Après Santõka

an ghaoth sa mbile
ar maidin is san oíche
is guth chlog cille

the wind in the tree morning and night and the sound of a church bell

ar chonair chaol chúng,
cluinim guth cléireach is cloig
thall i dTigh Moling

on a narrow road I hear the sound of clerics and a bell over at Moling's house in St Mullins

ar foluain liom féin
ag éisteacht leis an abhainn
chomh geal agus glan

wandering on my own listening to the river bright and pure

liom féin gan seise,
siúlaim ar fud an tsléibhe
faoi néalta neimhe

on my own without a friend I walk all over the mountain under the clouds of heaven

gan choirm gan leann,
siúlaim liom i m'aonarán
ag rá mo chuid rann

without a drinking party or a drink I hermit-walk reciting my verses

gan taobh le duine,
siúlaim ar fud an tsléibhe
ó chill go chéile

trusting nobody I walk all over the mountain from churchyard to churchyard

i mBinn Fhoibhne
codlaím liom ar adhairt chloiche
faoi néalta neimhe

on Binevenagh I sleep on a stone pillow under the clouds of heaven

ar mo thuras dom
in Eachtaí stadaim dem réim
go n-ólaim coirm

on my journey in Slieve Aughty I stop and drink at a party

álainn – gáir na dtonn
is ceiliúr an loin den bhinn
is an t-uisce glan

beautiful the roar of the waves and the blackbird warbling in the mountain and the pure water

ag dul níos doimhne
agus arís níos doimhne,
na sléibhte uaine

getting deeper and deeper still the green mountains

chomh fliuch ar maidin
leis an drúcht – dul mo shlí féin,
is é ár mian

so wet in the morning with the dew I want to go my own way

liom féin ag feitheamh
leis an ré thall ag lúbadh
mar sin faoin sliabh

on my own waiting and watching the moon over there going down like that under the mountain

och, cách faoi shuan
agus oíche lán ré ann
is í chomh glan glan

och everybody asleep the night of a full moon so pure

ag bonn an tsléibhe,
luíonn leachtáin le chéile
faoi theas na gréine

at the foot of the mountain grave mounds lie together under the heat of the sun

an lá go hiomlán
níor dhúirt mé aon fhocal féin –
fuaim is gáir na dtonn

all day I didn't say a single word the sound of the waves

éiríonn an sliabh
chomh dorcha duairc dubh,
éistim lena ghuth

the mountain gets so pitch-dark and gloomy I listen to its voice

i ndiaidh mo bháis,
de luibheanna fúm ag fás
is fearthainn gan sos

after my death all those weeds growing around me and endless rain

Ceithearn

Amuigh go maidin i mbarra crann,
I m'aonar i mbarr eidhinn,
I mboth fhuar sa gcoill chiar,

I ndoirí dorcha nó sa bhfeá mór
Ó Dhoire Cholm Cille go Fiodh Gaibhle,
Is iad mo chairde mo chrainn –
Dair, caorthann, draighean, airne,
Crann úll, crann creathach, coll, cuileann,
Fuinseog, beith, fearn, saileach –
Mar a bhfuil na leannáin ar a dteitheadh,
Na dásachtaigh, na fir allta
Le craobhacha, na fir fógartha,
Na díthreabhaigh, na naoimh féin
Cruinn le chéile,
Crainn Éireann agus gealta Éireann
Ina gceithearn amháin choille.

The Men of the Wood

Out until morning in the creamcroptops of penis-shaft-vault-trees, on my tod in the creamcroptop of an ivy, in a rawcold bothy in the waxdark Kalendscastrationwood, in dark oakgroves or in the great wood from Derry to Figile, my respitefriends are my stocklotshaft-trees – oak, rowan, blackthorn, kidneysloe, apple trees, aspen, oghamChazel, holly, ash, beingbirch, alder, willow – where the eloping afflictionlovers are, the mad men, the wild men of the wood, the outlaws, the puny hermits, the holysaints themselves gathered round together, the stocklotshaft-trees of Ireland and the nakedwood-grazingbattle-fugitivebirdbeastpan-iclunatics of Ireland as a single band of woodkernes.

An Scriostóir

Tháinig do m'ionsaí an scriostóir sin
Agus a mhuintir na cléirigh
Gur chuir siad teorainn
I m'fhearann agus i m'chrích
Gur dearnadh m'iamh

Nó gur éirigh na doirí dorcha
Agus an choill chiar
Agus crainn Éireann uile
Ón muir mhór go mullach na mbeann
Ó Shliabh Eidhneach go Ros Earcáin,

Ó Fhiodh Gaibhle go Bile Tiobradáin
A bhí lán le luibheanna is torthaí troma
Ag cromadh go talamh
Ina maoil agus ina machaire
Agus rinne mé dán dubhach

Agus ceol ar chruit mhín
Go ndeachaigh mé thar sáile
I m'long gan laoi go hInis Muirígh
Thar craos na mara go hÍle go hEige
Go Carraig Alasdair cian ó m'mhuintir.

The Destroyer

That scrapedestroyer and his familycommunity of altar-boyclerics attackapproached me and set a border in my endlands stopenclosing me and the dark oakgroves and the waxdark desecrationwood and all the stocklotshaft-trees of Ireland from the ocean to the rooftops of the regardpeaks from Slieve Inagh to Rasharkin, from Figile to Toberdan which were tidefull of herbs and fruits bending to the ground and rose-became baldround hills and battleplains and I made a blacksad dawnhal-terfatepoem and songmusic on a sweet lute and went off overseas in my boat without a laytiller to Inishmurray across the gluttonygullet of the sea to Islay to Eigg to Ailsa Craig longingfar from my familycommunity people.

Bréagaireacht

B'fhearr liom ná coimirce
Rí neimhe nó talún,
Agus muintir na heaglaise
Dul i m'aonar ar fud Éireann
Ar fáinneáil is ar foluain
Ar seachrán i mo réim baoise
Mar a bhfuil ceiliúradh na gcon,
Crónán is dord na ndamh,
Bréagaireacht na sionnach
Is donáil na mac tíre
Faoi chranna sa gcoill chiar,
I bhfolach sa bhfeá mór,
Ar feadh na ndoirí dorcha
Sa *sylva sacrosancta.*

Liecoaxing

I would rather than the protection of the king of non-skyheaven or earth, aye, or the people of the church to go on my tod all over the Irelandworld fannelflutterloitering and full-on floathovering derangementerrorwandering on my wild career where there's the farewell celebrationwarbling of the hounds, the droning and chanting of the oxchampionstags, the liecoaxing of the foxes and the howling of the landsonwolves aboutunder stocklotshaft-trees in the waxdark Kalends-desecrationwood, sackhidden in the great wood, throughout the dark oakgroves, aye, in the *sylva sacrosancta*.

Trua Sin, a Chléireacháin

Ag Droim Damh is ag Droim Fraoch
An lá sin, b'é mo shlua
Deichniúr is deich gcéad laoch
Is is mairg mar a dh'fhuirigh mé leis an dáil,
A fhir an cheoláin lán de thnúth

Is d'fhormad agus is trua
Suibhne Ros Earcáin ina luí sa tuar
Sa mbuaile nó sa bhfál sin thoir
Sa mbualtrach is a thaobh leis
Mar a mbím is a bhím ag caitheamh mo phroinne

Nó ar fáinneáil is ar foluain i mo réim reatha
Gan sos i sneachta, sioc nó síon
I mullaí beann, sa gcoill chiar dhlúth
Ó Shliabh gCuilinn go Luachair Deá,
Ó Shliabh gCua go Sliabh Breá,
Ó Mhaigh Linne go Maigh Feá

Nó sa muir mhór i mbarr na toinne
Trí bhriathra Rónáin Dhroim Geis
Ó d'imigh mo bhean is mo mhac is m'iníon
Is mo bhuar mo bhiolar is mo mheá,
Mo mhairg, m'uisce fuar
I m'gheilt ghlan gan chonn gan choir
Gan chairde gan chabhair is is mise dúil
Nach sóúil ná sáil is nach n-iann súil
Agus ní suanach sóúil ná socair sáil,
A chléirigh na cille, mo bheatha.

That's a Lean-meatpity, Little Altar-boycleric

At Drumdaff and Drumfree that day, my fairyarmycrowd was 1010 lay-warriors and more's the pity that I delaywaited for the nearjudgement-meeting in the Dáil, little belltinklewhimpererman tidefull of envylonging and rivalry and another lean-meatpity is Sweeney of Rasharkin lying in the bleaching-greencattle-fieldomendung in the dung-yardmilking-place or in that fieldwallhedge in the east in the cow-dung with his side thighexposed also where I waste-eat my prandium or fannelfluttering and full-onfloatflying in my headlong runningsway without rest in snow, frost or stormy weather on the roofsummits of regardpeaks, in the warpthick waxdark castrationdesecrationwood from Slieve Gullion to Slieve Luachra, from the Knockmealdowns to Slieve Breagh, from Moylinney to Moyfea or on the great sea on creamcroptop of the blisterwaves through the words of Ronan of Drumgesh since my wifewoman and my son and my daughtergirl went away and my kine is my watercress and my measure of mead is my rawcold rainwaterpis-stears and I'm a pureclear nakedwood-grazingbattle-fugitivebirdbeast-paniclunatic senseless and harmless without respitefriends or succour for I'm a desirehope-elementcreature not heelcomfortable and who doesn't joinclose a hope-eye and my sustenancelife is not reststeady or heeleasy, altar-boycleric of the cellchurch.

Faoi 3

Lean cailleach an tí
Is Loingseachán is teaghlach an rí
Ar mo shliocht coicís ar mhí

Is na cinn gan chorp gan cholainn faoin slí
Ó Mhá Linne go Má Lí
Agus an mhá atá sa Mí

I mo bhochtán gan bhrí
Gan chairde gan ní
Ar fáinneáil is ar foluain is ar gealtacht faoi thrí.

X3

The nunhag of the house and Lynchehaun and the royal household followed in my footsteps for 3 weeks and the heads without a body or a corpse between them all the way from Moylinney to Moylee to the plain in Meath and I a weak and meaningless poor sicko without friends or respite or anything fannelflutterloitering and full-on floathovering in nakedwood-grazingbattle-fugitivebirdbeastpaniclunacy 3 times over.

Mo Bheannadáin

Is amhlaidh atá mo bheannadáin
I ngach coill chiar,
Gach dionn is fothair,
Toll, cluthar is dlúth,
I mullach sceiche,
I mbarr na ngéag in Imleach Iúir,
Sa bhfraoch ar lár Ghleann Bolcáin,
I ndosanna crann eidhinn sa ngleann,
M'áras, mo dhaingean, mo dhún
Is mo dhíon ar dhoineann is ar fhearthainn,
Reo, sioc, sneachta is síon,
Mo sciath dhídine, m'fhoscadh,
M'fholach im' chríoch is im' fhearann,

Ar shiúl ó shluaite na cruinne,
Leis na héin i gcoll is i gcuileann,
I nglac Bhile Tiobradáin,
I m'aireaglán i dTuaim Inbhir,
I bhfáisteach folamh sa ngleann,
I bhfargán ar fhorléas na bruíne,
Sa ros i mBeanna Boirche,
I mullach Shliabh Eidhneach,
I gcuas caol crainn i mBeanna Broc,
Ar chlúmh i gcíocha cnoc,

Agus ó dhíthreabh go díthreabh
Ar fud Éireann go cruinn
Ó Dhún Sobhairce go Teach Doinn –
I muine nó i mothar nó i gcabhán,
I gcuasa cúnga cloch,
I scailpeanna crua carraige,
Ar Charraig Alasdair thar loch amach,

Sa mboth fhuar i leith leapa le mo leannán,
Faoi ghlas i ngéibheann
Is i gcuibhreach i dtolg Loingseacháin,
Sa Ráth Mór,
Sa teach mór,
I dTeach Moling faoin bhfál,
Faoi chraobh san eas thall,

Faoi bharr doire,
I mbile
I bhFiodh Gaibhle,
In uaimh Dhonnáin Eige thar tuile,
Sa mbuaile,
I gCluain Chille
Is i gCill Deirbhile
Agus gach ionad eile,
Na hionaid is dile
Liom féin in Éirinn uile,
Ar gealtacht is ar ginideacht is ar mire
Ar fáinneáil is ar foluain is ar buile
Is ar dásacht is araile,

Agus i ndeireadh, thall i mo thír féin,
Mar atá i ndán, i reilig fíréin.

Topophilia

It's apparitionlike this, Olaf – my topophilia is for every waxdark desecrationwood in Kill and Kyle, every hillfort in Dinn and every steepwoodedpasturehollow in Foher, holehollow, warpclose and secret sheltered, the rooftop of a hawthorn in Mullagh or Skeagh, the creamcroptop of the yew branches in Emly, the furyheather on the centreground of Glenbalkan, dronethicket-tufts of ivy stocklotshaft-trees in the smoke-cloudhollowglen, my wombabode, my firmfort in Dingle and Dangan, my downclosefort and my roofprotection against stormwintriness and rain, frost, snow and stormy weather, my wing-shieldbasket of shelter, my shadowshelter, my hidecover in my endlands in Farren and Creagh, away from the fairmyarmycrowds of the exactround universe with the birds in oghamChazel and in holly, the handrecess of the sacredscionbordertree in Tipperton, my plumpasture summer-shieling in Toominver, an empty house in the smoke-cloud-hollowglen, a ledge on the skylight of the strife-fairydwelling, the flax-wooded headland in Ross in the Mourne Mountains, the roofsummit of Slieve Inagh, the kyletwignarrow cupcovecavity of a stocklotshaft-tree in Pennybrock, featherdown in the paps of the hills in Knock, and from hermitagewilderness to hermitagewilderness in Derrew – a Jovecover-thicket in Munnia or dark-cloudbrush-woodjungle in Moher or little maimhollow in Cavan, narrow cupcovecavities of castleshorestones in Coose and Clogh, hardrock clodbank-caveclefts in Carrick, Ailsa Craig across the pond, the rawcold bothy in bed with herself in Scotstown, aboutunder green-greyrivuletlock in shieldingself-isolationquarantine-shackle and captivityfetter in Lynchehaun's thrustcouchbed, the great rampart in Rathmore, the Big House in Ballinteemore, underabout the fieldwallhedge at Moling's house in St Mullin's, underabout a heathertresstree in the stoatwater-fall over there, underabout the cream-croptop of an oakwood in Barraderry, in a sacredscionbordertree in Figile, in the cave of St Donan in Eigg across the sea, in the enclosed dung-yardmilking-place in Boola, in a cellchurch-yard in Clonkilly and Kildervila and every other place, the places I like most in all of Ireland, on my own in nakedwood-grazingbattle-fugitivebirdbeastpaniclunacy and in goblinmadness and in a frenzy fannelflutterloitering and full-on floathovering and fury et cetera and, in the heel of the hunt, in my own country, as is dawnhaltergiftfated, in the relicgrave-yard of the just.

Erin

Och, a Erin, a chroí
Níl ar do chorp méid orlaigh
Nár fhág mé gan taisteal

I m'gheilt ó bhonn go baithis
I ngach cabhán is clais is cuas caol
I gcíocha cnoc is in ucht ard an tsléibhe
Ón nGabhal go Sliabh Uillinne
Go Droim Lorgan go hÉadan Tairbh,

Na géaga, do dhá láimh, do dhá chos,
Do bhosa, do thaobh, barr do throighe,
Do dhá shúil agus do bhéal,
Do leasracha, do shlinneáin is d'ioscaidí,
Do mhuin is do chlúmh, do chneas is do chúl,
Gach craobh cheangailteach i mullach do chinn,
An gleann, m'anam, is a bhfuil ann
Ó Theach Doinn go Dún Sobhairce.

Erin

Och, Erin, dearheart, there isn't as much as an inchbit in Orlagh on your corpsebody that I've left unhackletravelled as a nakedwood-grazingbattle-fugitivebirdbeastpaniclunatic from tip to toe in the Bonn, in every maimcavity in Cavan and groovegulletgully in Clash and Closh and cupcove in Coose and Coss and Cove and twigslenderkyle in Keale and the paps of the hills in Knock and the high breast of the Jovemountainmoor in Slieve from the Figile to the Hill of Ushnagh to Drumlurgan to Edenterriff, the branchlimbs in Gaigue, your two armhands, your two legfeet, your slap-palms, your aspectflank, the creamcroptop of your vampfeet, your two hope-eyes and your frontlipmouth, your exposed thighs, your sleyshingleshoulder-blades, your tiny kneehollows, your vinetopback and your body hair, your skinside and your hairback, every connected lingbranchtress on your endhead in Cuss and Cush and Barr and Cool Lodge and Creeve and Mullagh and Aillyhaloo, in Glan and Glen and Glynn and Glin Demesne and Glenbevan and Glenfield and Glowens, aye, the whole lot from Mizen Head to Malin Head.

Loci poesis

I mo réim is mo raon maidhme,
Codlaím san eas thall
Nó le cluas le cloch adhairte
Thuas ar ucht Bheanna Boirche
Nó i mullach Shliabh Eidhneach,
Gach conair agus gach caoi
Gach lá dom ag taisteal na mbeann
Ó bhinn Shliabh Nia go binn Shliabh Eibhlinne,
Ar ginideacht agus ar fáinneáil
Is ar dásacht i m'gheilt idir ghealta

Nó i mbile le craobhacha
I m'aonar dom i mbarr eidhinn,
I mbarra craobh críon,
I mullach crainn dosaigh dhlúith
Nó i mullach an iúir i nGleann Bolcáin
Idir lár talún agus néalta neimhe
Gan sos ar feadh na hoíche
Go ngabhaim rann agus laoi.

Loci poesis

On my swaysuccessioncareer and my headlong rangerout, I sleep in the stoatfall over there or with my ear to a pillow stone upon the breastface-slope of the Mournes or on the roundsummit in Inagh, everywhich way every day as I hackletravel the regardpeaks from the cornerpeak of Slievenee to the cornerpeak of Slieve Felim, goblin-mad and fannelflutterloitering and frenzied as a nakedwoodgrazingbattle-fugitivebird-beastpaniclunatic amongst nakedwood-grazingbattlefugitivebird beast-paniclunatics or raging mad in a sacredscionbordertree on my tod in the creamcroptop of an ivy, in the creamcroptops of decayed lingbranches, in the roundsummit of a bushy warpdense penis-shaftvault-tree or in the roundtop of a yew in Glenbalkan eitherbothbetween the centreground of dry-landearth and the trancenebulae of non-skyheaven without rest all night and make partitionverses and rudderexhortationlays.

Mo Chairde

Ó tá mé gan iníon Choinn Chiannachta
O saobhadh mo radharc is ó chlaochlaigh mo ghné,
Rithfidh mé leis na coin is an damh rua
Thar Mhaigh Luirg, thar Mhaigh nAoi,
Ó Ghleann Bolcáin go Teach Doinn,
Ó Shliabh Mis go hInis Bó Finne,
Ó Ros Bearaigh go Beanna Broc,
Ó Loch Léin go Cill Cua,
Gach conair agus gach caoi,
Thiar, thoir, thuaidh, theas
Le gealtacht gan chairde gan sos
Is tabharfaidh mé taobh ní le mo dhaoine féin
Is ní le cléirigh na cille ná na heaglaise
Ach leis an Seoigheach is le Mac Uí Éanna,
Leis an mBéarrach is le Seán Ó Sé,
An Searcach is Mac Uí Chaoimh,
Ag Snámh dhá Éan le Flann Ó Briain
Is Brian Ó Nualláin mar an gcéanna,
Seán Ó Ríordáin is Pádraig Ó Fiannachta,
Ó Colaim, Ó Maoldúin, Ó Foghlú,
Mac Suibhne, Mac an tSaoir is Ó Floinn
(Is a' triall gun chonn gun chèill
An Alba le Caimbeul is Uilleam Nèill),
Sa bhfál sin thoir ag taithí le bliain
Is ag feitheamh le Moling de chéin,
Dom leanúint ar mo shliocht go dílis ó thús
Go deireadh na ré gan bhean agam gan chú,
Go néalta neimhe mar a bhfuil na naoimh,
Cléirigh na coille, cléirigh na gcnoc,
Cléirigh na ngleann, cléirigh na binne,

Cléirigh an tsléibhe, cléirigh na glaise
Cléirigh na loch, cléirigh na n-eas,
Cléirigh na má, cléirigh na ros,
Mo chairde, mo mhuintir is mo bhunús.

My Respitefriends

Since the girldaughter of King Kong of Keenaght is longingabsent since my sight has been distorted and my speciesform translationjourneyshifted, I'll run with the hounds and the red championox-stag across Moylurg, across Moynee, from Glenbalkan to the Bull Rock, from Slemish and Slieve Mish to Inishbofin, from Rossberry to Pennybrook, from the Lakes of Killarney to Kilcoo, every whichway, backwest, fronteast, north, south in nakedwood-grazingbattle-fugitivebirdbeastpaniclunacy without respitefriends without rest and I'll sidetrust not my own menpeople and not with the altar-boyclerics of the cellchurch-yard in Kill or the church in Eglish but with Joyce and Heaney and O'Keefe, at Swim-two-Birds with Flann O'Brien and Myles the same, O'Donovan, Ferguson, Yeats, Clarke, Colum, Graves, Snodgrass, Montague, Skelton, MacIntyre, Meehan, Muldoon, Foley, Ennis, Monaghan, Batchelor, Kinsella, Hewitt, Sweeney and McSweeney, etc. and in Scotland with Campbell and Neill and Finlay, in that fieldwallhedge in the fronteast hauntvisiting for a year and waitwatching Moling from afar, following me properfaithfully on my progenytrack from the start to the end of my moonspacetime and me without a wifewoman or a dog, *les clercs* of the castrationwood in Kyle, *les clercs* of the hills in Knock, *les clercs* of the smoke-cloudhollowglens in Glynn, *les clercs* of the gableregardhornpeaks in Bing, *les clercs* of the mootmountain in Sleaty, *les clercs* of the chillygreygreenstreams in Glasha, les clercs of the Lakes, *les clercs* of the stoutwater-falls, *les clercs* of the plains of Eglinton, *les clercs* of the linseedwoodedhead-lands in Ross, my respitefriends, my familyfolk and my majorityorigins.

Moladh

Agus tú féin, a fhir chráifeach,
Ag gabháil na salm i saltair Chaoimhín
I bhfianaise lucht an léinn
Agus ag croitheadh uisce choisricthe
Mar bheannacht ar chách,
Bím féin ó dhíthreabh go díthreabh
Gan taobh le mnaoi ná gan chairde,
Gan bhróg is gan éadach,

Gan bhia, gan deoch
Ach mo chuid lus bian, sméara,
Caora cuilinn is eidhinn
Agus cnónna coill
Agus an breac bán
Agus deoch d'uisce fuar as glaise ghlan
Agus i m'chodladh san aill
Os cionn an locha mar aon leis na héin
Agus mo leaba cloch adhairte
Nó cuas caol crainn
Agus thuas ar cholbha chrua
Mar a bheadh Uaimh Dhonnáin

Agus i m'aonar i m'aireaglán
Agus i m'fhianaise
Dobhrán sa loch lán
Agus, éist, scol is ceiliúr an loin
Den bhinn, crónán is dordán
Is gáir is búir na ndamh
Agus donáil na mac tíre
Go hard ag teorainn do chille
Sa ngleann agus na cléirigh
Ag moladh rí neimhe naomh.

Molypraising

When you yourself, holy man, are goreciting the psalms in St Kevin's tramplepsalter in the witnesspresence of the scholars and aspersing holy rainpisstearswater on everyChristperson, I'll be going from wildernesshermitage to wildernesshermitage without sidetrust in women, without respitefriends, without a sandalshoe or clothes, without ale or aliment, just for my lot loose bean peltplants, smearberries, sheepberries of holly and ivy and hazelwood-nuts and fallow-white psaltertrout and salmon and a drink of rawcold rainpisstearswater from a clearclean greenness-stream and sleeping in the cliff above the lake at one with the birds and for my bed a shorecastlestone pillow or the kyletwignarrow covecavity of a penis-shaftvault-tree or up on a hard ledge as in St Donan's cave and on my tod in my little oratory and in my witnesspresence a dim-witotter in the tidefull lake and, listen, the call and farewell-celebrationwarbling of the elkblack-bird from the regardpeak, the droning and fameshouts and boorbellowing of the championox-stags and the howling of the land-sonwolves in the smoke-cloudhollowglen and the altar-boyclerics mollyprasing the king of holysaints' non-sky-heaven.

Caoineadh Shuibhne

An gníomh a rinnis is faram
Cléirigh na cille gur mairg
Agus fágaim ort mo mhallacht –
Beidh do chorp agus t'anam,
T'intinn agus t'aigne
Ag deamhain agus gabhfar sailm
Don té nach ndearna t'aimhleas
Ná do dhuine eile ar thalamh

Ag imeacht liom trí aiteann
I mo gheilt ghlan ar gealtacht
Ó Theach Doinn go Ros Bearaigh,

Ón mBuais go hÉadan Tairbh,
Ó Chríoch Gháille go Críoch Bhreatan,
Go Dairbhre nó don Daingean
Is gach aird i mo réim reatha
Le huamhan agus le heagla

Gan feoil is gan choirm leanna
Ach ag ól uisce de mo bhasa
Seachas deoch meá ná bainne,
Gan ghuth cloigín im fharradh
Ná donáil na gcon alla
Ná ceiliúr an loin ar maidin
Gan mhná áille, gan leaba,
Gan neamh, gan saol agam,
Gan Corp Chríost a chaitheamh

Agus ó tháinig bhur gcealg
Im thimpeall, beidh mé marbh,
A fhir, ón ngoin a radais.

Sweeney's Lament

That deed you did when the cellchurch-yard altar-boysextonclerics were in my company was woebad and I curse you and your corpsebody and your soul and your mind and all will be possessed by demons and psalms will be recited for the one who never did you or any other man-person on dry-landearth any harm going through the whins as a pure wildnakedgrindgrazingbeastwoodbirdbattle-fugitivepaniclunatic in nakedwoodgrazinglevitationlunacy from the Bull Rock to Rossberry, from the Bush to Edenterriff, from Galey to Dumbarton, to Valentia or to Dingle and every airt in my wild pursuit with terror and fear without flesh or alefeast, drinking rainwater out of my palms and not mead or milk, without a voice or the sound of a clusterbell or the howling of the wild dogs or the farewellcelebrationwarble of the the elkouzel in the morning without wifewomen or a bed, without heaven or the lifeworld and not wastethrowhankergetting *Corpus Christi* and I'll be dead from the guilesting and scrapwound that you've kickgiven me.

Guí

Ar bhruach Uisce Bhearú
Le taobh na conaire, cian
Ó m'eol is ó m'thír féin,
Mo chríoch is m'fhearann is mo dhú
Mar a bhfuil iomaí eidheann is sceachóir,
Iomaí cnó coill, caor is creamh,
Sméara, sú craobh is dearcáin darach,
Agus Moling is Loingseachán,
Mo sheise Congal,
Ailín, mo bhean,
Mo chairde is mo chumainn
I mbeannad ina sionad naomh
Ag an tobar úd thall,
Go n-adhlactar mé i reilig fíréin
Faoi dheoidh le honóir
Go bhfaighidh mé ionad ar neamh.

Prayer

On the swollen bank of the Barrow beside Connery's path, longingfar from where I know best and my own country, my endlands and my proper native place where there's ivy and haws, treeoghamCwordhazelnuts and wild crave-garlic, black smearberries, raspberries and oak thistlecavityacorns, and Moling is there and Lynchehaun, my companion McGonagle, Allan, my woman-wife, my respitefriends and my friend-shipsweet-hearts in a blessed place as a holy synod of saints at that well over by, may I be sepulchreburied in the relic-grave-yard of the just at last with honour and gain a place in non-skyheaven.

Ag Tobar na nGealt

Bhí mé i mo rí maith mór ar Dhál Araidhe
Gur scar mé le mo riocht is mo chruth
Gur chlaochlaigh mé deilbh is dath
Trí bhriathra Rónáin Fhinn
Gur theith mé as an gcath le huamhan
An lá sin i Magh Rath
I mo mheatach gan bhrí gan ghiolla
Go ndeachaigh mé lom nocht ar craobhacha
I m'bhochtán gan chairde gan folach
Gan díon im'aonar i mbarra crann
Sa gcoill chiar, i ndoirí dorcha,
In imeall an fheá, trí gach díthreabh
In Éirinn, i seascann is mothar,
Gan bhia gan deoch ach biolar is uisce
Gur fhás clúmh ar mo thaobh
Gur tháinig mé romham faoi dheoidh
Go Tigh Moling nó go ndearna mé dán
Sa mbuaile gur adhalacadh mé le honóir
I reilig fíréin go bhfuair mé m'ionad ar neamh
Is gurb é sin críoch mo bheatha.

At Tobernagalt

I was a great and good great king of Dalnaria but I parted with my creationform and became disfigured and changed warpshape and colour by the cursepledgewords of Ronan Finn and fled out of battalionbattle in horror that day in Moira as a coward without meritsignificancestrength or a gillieboy and went stark mad as a meanbeggar without respitefriends without sackcovering without roofshelter on my tod in the creamcroptops of stocklotshaft-trees in the waxdark castrationwood, in dark oakgroves, at the edge of the wood, three times through every hermitagewilderness in Ireland, on my tod in a sedgeswamp and a darkcloudbrush-woodjungle, without ale or aliment but watercress and rainpisstearswater and then egrethairfoliagefeatherdown wastegrew on my side and I came at last to St Mullin's and said a dawnhalterfatepoem in the dungmilking-grazingfield and was sepulchreburied with honour in the relicgrave-yard of a rarejust-man and I found my place in nonsky-heaven and that's the end of my life.